The Human Side of Japanese Enterprise

To my father,
Masao Tanaka,
who gave his life to
the Japanese business world

The Human Side of Japanese Enterprise

Hiroshi Tanaka

upp University of Pennsylvania Press
Philadelphia

First published in Great Britain in 1988 under the title *Personality in Industry: The Human Side of a Japanese Enterprise* by Belhaven Press (a division of Pinter Publishers), 25 Floral Street, London WC2E 9DS.

First published in the United States in 1988 by the University of Pennsylvania Press.

Library of Congress Cataloging-in-Publication Data

Tanaka, Hiroshi, 1943–
  The human side of Japanese enterprise

  Includes index.
  1. Ashikkusu, Kabushiki Kaisha—Management.
2. Sporting goods industry—Japan—Management.
3. Industrial management—Japan. 4. Onitsuka, Kihachiró, 1918–   I. Title.
HD9992.J34A837   1988   302.3′5   88-11399
ISBN 0-8122-1276-2

Printed in Great Britain

Contents

Preface   ix

1. Rebirth   1
   Prologue   1
   Desolation   1
   The Formative Years   3
   Promise to a War Comrade   8
   Defeat   11
   To Kobe   14
   Renamed 'Onitsuka'   15

2. Learning Through Experience   17
   The Dark Side of Business   17
   Changing Direction   20
   Postwar Managerial Ideology   23

3. Onitsuka Corporation   26
   Corporate Assets   26
   Rising to the Challenge   28
   Strategy for the Novice   31
   On the Road   32
   Marriage Arranged   37

4. Corporate and Personal Survival   41
   Work is Everything   41
   Tiger Brand   45
   A Brush with Death   46
   The Saviour   50
   Changing Fortunes   51

5. Solidarity   54
   Retailer Support   54
   Employee Dedication   56
   Personnel Training   58

6. Growth and Greed   66
   Olympic Involvement Begins   66

Accused of Tax Evasion 67
An Obligation Fulfilled 69
Search for Happiness 69
A Fair System of Merit 78
Managerial Training and Advancement 80
A Promise Fulfilled 82

7. Broadening Perspectives 84
Travelling Abroad 84
Product Innovation 86
Distance Running Shoes 87
Early Research 91
Marketing Strategy 94
The Onitsuka Circle 96

8. Diversification Disaster 99
Stock Exchange Listing 99
Diversification Out of Control 100
The Circle Stands Firm 104
Dealing with the Banks 106

9. Point-of-Focus Management 110
Parting with the Heir Apparent 110
'Glass Pane' Management 115
Importance of Point-of-Focus Management 116
The Olympics in Japan 119

10. Consolidation and Expansion 131
Fiscal Control 131
Domestic and Foreign Expansion 135
Business Culture Differences 142
International Rivalry 148

11. Strengthening the Corporation 152
The Oil Crisis 152
The 'Diet' 154
Functions of Profit 157
Diversification Rechallenged 160
Success 162
Corporate Olympics 165

12. The Birth of ASICS 170
Totalization Advances 170
Mitsuji Teranishi and GTO 171
Kazuma Usui and Jelenk 174

From Co-operation to Amalgamation 177
ASICS 184

13. Growing Pains 189
Corporate Adjustments 189
A New Role for Onitsuka 194
Labour–Management Unity 196
'ASICS Innovation' 200
Becoming Number-1 in Profitability 203
Winter Olympics 205
Recognition 207
National and International Association Involvement ... 208

14. Meeting the Escalating Competition 211
Modernizing Garment Production 211
Changes in Merchandise Distribution 217
Marketing Lessons from Descente 218
R & D in Sports Shoes 220

15. Ongoing International Expansion 230
Taiwanese and Korean Licensees 230
German and Brazilian Subsidiaries 235
A New Corporate Office 237
Research Institute of Sports Science 239
Sound Minds in Sound Bodies 241
The High Cost of Corporate Success 242
Epilogue 244

Appendix: Onitsuka's Speech 246
'Theories and Practices of Japanese Management' ... 246
Matsushita's Comments on Onitsuka's Management Philosophy ... 250

Notes 252

Index 263

Preface

My work on this book began shortly after my first encounter with Kihachiro Onitsuka in Tokyo in 1982 but its origins lie in my upbringing as the son of a Japanese businessman and my own later experience of the Japanese business world. Educated in postwar Japan, I worked for a major Japanese electronics firm for two years after graduating from university, before disillusionment with the Japanese business world led, by a somewhat circuitous route, to my pursuing graduate studies in cultural geography at two Canadian universities. Perhaps it is my *karma*, but strangely enough I now find myself teaching not geography but management.

In my view, the ultimate goal of management as an academic discipline is the development of a body of reliable public knowledge about managerial phenomena—how these come into being, how they are maintained or altered over time, and how they interrelate. In recent years, with the increasing curiosity about, interest in, and scrutiny of Japanese management, I have become uncomfortable with the gap between my image of Japanese managerial processes and my perception of the Western view of these processes emanating from their portrayal by the publishing world and the media. This book is my modest attempt to provide a rounded picture of one corporation's progress showing the human difficulties of the man at the helm as he attempted to find the path to business success, and the evolution of his personal management philosophy that gave the corporation a sense of direction through its difficulties, allowing it to act as a catalyst for social progress.

Japan's rapid economic progress since the end of World War II has attracted much attention from Western business concerns, almost to the point of a tendency to emulate the perceived Japanese approach. Western publications, I feel, have collectively created a myth that the Japanese hold the key that magically unlocks the door to entrepreneurial success. I, however, think there is no one distinct Japanese formula or set of management practices—be they the often discussed lifetime employment, seniority system, consensus decision making, quality control circle, suggestion system, god-father system, just-in-time production, or robotization—that will automatically guarantee a viable enterprise.[1] Just as there are many commonalities shared by successful Japanese businesses, so is there much diversity among them in their corporate philosophies and practices: each corporation has its own distinctive style and tradition.

This book concentrates on how one organization and managerial system evolved and the role that entrepreneurial values have played in this development. Often neglected in discussions of Japanese management is the underlying value system which permeates the whole society, of which business is a part. The corporation is the precinct in which managers and workers alike search for the meaning of life. The bond that unites all personnel is this shared mission of the heart and soul. This must be borne in mind if one is to understand the essence of managerial practice in Japan.

The purpose of this account is not to propagate the notion of the often alleged general superiority of Japanese business behaviour, nor is it to argue the transferability of such managerial practices to other parts of the world. Rather, it is to shed light on the reality of corporate progress by describing the evolution of one particular corporation, ASICS, as it was guided by its founder and president, Kihachiro Onitsuka. Within the evolutionary framework, I hope to provide a sense of perspective, to show how Mr Onitsuka's decisions and actions as well as the subsequent corporate activities fit within the socio-economic context. By describing a sequence of key events as they are remembered and perceived by Kihachiro Onitsuka and his close business associates, an attempt is made to paint the picture as it is seen and experienced by the Japanese manager himself, thus making explicit what is implicit in managerial action.[2]

It is widely acknowledged in Japan that managerial responsibility lies towards three constituent groups: employees, society (especially customers) and shareholders. As seen in this account, managerial responsibility encompasses the satisfaction of the needs of committed employees through the provision of rewarding work. Corporate responsibility to society is fulfilled through the provision of quality products at a fair price, as well as through taxation, donation and support of community activities. The outcome of the effective performance of various functional activities, including product research and development, marketing, production and finance, is profit. The appropriate distribution of profits to shareholders, employees, subcontractors and for corporate development is the third area of managerial responsibility. The events portrayed herein directly or indirectly relate to one of these three areas of managerial concern.

It has frequently been suggested that the Japanese apply textbook management principles in their daily business operations. Be that as it may, as this book illustrates, Japanese entrepreneurs (like their counterparts in any other part of the world) are catalysts of change, continually interacting with a changing environment. They are constantly rewriting the textbook. The validity of the textbook can only be tested and appreciated within particular contexts and situations. This book shows that the reality of the practice of management is more than the simple application of theories. Commitment, co-operation and persistence are required to successfully implement policies. In addition to the ubiquitous managerial resources of capital, material, people, time and information, insight and spiritual guidance attained from Asia's rich depository of historical figures and events is effectively utilized by entrepreneurs.

Corporate culture, no less than culture in general, is cumulative, learned, shared and dynamic. Corporate cultures progress, regress, revive or pass into history. Behind such dynamic corporate processes are the entrepreneurs' relentless efforts. The relationship between corporate performance and such effort is, however, not necessarily consistent. Active, well thought-out, well intentioned and persistent managerial effort often positively influences the extent to which the social mission of the corporation will be fulfilled. On other occasions, the results of such efforts cannot be fully harvested. The milieu of corporate behaviour and the subsequent expressions of it are diverse and complex.

The commonly held perception of Japanese management is, I feel, based on the practices of large corporations. In reality, however, large enterprises make up only a small fraction of the Japanese business world in terms of both numbers of establishments and employees. According to a 1985 government White Paper, small firms in Japan, excluding those in the primary industry, account for 99.4 per cent of all industries and 81.4 per cent of the number of employees.[3] The corporation initiated by Kihachiro Onitsuka in 1949 evolved through his hard work, mistakes, painful decisions and personal sacrifices. Initially a three-man operation, Onitsuka Corporation evolved into a thriving middle-sized firm entering into the international market and eventually, through tripartite amalgamation, into ASICS, a major sporting goods manufacturer in Japan.

Today ASICS has a workforce of about 1,900, its subsidiaries employ another 3,400, and it is listed on the Stock Exchanges in Tokyo, Osaka, Nagoya, Luxembourg, Vienna, Frankfurt and Singapore. The annual net sales totalled 120 billion yen for the fiscal year 1986. The operating income for the same year was 6 billion yen. Onitsuka and his company have come a long way. The evolution of Onitsuka Corporation into ASICS is one example of the development and growth of postwar established corporations, which are the backbone of Japanese economic recovery and progress.

I first encountered Kihachiro Onitsuka's name in the *Mainichi Daily News* in Tokyo when I was looking for a keynote speaker for the conference on Japanese Management held at the University of Lethbridge, Canada, in March 1983. Mr Onitsuka graciously accepted our invitation and subsequently delivered a stimulating address. Captivated by his enthusiasm, his belief in the ability of individuals to make their dreams come true, his social commitment and his willingness to share his hard-earned management know-how, I determined to learn more about him and his company and, through this book, to share what I discovered.

Kihachiro Onitsuka likens his life to the Buddhist proverb *nanakorobi yaoki* ('fall seven times, rise eight times'). 'Truly,' he says, 'my life has been a tale of ups and downs. There is much I hesitate to disclose. However, I cannot pretend to be more than what I am. Honesty is far more important than "looking good". I will share my experiences, my stumbling, my falling and my getting up again as it happened, in the hope that others may learn from them.'

Mr Onitsuka's own writings, speeches, my conversations with him over the past five years, both in person and by letter, and corporate documents which he provided, form the core of this book. At his request, three names have been changed and appear in the text as Shigeru Higashida, Minoru Ishibashi and Mamoru Okitsu. In the text, quotation marks around Mr Onitsuka's words or a displayed extract indicate that they are a direct translation from his writings, including his letters to me, and our recorded conversations. The omission of quotation marks from statements attributed to Mr Onitsuka indicates a paraphrasing of his written documents or summarized excerpts from our conversations. I have tried to synthesize this information with that gleaned from interviews with ASICS' executives and employees in Japan, Taiwan, the United States and West Germany; with personnel from its subcontract factories in Japan, Taiwan and Korea; and with Mr Onitsuka's wife and daughters, other family members, business associates and friends.

To all of these individuals I am deeply indebted for their willingness to share their experiences with me, to answer my questions, and to make the writing of this book an educational and enjoyable experience. I am particularly grateful to Mr Kihachiro Onitsuka for the many patient hours he has given me out of his busy schedule on the several occasions that I have been in Japan and Korea and for his lengthy and detailed correspondence in reply to my many written enquiries. Without his blessing and also his concrete assistance along with that of the staff of ASICS' Office of the President, especially Mr Koichi Shiba, I could never have carried out the extensive interviews with ASICS' personnel and associates around the world in the limited time available.

I am also indebted to many people outside ASICS Corporation for their assistance in making the completion of this project a reality. In particular, I would like to express my gratitude to the following persons for their assistance with data collection: the late Professor Emeritus Ryukichi Ito of Seikei University, Professor Ken Kageyama of Aichi University of Education, and Dr Osamu Asano of the Asano Clinic. Miss Eriko Onoda, a graduate student at Kyoto University, translated one of Mr Onitsuka's major writings into English. A number of people have read the manuscript and offered constructive criticism. I am indebted to Professor Geoff England of the University of Lethbridge and Mr Aldo Opel for their assistance in the revision of an early draft. Additional suggestions came from my friend and mentor, Professor Emeritus Philip Wagner of Simon Fraser University, as well as from Professor Paddy Tsurumi of the University of Victoria, Mr Dennis O'Connell, Economic Development, City of Lethbridge, Mrs Edna Smith, and Dr Marilyn Nefsky of the University of Lethbridge. The assistance offered by all of these individuals was invaluable. Any shortcomings of this book, however, are solely my responsibility.

From the inception of the project I have been grateful for the support of my colleagues in the School of Management at the University of Lethbridge, particularly, Dr George Lermer, Director, and Mr Larry Merkley, Associate Director. The many drafts of the manuscript were typed by Mrs Gail Kembel and Mrs Marlene Lapointe. Their competence, efficiency, cheerfulness and ability to meet tight deadlines is truly appreciated.

Finally, I would like to express my appreciation to my wife, Beverly, who worked with me throughout the course of this project and to our son, Ranken, who sacrificed hours of play time with his father while this work was in progress.

1 | Rebirth

Prologue

ASICS—*Anima Sana In Corpore Sano*, 'a sound mind in a sound body'—was Kihachiro Onitsuka's dream for the youth of Japan; now it is his dream for mankind. Through his business endeavour, Onitsuka took the first step to actualize this dream nearly forty years ago. He was thirty years old, a survivor of the Pacific War. Three years with a newly formed company had exposed him to the widespread corruption of postwar Japan. If his country was to rise from the physical devastation, economic ruin, and spiritual deflation the war had inflicted, its young people needed hopes and dreams; they needed jobs. Onitsuka saw in the manufacture of sports shoes the opportunity to provide both.

He established his company with two employees, a desk and a telephone. It was one of a few hundred minute business establishments involved in the rubber footwear business in Kobe. Today, ASICS' (Tiger) products are known globally, and include, as well as footwear for most sports, a wide variety of sports equipment and apparel—over 200,000 items in all.

Onitsuka acted on his dream and actualized it. The backbone of his corporate success has been the consistent application of his corporate ideology that the company exists for the benefit of society—consumers, employees, shareholders, and all those affected by the corporation's existence. He formulated his ideas through his experience of personal hardship. ASICS' evolution is Kihachiro Onitsuka's life itself.

Desolation

'*Nippon wa maketa*—Japan is defeated.' On hearing these words, broadcast on 15 August 1945, Kihachiro Onitsuka felt as if his soul had been torn from his body. He was disillusioned, desolate—a young man adrift.

On his discharge from the disbanded Japanese Army, Onitsuka, whose name was then Kihachiro Sakaguchi, returned to his home in Tottori prefecture, a rural district in western Honshu, Japan's main island, bounded on the north by the Japan Sea and on the south by the Chugoku mountain range. It was to Kihachiro Sakaguchi's Tottori address that, in the closing days of 1945, a letter from Seiichi and Fukuya Onitsuka was to arrive. The letter, though simple in its content, marks the initial step in the remarkable history of Kihachiro Sakaguchi who was to become Kihachiro Onitsuka, founder and president of ASICS Corporation.

Sakaguchi had come to know the Onitsukas well during their frequent visits to the military base at Himeji where he had been stationed. They were a middle-aged, childless couple from Kobe who were to have adopted Sakaguchi's close friend and fellow soldier. It would be another eighteen months until word reached the Onitsukas that their chosen son had been killed in action in the latter days of the war.

The letter conveyed the loneliness of the couple and suggested that Sakaguchi come to Kobe, a major international Pacific port, to work and to live with them. The news of the Japanese surrender had left him in such a state of disbelief and shock that for sometime he had not thought about his commitment to this couple on behalf of his friend. No sooner had their letter arrived than the Onitsukas themselves came to Tottori to plead their case.

In January 1946, with the New Year celebrations barely over, Kihachiro Sakaguchi bid farewell to his parents and relatives and left for Kobe. Respecting his mother's wishes not to wear his Army uniform, he wore the khaki-coloured *kokuminfuku*, the national wartime uniform for male civilians. Made of cotton (wool was reserved for the military) and worn without a tie, it had a high-buttoned neck with a stand-up collar—resembling the outer jacket of the Communist Party of the People's Republic of China. 'You would look too much like a remnant of the defeated army in your officer's uniform', she had said.

Sakaguchi walked twelve kilometres along the snow-packed roads to Tottori station. He managed to get on an overcrowded train by scrambling through a window, but it was so congested that once inside he was unable to stick out his arm to wave goodbye to his eldest brother who had come to see him off. Inside the rail car it was impossible to move. Getting to the toilet was out of the question. Adding to the discomfort was the soot-laden air. As the line that linked Tottori to Kobe passed through numerous tunnels, soot stung eyes and turned faces black. When the train arrived at Kobe's Sannomiya station, it was almost dusk. Kihachiro Sakaguchi was then twenty-seven years old. This was the starting-point of his new life.

Nineteen forty-six was also the starting-point of Japan's recovery from defeat and its development into a dominant economic nation. Its present Constitution, drafted by the United States and put into effect in 1947, renounced not only war but even the maintenance of armed forces. In retrospect, far from harming Japan, the compulsory demilitarization freed the nation from the burden of military expenditure and enabled resources to be channelled into economic growth. The country could begin to revive its industries, the initial step in its subsequent rise to its present position as the world's second largest capitalist economy.

The Formative Years

In 1918, Kihachiro Sakaguchi was born in Meiji, a mountain village in Tottori prefecture situated deep in Japan's snow country. Now the Matsugami district of Tottori city, at that time Meiji village consisted of eight scattered hamlets with a combined population of 2,500 people (400 households). His grandfather had chosen his name, calling his grandson after Kihachiro Okura (1837–1928), an entrepreneur who, during the Meiji (1868–1912) and Taisho (1912–1926) periods, accumulated tremendous wealth and made a lasting contribution to Japanese society.[1]

Like Kihachiro Okura, Kihachiro Sakaguchi was the youngest in his family. He had two brothers and two sisters. His father was Dentaro Sakaguchi, and his mother, Kame Takahashi. Middle class for several generations, the Sakaguchi family was quite well-off. Kihachiro's grandfather was the county chief and Kihachiro's eldest brother the leader of the young men's association of the village and later the mayor. In addition to farming, his grandfather had been a broker dealing in Inaba paper, a regional product used for calligraphy and in the manufacture of interior sliding screens. The profits of the brokerage had allowed him to purchase additional land which was subsequently farmed by Kihachiro's father. Of course, being well-off in a rural area like Tottori meant only that one was not scrambling to make ends meet day to day. Compared to many of their neighbours, the Sakaguchis were able to enjoy a fairly comfortable way of life.

Kihachiro, as a young child, was sometimes mischievious and wayward. One particular morning he persuaded some of his first grade classmates to go fishing before school started. They became so engrossed in their fishing exploit that they completely forgot about school. Unfortunately it began to rain—not that Kihachiro noticed. However, his father did, and decided to take an umbrella to his son for use on his return from school. Only then was it discovered that Kihachiro and some of his classmates were missing. A search was quickly organized and joined by the teacher, Harue Yasuda, who had just begun her teaching career that year. The children were found still fishing happily at the river, oblivious to the consternation they had caused. Kihachiro's father, in his displeasure, gave his son the scolding of the young man's life. The incident is significant in that it demonstrated Kihachiro's early ability to become totally absorbed in the matter at hand, an attribute that was to serve him well in later life.

Despite his occasional waywardness, Kihachiro succeeded in gaining entrance to the prestigious Tottori Ichichu Middle School, now Tottori West Senior High School. He was one of only four students from his graduating class of sixty-two to do so.

Today, all Japanese children continue on to junior high school under the nine-year compulsory education system introduced after the war, and nearly 95 per cent go on to high school. In the 1920s, however, only about 10 per cent of elementary school graduates continued on to a four-year middle school programme and the applicants had to be selected for entrance. Admission to middle school was not open to the majority of those completing the compulsory six-year elementary education programme, a programme that had as its core the virtues of the family tradition, loyalty to the nation, and diligence. Kihachiro was among the handful of students allowed to advance to a higher level of learning.

Much of the credit for Kihachiro's success in passing through the narrow gate to higher education may be attributed to the tuitionary skills of his grade six teacher, Tokichi Fukuda, a man dedicated to his vocation. Like many teachers who recognized exceptional qualities in particular students, Fukuda took a personal interest in Kihachiro and five or six of his classmates who wished to advance to higher education, often tutoring them after school. He received no pay for his work, however, his teaching performance and the quality of the school would be assessed according to the success rate of the students who attempted the middle school entrance examination. A newly qualified teacher, Fukuda was striving to establish his reputation and that of his school. He often worked with Kihachiro and the others until very late at night. He was strict and demanding. Kihachiro was a little afraid of him but at the same time he respected and trusted him and placed himself whole-heartedly under Fukuda's guidance.

Fukuda remembers Kihachiro as an outstanding student, always at the head of the class and very popular with his classmates. 'Rural students at that time', says Fukuda, 'lacked the competitive spirit of their urban counterparts and could not compete on an equal footing. I wanted to help them overcome this disadvantage.'

Having been accepted at Tottori Ichichu Middle School, Kihachiro set as his goal the Military Academy. Although the Sakaguchi family may have been a wealthy family for the region, they were none the less farmers. It is doubtful that there would have been enough money to send all five children on to higher education. Kihachiro understood this even as a child so he chose the academy, where the government would be paying his tuition fees. The Military Academy had another attraction for him: past graduates from Tottori Ichichu Middle School who were now Naval and Army officers returned to Tottori occasionally and Kihachiro longed to wear a uniform like them.

Two years after Kihachiro entered middle school, his former teacher, Fukuda, transferred to a primary school on the outskirts of Tottori city. At the time, Kihachiro was bicycling the twelve kilometres between his home and his school every day. There was a return bus once a day but its schedule did not correspond to that of the school. In the winter, all means of transport from the village to the city came to a halt because of the deep snow. It snows frequently in this part of Japan and drifts are deep— between one and three metres on average throughout the winter. Accordingly, until the advent of modern snow removal equipment, students who lived outside the city found it necessary to take up lodgings in Tottori city for the winter months. When Fukuda moved, Dentaro Sakaguchi asked if his son could board with him. 'I was surprised and aghast at first', says Fukada.

He had just married Sadako Kishida, also a school teacher. 'Our rented lodgings were very small, barely big enough for two, never mind three', Fukuda recalls, 'but I realized what an advantage it would be for Kihachiro to live with us so I persuaded my wife to agree to the arrange-ment.' Kihachiro and the Fukudas lived together in one ten-mat room (approximately 20 square metres). The desk and wardrobes (Japanese rooms are without built-in storage space except for the accommodation of bedding) occupied one-third of this area, however, leaving a 14 square metre multi-purpose living space.

It was not only because the Fukudas were newly-weds and living in rented quarters that space was limited. The traditional Japanese house is characterized by the absence of privacy, by the lack of inviolable space for each of its inhabitants. If the space is sufficient it may be subdivided by sliding screens, but these afford no barrier to any sound above a whisper. In the summertime they are often removed altogether. There is no bedroom, dining- or living-room as such. Sleeping mats are spread on the floor at night; in the morning they are stored in a cupboard, and the table around which the day's activities take place is returned to the centre of the room. Fukuda recalls:

I felt so strongly about Kihachiro becoming an officer that my wife and I did all we could to help him. We took turns keeping him awake to study. The light often stayed on all night. I did feel sorry for Kihachiro at times, but I did not hestitate to shout at him should he start to drowse, and wake him up with cold water from the well in the backyard. Not once did he complain. He always did as he was told. I was surprised by his strong will and determination. Somehow I did not expect it of him. I expected him to have been spoiled as his family was well off.

Kihachiro's grandfather had been in charge of his grandson's upbringing from early childhood. He woke Kihachiro early every morning, telling him that if he overslept he would never get ahead in life. When Kihachiro misbehaved his grandfather would confine him to the rice storage shed. Here Kihachiro would listen to the mice and occasionally fall asleep crying. Then, when the punishment had lasted the appropriate length of time, his mother would let him out, comfort him and give him a hot dinner. Thinking back, Onitsuka is grateful for the way he was raised—for the affection of a kind and loving mother and the discipline of a strict but equally loving grandfather.

Reflecting on the time he spent with Fukuda and his new wife, Onitsuka realizes how much he intruded upon their privacy. However, he says, 'I was but a child then, and much more naïve than the children of today. I did not really understand the intimacies of married life, so, in my ignorance, I did not feel at all awkward living with newly-weds.'

Years later, when Fukuda and Onitsuka were having a drink together, they joked about it.

'By the way, when was your eldest son, Ken, conceived? I never realized . . .'

'Well, I can tell you it wasn't easy!'

Such was the depth of their relationship that it was to become lifelong. For a time after the war, however, Onitsuka and Fukuda lost track of each other. Hearing that Onitsuka was in Kobe, Fukuda and his wife visited the city and searched in vain to find him. A few years later, the basketball inter-high school championships were held in the Tottori high school where, unknown to Onitsuka, Fukuda was principal. The day before the games, Onitsuka, in accordance with his policy of promoting his basketball shoes through his attendance at games, arrived at the school. Immediately, the two men renewed their friendship. Several years later, upon his retirement, Tokichi Fukuda was invited by Onitsuka to become an adviser to ASICS' newly established Tottori factory—a position he still holds.

As with much of Onitsuka's life, things were not to proceed smoothly for long. He was to find that the one major career objective behind the support given him by the Fukudas—support that could not have been greater had they been his own parents—was suddenly to crumble: he was forced to give up his dream of becoming a military officer by entering the academy as a cadet.

During the summer of his fourth year at middle school, Kihachiro took part in a sumo wrestling tournament at the village *bon* festival. *Bon*, celebrated in mid-August throughout Japan, originated as a Buddhist religious observance but is now a joyful social occasion as well. It is believed that at this time the spirits of the dead return to their earthly homes. Kihachiro was doing well winning all his matches—until the last one. He had been practising judo and kendo and had reached the second *dan*, or level, in kendo, so he entered the last match with confidence in his strength. His opponent, however, was very big and threw Kihachiro to the ground. He landed on his chest and this resulted in pleurisy.

Two years of convalescence followed. Kihachiro had no choice but to give up his dream of going to the academy to become an officer. This twist of fate may well have saved his life. His three classmates, Setsuo Kuno, Tadashi Motogi and Kameji Koshiba, who were accepted into the academy, were all killed in the war.

Following his convalescence, Kihachiro had to undergo a physical examination for military conscription which was then compulsory for men of twenty years of age and over. Kihachiro's health had recovered better than expected thanks to his two years spent in the fresh air of the countryside, and, at 164 centimetres and 66 kilograms, he attained first rank in the examination. To be included in this class one had to have a minimum height and weight of 164 centimetres and 60 kilograms and be in excellent physical and mental condition. Those who could not meet these criteria were relegated to second or third rank, depending upon the extent of their deficiencies. The last-named were excused from military service entirely while second-rank men were only called up for active duty in wartime. In January 1939, at the age of twenty, Kihachiro Sakaguchi joined the Japanese Imperial Army's Tenth Regiment of the Himeji Tenth Division of the Transport Corps. Shigeharu Kunitomi, a classmate from Tottori Ichichu Middle School, joined the regiment at the same time. Like so many of Sakaguchi's Army comrades, Kunitomi was killed in action.

At that time, the Tenth Regiment consisted of about 1,500 men. The function of the Transport Corps was to deliver food, arms, ammunition and medical supplies to the front lines. Here, in a three-month training period, Kihachiro Sakaguchi received his initiation into the Army. Morning and evening, the new recruits were assigned to the stables to air and dry the straw, dispose of the horse manure and clean the horses' hooves. Each morning, Sakaguchi would have to break the ice on the bucket and then wash the horses' hooves in the freezing water. His hands had open cracks from the cold and the manure would get into the sores. If dirt remained on a hoof the inspector might command the recruit responsible to lick it. Any recruit, Sakaguchi's superiors postulated, could be replaced for the price of the postage on a conscription notice. The horses were much more valuable and had to be properly cared for.

For Sakaguchi learning to ride was a painful experience. Frequent falls and remounting bruised him and staying on the horse took the skin off his buttocks. Often after a day of 'riding' he could only get up the dormitory stairs on his hands and knees. One Sunday, after having been confined to the regimental training area for sometime, the recruits took the horses into town. Sakaguchi enjoyed the excursion but when he got back to camp he was reprimanded and hit on the face with a horse whip for having been too much of a sightseer during the exercise. Shortly thereafter, his parents came to visit, but Sakaguchi was ashamed to show them his face and made an excuse not to see them.

Many times Sakaguchi felt that he could not endure any more, that he had reached his physical and mental limits. At the same time, however, he knew that soldiers had to undergo the necessary training, that orders were absolute and obedience mandatory. The individual soldier had to survive in adverse conditions and to relentlessly attack the enemy.

Reminiscing about this time, Onitsuka says, 'It was a hard life but it taught me perseverance and endurance and how to recognize people's good qualities, and developed my fighting spirit and positive outlook.'

Konosuke Matsushita, the founder of and now adviser to Matsushita Electric Industrial, today one of the world's largest consumer electronics manufacturers producing such well-known brands as Panasonic, National, Technics, and Quasar, is considered to be Japan's foremost management guru. Matsushita once said, when asked by one of his executives what the secret of management was: 'Such a thing cannot be understood through words alone'. Later this same executive, charged with executing a major project by the following morning, called into being all his resources and, in so doing, met the deadline. Congratulating the executive on a job well done, Matsushita said: 'This is it. No matter how difficult the task at hand, you must follow through. That is the secret of management. This knowledge is priceless.' With that Matsushita held out his hand and asked for a lecture fee.

Onitsuka learned this very important lesson—the importance of follow-through to good management—from his military experience.[2] Through his military experience, too, Onitsuka made many friendships, upon which he would later draw in his business career.

Promise to a War Comrade

At Himeji, Sakaguchi met a man who was to greatly alter his life. His name was Terutoshi Ueda. He was the same age as Kihachiro Sakaguchi. As a graduate of the Military Academy he had been promoted from a cadet to a second lieutenant, then immediately to a first lieutenant. Lieutenant Ueda was Sakaguchi's superior, but they got along very well together as friends.

Remembering Ueda today, Onitsuka says, 'He had none of the elitism of his brother officers of the academy. Though somewhat unconventional, he was a highly considerate man, an attribute that attracted me to him.'

Ueda was from Hagi city in Yamaguchi prefecture in western Honshu. His mother was remarried and she and his stepfather and Ueda's sister comprised his immediate family. Ueda was very kind to Sakaguchi while he was studying for the examinations to qualify as a military cadet. The examinations, which followed the three months of initial training, consisted of tests of leadership ability, war tactics using scale models, moral character and personality and investigation into the individual's background and ideology. Sakaguchi passed them. Unfortunately, however, he contracted pleurisy again, this time from a cold, and had to be hospitalized for some time. Consequently, he was no longer eligible for the highest rank, being appointed instead as a military cadet of the second rank (a non-commissioned officer). Since he had passed the written exam, however, he was given a certificate of competence for officership. This enabled him to be commissioned as a second lieutenant only one year after the others in his entry class.

Following his commission, Sakaguchi and Ueda became even closer. Ueda nearly always asked Sakaguchi to accompany him if he was going drinking or out on the town. Unlike Sakaguchi, Ueda was a dedicated partyer. The fact that his pay was higher than Sakaguchi's also helped. They spent many evenings together, sometimes boisterously in the company of geishas in Himeji, and on other occasions they would philosophize well into the night with equal intensity. They became virtually inseparable—as close as true brothers.

The conduct of the war worsened with each passing day. Although it was not widely acknowledged in Japan, the country was rapidly moving towards a disastrous defeat. In October 1943, the Student Mobilization Law was proclaimed and all the university and technical school students for whom conscription had been deferred were called up. Sakaguchi was appointed as instructor of the first group of student soldiers who were enrolled in the Himeji Regiment. Among these young men were a group from Keio University in Tokyo. Kunikichi Sato, who later became chairman of the Japanese Coastline Ship Owners' Association, was one of the Keio students.

It was during this period that Sakaguchi first met the couple from Kobe, Seiichi and Fukuya Onitsuka, whose name he later adopted. They had come to pay their respects to Kunikichi Sato as friends of his parents. Lieutenant Ueda, who was acting captain, and Sakaguchi both met the couple. Subsequently, there developed a very close relationship between the Onitsukas and the lieutenant. Occasionally, Ueda would visit Mr and Mrs Onitsuka in Kobe, and at other times one or both would visit the lieutenant. The relationship appeared to become one of parent and child. The couple were childless. They called Ueda *bon*, beloved child.

When the Onitsukas came to Himeji, they would often ask Sakaguchi to join them for a Chinese meal, a favourite treat. Before long they had begun to call him *shobon*, small beloved child. Sakaguchi did not know it at the time but the Onitsukas were hoping to adopt Lieutenant Ueda as their son.

The system of adopted children has a long history in Japan. In order to maintain the family and protect the spirits of their ancestors, families would adopt a child, often already full grown, if they had none of their own. If the family only had daughters, a man would often be brought in to marry one of them and take over as the family head, assuming the family name in the process and relinquishing his responsibilities and ties to his natural parents. Men who accepted such invitations were generally poor but with good promise and potential, given proper backing. Marrying into a well-off family with good connections would give the man the prestige, wealth and position of his adopted parents. On the other hand, he could also be the target of much ridicule, and considered a henpecked husband.

Sadly for the Onitsukas and Lieutenant Ueda, the ravages of war were to interrupt and eventually end their relationship. In November 1943, it was decided that a new troop would be dispatched to Burma. Sakaguchi's regiment was divided into two groups; one to go and the other to stay. Both Lieutenant Ueda and Sakaguchi were in the group destined for the front. The new commander chosen for the regiment that remained, however, was young and inexperienced. It was thought that he would need a seasoned regimental adjutant to assist him and it was decided that Sakaguchi should be that person.

Sakaguchi protested the decision to Ueda, but to no avail. Well versed in regimental matters, he was the officer best suited to the post. He would remain at Himeji. The pronouncement meant saying goodbye to many fellow soldiers, probably for good. That was what war was all about.

Ueda came to Sakaguchi's room to have a farewell drink on their last night together. There he confided to Sakaguchi that he had promised the Onitsukas he would be their adopted son and would attend to them on their death-beds. He entreated his friend to look after the couple until he returned from the front. Sakaguchi gave him his word. On the following day, Lieutenant Ueda left with the regiment, one of some 300,000 Japanese soldiers to be stationed in Burma. It was the last time Sakaguchi saw him.

The war in Burma was particularly grim. At times, the terrain and the climate made combat conditions almost unbearable, with no quarter given or asked on either side. For the Japanese, the intention was to cut Chiang Kai-shek's overland supply route. The Navy had already blocked access through the South China Sea. The Japanese Army suffered its greatest defeat ever in Burma. Few soldiers were to return home from the fronts at Imphal, Kohima, Mandalay, Meiktila and Sittang.

Defeat

After half the regiment had departed for Burma, other detachments were dispatched to Okinawa and Manchuria. Sakaguchi, however, was left out of these corps for the same reason that he had remained at Himeji when Ueda was sent to Burma. He was never to experience combat—a great disappointment to him at the time. His only mission outside Japan was to north-eastern China to deliver soldiers, horses and ammunition to the Japanese forces there.

The fall of Saipan in June 1944 provided the United States with the air base it needed to attack Japan directly. In preparation for fighting to begin at home, the remainder of the regiment at Himeji was reorganized as the Tobu 54th Corps and was eventually moved to Nagano city in the interior of central Japan. The first Tokyo air raid came on 24 November, two weeks after commencement of the construction of an underground fort on the outskirts of Matsushiro town near Nagano intended to house the Imperial headquarters and also to provide residential accommodation for the Imperial family. The site was chosen because of its remoteness, its solid geological base, its proximity to a site on which an airport could be built and, finally, because the names of the mountains under which the headquarters was to be constructed suggested divine protection.[3]

Sakaguchi went with the regiment to Nagano. Although he was charged with guarding the Imperial headquarters, he never actually saw the underground fort as details of its exact location and layout were top secret. Even many senior army officials, the Nagano military police, and members of the Imperial household remained uninformed as to the details of the plan.

The war ended when the headquarters was only 70 per cent completed. The construction involved 800,000 people and cost 60 million yen. Today, the former intended underground Army headquarters at Matsushiro is the Seismological Observatory of the Japanese Meteorological Agency.[4]

People could sense that the tide of the war was fast turning against Japan. The transfer of the Imperial headquarters from Tokyo to Matsushiro, for Sakaguchi, was symbolic of Japan's plight. Most of the cities in Japan were in ruins from the showers of incendiary bombs. On top of this, in early August 1945, there were rumours of an extraordinary bomb dropped on Hiroshima. A contemporary of Sakaguchi's, who had been dispatched to a school for arms development, returning from Hiroshima, substantiated secret reports of a bomb far more destructive than any Japan had seen before. Japan, he told Sakaguchi, had been planning to make a similar kind of bomb.

As early as 1942, Dr Yoshio Nishina, a leading Japanese physicist, had addressed the Diet about the possibility of manufacturing a small, highly portable bomb with incredibly destructive powers. The Japanese, however, never followed through with the project. Unable to appreciate fully the gravity of the Hiroshima bombing, Sakaguchi could only imagine something like a very large incendiary bomb. Yet something dark and foreboding in the eyes of his friend told him that this was no ordinary bomb.

As we now know, the first atomic bomb was produced at the Los Alamos, New Mexico laboratory and successfully tested in New Mexico on 16 July 1945. Three weeks later, on the morning of 6 August, when the atomic bomb, with its estimated explosive force of 20,000 tons of TNT, was dropped on Hiroshima—a virgin target—about 236,600 of the 400,000 people who were within the city environs were directly affected. Of these, 63,600 were missing or killed, according to a survey taken on 25 August 1945. Ninety per cent of the city was levelled. Three days later a second more powerful bomb was dropped on Nagasaki where 75,000 people were killed or injured.[5] It was some days before the horror of the bombings became widely known even among the military. The possibility of so rapid a defeat was something neither the military nor Sakaguchi had contemplated.

At noon on 15 August 1945, in a recorded message broadcast nationwide, Emperor Hirohito announced Japan's unconditional surrender to the Allied nations. Grand Chamberlain Sukemasa Irie, who served the Emperor for fifty-one years until his sudden death in 1985, recalled the night of 14 August 1945 when the Emperor prepared the speech in the bomb shelter of the Imperial Palace while Tokyo air raid sirens screamed and a contingent of B-29 bombers flew over the city. Irie fully expected the Emperor to be downhearted because the proclamation of defeat was imminent. When Irie thought the recording of the speech was finished, the Emperor said with a great deal of vigour and spirit, 'Let's try it again'. It seemed to Irie that the Emperor realized that although Japan had been defeated in the war the nation must and would make a new start.[6]

Despite the fact that the Commander of the Imperial Guard was assassinated by Army personnel trying to prevent the Emperor's message from being put on the air, it was in fact broadcast. Sakaguchi heard the Emperor's speech over the radio in the Army lecture hall in Nagano. He was unable to decipher the words. He could not understand whether it was that the Japanese were defeated or that they were to fight to their deaths. He could only hear static. Excitement blurred his thoughts.

Sakaguchi immediately called the division headquarters. Before he finished asking his question, the voice shouted, 'You idiot! *We lost!* All right? What else do you want?', and the telephone was slammed down. He did not try to call again. The voice on the other end was trembling, obviously in tears.

Later, headquarters phoned to confirm Japan's surrender. The order was given that under no circumstances were the Japanese soldiers to fight, resist, or engage in any military activity whatsoever. Headquarters were taking precautions to guard against unexpected, reckless action. Nevertheless, there were some unfortunate events. Even though the war was over, the next day a young officer at Nagano forced his fully uniformed troops to engage in an exercise crossing the Chikuma River without first checking the depth and rate of flow of the water. Because the officer disobeyed the command, five men drowned needlessly.

It was about eleven o'clock when Sakaguchi returned to his room. His landlady mused aloud about what would become of them now that the war was over as she prepared a meal of boiled bean curd with ingredients purchased on the black market. Having nothing to say to her, Sakaguchi ate his meal alone in silence. The radio was playing an unfamiliar *koto* melody. He could not longer hold back the tears. Suddenly they poured down his face, as if a tap had been turned on somewhere deep inside. They would not stop. Rage and frustration took over.

For the Japanese, the defeat was a profound shock. Since the latter part of the nineteenth century, they had undergone an effective programme of indoctrination. Many still perceived the nation to be invincible. Amidst Sakaguchi's tears, many faces appeared. Blurred, they would appear, disappear and reappear. They had all given their lives for their country—in mid-China, north China, Burma or in the south. Sakaguchi had been prepared to do the same but now he would not have the chance. What would he do with his life? He felt compelled to do something for those who had sacrificed their lives, so that they might rest in peace. The question was what could he do? He had no idea. He only knew that he had to do something. He could only feel the gnawing emptiness and the thoughts of 'nothingness' that dominated his troubled mind. The military had been his life.

When the war was over Sakaguchi heard many negative comments, such as, 'The Japanese were very reckless in this war'; 'I did only what I had to do to get by'; and 'From the beginning I knew the Japanese were going to be defeated anyway'.

Yet of his own feelings he says:

I have no regrets. I did my very best as the adjutant of my regiment with 1500 soldiers. For me, then, there was no alternative but to fight to defend my homeland. Through military life I acquired invaluable assets. I learned to challenge my own limits and to overcome extreme difficulties. Today, though, I am totally against war.

After the end of the war, Sakaguchi stayed behind to tie up loose ends. By the time he was discharged it was December 1945. He returned to his home in Tottori and for a short time steeped himself in the warmth of his family and the beauty of the familiar landscape. Here he came to feel himself again. It was at this time that he received the letter and the visit from the Onitsukas asking him to live with them in Kobe until Lieutenant Ueda returned.

To Kobe

Five months after Japan's defeat was announced, Sakaguchi arrived in Kobe. He looked around as he stepped off the train. The entire city had been razed. Fifty-five times, from January 1945 until the war's end, Allied planes had dropped their bombs on or near the city.[7] Only the *torii*, the sacred arch of the Ikuta Shinto shrine, stood among the debris. It had an eery glow, as it reflected the light from the setting sun. Between the Maya mountains to the north and Osaka Bay to the south were the rolling mounds of rubble, with the ruins of buildings scattered sporadically among them. The elevated railroad cut a straight line through this desolate scenery.

Stepping into the streets of Kobe, one entered a lawless land. Homeless soldiers and repatriates from overseas territories roamed aimlessly about. Kobe was, as it is today, a multi-ethnic city. Its calm harbour and proximity to Japan's commercial hearth had attracted many foreign settlers after Japan reopened its doors to foreign trade in 1868. Many of the city's foreign residents had been oppressed during the war and now some were taking advantage of the deflated Japanese public. The local police could not cope with the chaos. The American military police, armed with heavy machine guns mounted on amphibian tanks, patrolled the streets.

It was not surprising that the Onitsukas felt anxious living on their own. Sakaguchi headed for the house and found it still standing, as he had been told, although some 70,000 homes had been burned to the ground. Seiichi Onitsuka had worked some years earlier for one of Japan's major shipping companies. A three-year posting in London had left him with a working knowledge of English and an appearance reminiscent of a tidy, well-groomed British gentleman. On his retirement he had assisted in a small trading company and was still engaged in this when Sakaguchi arrived in Kobe. Sakaguchi had kept in close touch with the Onitsukas in the two years since Ueda's departure for Burma. Now they welcomed him with open arms, as though their own son had returned. It was agreed that he would board with them.

Before many weeks had passed, Sakaguchi had decided to start his life anew in Kobe. His familial obligations were minimal. Shortly after he came to the city his mother had been stricken with pneumonia and died. She was sixty-five. Sakaguchi had returned to Tottori for her funeral. Memories of his mother had flooded back: her infinite patience as she and his grandfather taught him calligraphy in preparation for his entry into primary school; her faith and care when he was hospitalized with pleurisy; and, later, when he was in the Army, the talismans she had sent him, each one purchased when she went to pray for his safety at the local Shinto shrine. Now Sakaguchi's father had his eldest son and the next eldest to look after him. Sakaguchi didn't feel he was needed in Tottori. Also, he had found a job in Kobe through friends of the Onitsukas.

More than eighteen months were to pass before the news of Lieutenant Ueda's death arrived: 'Staff Officer Terutoshi Ueda killed in action in Burma on 11 April 1945.' This meant that he had been killed a year and a half after he and Sakaguchi had parted at Himeji. In the meantime he had been promoted from lieutenant to major and, by the time of his death, to adviser to the Division. He had been shot while travelling to the front in a staff car at Mandalay. Sakaguchi reflected on their last night together. They had had the optimism of youth then but now all that remained for Sakaguchi was regret, a regret that he had been incapable of preventing their separation.

The effect of the news upon the Onitsukas was devastating. They had been living for the return of their son-to-be. Each day Mrs Onitsuka would go to the Repatriates Relief Bureau hoping to obtain information about Lieutenant Ueda—all to no avail. Sakaguchi was unable, try as he might, to find words of comfort for the grief-stricken couple.

Renamed 'Onitsuka'

The Onitsukas were alone in the world. They had no relatives, the house they lived in was rented, and there was no inheritance or savings to ease their old age. The rampant postwar inflation rendered what little money they had almost valueless. Their situation was desperate. They had just managed to survive, thanks to the generosity of Sakaguchi who gave them all his earnings. He had been intending to leave when Lieutenant Ueda arrived: he was staying with the Onitsukas because of his promise to his deceased friend.

When they asked Sakaguchi whether he would mind looking after them for a while, he gave them his word that he would look after both of them till their death, in the lieutenant's place. For a while, everything was fine.

Then again the couple began to show signs of worry—worry that some day Sakaguchi would leave them and get married. Sakaguchi promised he would remain with them as long as they wished, but this was still not sufficient to reassure them. Acknowledging that it was a great deal to ask of him, they implored Sakaguchi to become their adopted son, in Lieutenant Ueda's place.

While affection has gradually replaced authoritarian filial piety in postwar Japan, in those days, the ties of obligation between parents and children were strong. Whether they were parents by blood or not, absolute fidelity and loyalty were demanded of the children. Sakaguchi needed some time to think it over. It was said, at the time, that one should accept an offer of adoption only if the couple had a large inheritance or a beautiful daughter. The Onitsukas had neither.

Nevertheless, it did not take him long to decide to accept. Not only was he concerned about the Onitsukas, but he also could not help but feel that this was what his deceased friend would have wanted. He rationalized that, even if the Onitsukas had had a daughter, it was still possible that he would not like her. If the Onitsukas had had a larger inheritance, people would have thought that he was interested only in their money. Therefore, it was preferable that the Onitsukas had nothing to offer Sakaguchi.

'As well', recalls Tokichi Fukuda, 'there was no future in farming in Tottori. He could not have made a living if he had returned to his family home.' Sakaguchi accepted the Onitsuka's offer of adoption. He made a new start in life—this time as Kihachiro Onitsuka.

The Dark Side of Business

Kihachiro Onitsuka was able to obtain a position with the Higashida Company through an acquaintance of his adoptive mother, Hiizuru Tsunemi, a former Hyogo prefecture police chief. Onitsuka had been told that the company was situated in front of the Kobe Sannomiya railway station, but on arriving there he found nothing. Everything had been burned to the ground. He looked around and saw a tent. Inside, a few people were standing near a small fire. This was the company. The President, Shigeru Higashida, was among them. He was wearing a windsheeter, and struck Onitsuka as being a dauntless character.

Higashida informed Onitsuka that, the following day, they would begin to build a multi-purpose building that would also serve as an office, and invited him to assist with this arduous task. The idea of starting from scratch appealed to Onitsuka. The President seemed to be full of vitality and determination. Onitsuka resolved to put everything he had into establishing this company.

The next day, he and the other employees started construction, salvaging bricks from under the rubble for the building. There were not many labourers: the President, his brother, and brother-in-law, and Onitsuka. It had been some time since Onitsuka had worked so hard.

It was not long before the building, named the Kobe Culture Centre, was completed. The central hall was somewhat like a gallery. Many different activities, including lectures, exhibitions, flower arrangement classes and meetings, took place there. Through the distinguished members of the local government who gathered at the centre, Higashida became a Kobe celebrity almost overnight.

Even so, like many other business operations immediately after the war, the Higashida Company was forced to involve itself in several seemingly unrelated activities in an effort to survive the economic turmoil. In addition to managing the cultural centre, the company engaged in many ventures: buying and selling antiques, automobile repair, running a tea room, operating a beer garden for the Occupation Forces, and establishing a construction contracting firm.

Onitsuka's hard work in the company brought its own rewards. He was first made a senior manager, then an executive managing director two years later. By this time business was going well and the company had expanded to fifty employees. The higher Onitsuka advanced up the managerial ladder, however, the more aware he became of some unsavoury aspects of the company. The higher he climbed, the wider his field of vision became. What he saw was becoming more and more disappointing and unpalatable to him.

The beer hall was by far the most profitable of all the company's undertakings. Some of the beer obtained tax-free was sold on the black market for huge profits. Although he suspected the extent of the company's black market activities and its subsequent large profits, Onitsuka was unable to put exact figures to them. Those were known only to the president, who never divulged them to anyone, not even to senior executives. The lavish lifestyle of the president, however, was a fair indication of the company's success. He kept several mistresses and occasionally attempted to attract more from among the women employed by the company. Through his involvement with the female employees, he hoped to monitor the activities of his executives.

In those early postwar days, it was not uncommon for presidents of small-sized businesses to engage in activities similar to Higashida's. Onitsuka could have considered himself naïve in his attitude since these forms of moral turpitude were fairly commonplace. Nevertheless, they offended his moral upbringing. The enthusiasm he had had for the company waned; it was becoming increasingly difficult for him to hold back his feelings of disgust.

About this time, Higashida presented his plans for a sports centre to his employees. There was a 400 *tsubo* lot (about a third of an acre) available for purchase. It was suggested that this lot be bought in order to build a sports centre, including sleeping quarters for athletes and office space for various sports organizations. The concept excited Onitsuka.

The black market was flourishing and gang rule was everywhere. People were concerned only with living from day to day. Children growing up in such an environment emulated the behaviour of their elders, succumbing to all the evils around them. Many of Onitsuka's fellow soldiers had given their lives for their country, but certainly not to make it as degenerate as it was becoming. To Onitsuka this was plainly not right.

It was against this background that the concept of a sports centre was proposed. Onitsuka was enthusiastic: here was an opportunity to contribute to society in a small yet positive way. He resolved to make the idea a reality and in so doing to work so hard that his doubts about the company would be dispelled.

Onitsuka was appointed executive director of the project. As construction was about to begin, the company was faced with a problem. Owing to the strict postwar economic controls, construction materials were only distributed to those with permits. These permits were very difficult to obtain.

Onitsuka went to see his friend from his army days, Kohei Hori, who was now divisional head for health and physical education within the Hyogo prefecture Board of Education. He could possibly be of assistance in negotiations with the Ministry of Education, the government office concerned in this permit application. The men had been acquainted from the time when Onitsuka was regimental adjutant at Himeji. Hori had been the adjutant to the divisional commander and a second lieutenant. They had often seen each other through their duties, and had become close friends. After the war, through work, Onitsuka met Hori again and since then they had kept in touch.

Hori accepted Onitsuka's request for assistance willingly, and went immediately to the government office to negotiate a permit. Although reluctant at first, the authorities eventually granted permission on the grounds that Hori should be the guarantor for the company. They also added one more condition, namely that the building was not to be used for any purpose other than sport-related activities. The security of Hori's job depended upon Higashida Company's compliance with this condition. Finally, construction was permitted, and commenced.

Early in 1948, shortly before the completion of construction, Onitsuka heard a rumour that Higashida intended to sell the building. Several people, including some resident Chinese merchants, had come to view the project. It was rumoured that they were the prospective buyers. Onitsuka went to see Higashida and demanded to know the truth. Higashida's confirmation of the rumour dumbfounded Onitsuka.

Selling beer on the black market had been a profitable business, but was becoming very risky. Selling the sports centre would allow Higashida to settle his business accounts and disappear to parts unknown with the proceeds. This appeared to be his plan.

Onitsuka's dreams had been betrayed. While he had been working hard to honour his debts to his fallen comrades, his employer had been planning to make off with all the money he could lay his hands on. Onitsuka saw Higashida for what he was—a broker with a talent for making money. He was not worthy of being called an entrepreneur.

A controlled economy existed for some time after the end of the war, necessitating entry into the black market for personal and corporate survival. To keep body and soul together, people were forced to obtain food on the black market. One judge insisted, for example, because of his position, on surviving on allotted rations alone; he subsequently died of malnutrition.

For corporations, black market involvement was often equally unavoidable. A right minded entrepreneur who became involved in black market activities would only have done so to further the development of the company. Plainly, this was not Higashida's motive: he was merely a rogue out to make fast money.

Onitsuka knew he did not belong to Higashida's world. He could not accomplish his aims working under such a man. At the end of the war he had sworn to himself that he was going to live for his comrades, so that their deaths would not be wasted. He was determined to be faithful to this resolution. Onitsuka submitted his resignation. Higashida, fearing that Onitsuka would expose the company's wrongdoings once he was no longer an employee, rejected it. But Onitsuka had made up his mind. He left the company anyway, thereby forfeiting the retirement bonus due to him. But in this way the break was a clean one; he had no feelings of indebtedness or obligation. If his dreams were to be realized, Onitsuka would have to start a business of his own. He was resolute in his decision. It was now the end of 1948; he was thirty years old.

Changing Direction

The only outstanding issue was the resale of the sports centre. If it occurred, Hori's job would be in jeopardy. Accordingly, Onitsuka turned for help to Hiizuru Tsunemi, an adviser to Higashida Company and the acquaintance who had first introduced him to the company. Tsunemi was then a member of the Hyogo prefecture council—he later became chairman—and had close ties with the administration. He agreed that the best solution was to arrange for the prefecture to purchase the building if the resale could not be avoided. Approximately six months later, the prefecture bought the building and used it as a centre for social services.

Although his time as a company employee lasted only three years, Onitsuka had learned a great deal during this time. Higashida certainly had a talent for making money. In Onitsuka's opinion, however, there was very little in the organization that was worthy of the honourable title 'company'. Profits were used to satisfy the president's pleasures and there was no attempt to train the staff or to help them to achieve a sense of personal satisfaction. Higashida, once called the 'Star of Kobe Reconstruction', did as he had planned. He left Kobe, taking up residence first in Toyko and a few years later in Hokkaido.

Onitsuka's first incursion into the world of business had been without knowledge or experience. He had no predetermined management philosophy, nor even ideas about what constituted an 'enterprise'. His experience with Higashida was a sobering one. He had learned what not to do. It had also allowed him to begin formulating ideas compatible with his own moral tenets. Vague feelings that had lingered within him since the day the war ended began to shape into a resolution. He felt that he had now discovered the nature of his obligation as a war survivor: it was one of service to society. He would achieve this through business. Says Onitsuka:

> I feel indebted to Higashida. I do not mean this sarcastically in any way. If it had not been for the experience of these three years, the fuzzy feeling I had inside me would never have taken shape. Not only that, it is likely that I would have done exactly the same as Higashida in the years of business to follow. I have learned from Higashida's wrongdoing.

Onitsuka visited Kohei Hori shortly after resigning from the company. Explaining his desire to do something in the name of the country's war dead, he struck a responsive chord in his former fellow soldier. The question was 'what to do?'.

Onitsuka discussed with Hori his concern over the way the young people and the children were left to wander the streets while their parents worked all day and into the night just to feed them. He wanted to do something, however small, to furnish these young people with hopes and dreams. He envisaged providing them with jobs where he and they could work together and grow together, a business that they could turn into a success with their own hard work. He wanted to nurture the young people so that they would develop into responsible citizens, fit to lead the next generation.

Reminding Onitsuka of the adage 'a sound mind in a sound body', Hori suggested the manufacture of sports shoes as the vehicle through which Onitsuka might accomplish his aims. Through his work in physical education, Hori realized the importance of sports to health and predicted a widespread increase in their popularity as the country regained its stability. Hori's simple suggestion—that Onitsuka should make sports shoes—became the first step along the long and difficult road to eventual success for Onitsuka.

Onitsuka, like Hori, was dedicated to the promotion of sport. Both men felt that the characteristics of a good sportsman were also the characteristics of a good citizen. First, a sportsman must at all times abide by the rules of the game. In a sense, every citizen is like a sportsman in that he or she has to abide by and respect the rules, or laws, of society. Second, it is important that the spirit of fair play should dominate in achieving one's goals in sport; unfair measures should not be resorted to. Of course, some degree of 'gamesmanship' is acceptable in both sport and business. Third, the individual must try his/her best at all times. Fourth, harmony in the team always comes first in sport. Team spirit is essential: the individual must be ready to help others when necessary, and at times be prepared to sacrifice his/her own aims for those of the team. This spirit often leads to invaluable friendships. Finally, continuous training and practice are essential. The individual can aim for, and sometimes achieve, higher and greater goals in this way. All these qualities—important in developing good members of society—were, in Onitsuka's and Hori's opinion, what was needed for Japanese youth at the time.

Onitsuka recalled that Baron Pierre de Coubertin, father of the modern Olympics, was stirred to revive the Games and promote sport by the fact that the French were so badly defeated by the Germans in the Franco–Prussian War of 1870.

The young French soldiers had had no opportunity of participating in competitive athletics and sport through the French education system. Games were thought to interfere with study and were therefore prohibited. Coubertin observed that in many countries athletics and education were linked. There was a widely-held belief that competitive sport developed desirable character traits by promoting clean living, sportsmanship, mental and physical agility, and courage. Coubertin resolved to 'devote his life and modest fortune to the task of improving the youth of France through competitive sports and thus strengthen the manhood of the nation.'[1] In 1896, through Coubertin's diligent efforts, 1,503 years after the Olympics had been abolished by Roman Emperor Theodesius I— a convert to Christianity who considered the Games pagan—the first Modern Olympic Games were held in Athens.

The Americans had long recognized the value of athletic competition. Sport became an important tool in the restoration of Japan under the Occupation Forces. 'Olympic veteran [Douglas] McArthur ordered baseball competition [to be] renewed, and arranged for participation of Japanese swimmers in American meets. He used sport in a conscious effort to make sure that American values took hold at all levels of Japanese society.'[2]

Western sports had been introduced to Japan after the Meiji Restoration of 1868, but it was not until after World War I that they really took hold. Golf and baseball, in particular, became great favourites. This was without detriment to traditional Japanese activities. Sumo wrestling and martial arts such as kendo and judo were encouraged and flourished alongside the new sports. While the traditional Japanese sports were all performed barefoot, good footwear was necessary for basketball, volleyball and all the other Western sports that were gaining in popularity.

Talking with Hori, Onitsuka, for the first time in years, felt good inside. He had found the idea he had been searching for. Good footwear, Hori assured him, was the starting-point for sport. He would be providing the essential foundation. The overall shortage of goods in Japan, including shoes, made their manufacture even more desirable. But Onitsuka, knowing nothing whatever about shoemaking, questioned his ability to master the required skills. Hori reassured him. Kobe was a city of footwear, especially rubber shoes.

As an international port, Kobe was the point of entry for raw rubber and the point of export for rubber footwear to China and South-east Asia. The rubber footwear industry, begun just after World War I, utilized labour from Kobe's match industry. The latter was in decline owing to the loss of market caused by the establishment of the Swedish Match Trust. By 1921, about 70 per cent of Japan's rubber footwear was produced in the Kobe area. The great Kanto earthquake of 1923 destroyed most of the rubber footwear factories in the Tokyo area, making Kobe Japan's single major rubber footwear centre.[3]

Hori felt that Onitsuka could learn the craft of shoemaking. He knew that Onitsuka would not shy away from hard work, and Onitsuka agreed. He had always worked very hard; that was how he had progressed through school and the Army. Onitsuka's mind was made up. He would stay in Kobe and make sports shoes. Hori promised to introduce him to a few factories where he could learn the necessary skills.

Saying goodnight to Hori, Onitsuka headed home, oblivious to the clamour of the city. The cool winter wind soothed him as he ran, immersed in his thoughts, his plans and his hopes for the future. Onitsuka has always been motivated by the question, 'If I don't do it, who will do it? If I don't do it now, when can I do it?' That night he was certain of the answers to both questions.

In this way Onitsuka decided what his business would be. His company would provide the youth of Japan with the best sports footwear that could be manufactured. This objective was in accord with Onitsuka's desire to contribute to the reconstruction of Japan through its youth and to provide them with work that would enable them to grow into responsible members of society. It was this goal that enabled Onitsuka to plot his company's course and to set objectives that contributed to the realization of his dream.

Postwar Managerial Ideology

Managers of the type Onitsuka had encountered in his former employer notwithstanding—managers with an eye for their own personal gain only—there was, immediately after the war, a movement to formulate a managerial ideology appropriate to the postwar situation. It was spear-headed by a group of young, forward-looking executives disillusioned by past business leadership and ideology. In the spring of 1946, shortly after

Onitsuka moved to Kobe, about seventy such executives established the *Keizai Doyukai*, the Committee for Economic Development. Although it would be some years before Onitsuka learned of the organization's resolutions, three decades later he would become president of the Kobe chapter of the *Keizai Doyukai*.

The *Doyukai*'s pronouncements on business philosophy are, as M. Y. Yoshino points out, indicative of the major trends in ideological development in Japan for several reasons.[4] The *Doyukai*, with its membership of postwar-type professional executives, saw as its primary function the articulation of a business ideology appropriate to the postwar situation representing the viewpoint of the newly emerged managerial elite. The pronouncements of the *Doyukai* were, and continue to be, the outcome of thoughtful discussion, not only by the association's leadership but by its general membership as well. Serving as the main voice for Japan's new type of executive, the *Doyukai* has also profoundly influenced the executive's thoughts and ideologies. Today, membership has climbed to nearly nine thousand within the *Doyukai*'s thirty-five regional chapters. Takashi Ishihara, chairman of Nissan Motor, is the *Doyukai*'s director.

In early 1947, against a background of social unrest and chaotic economic conditions, the *Doyukai* put forward a proposal entitled 'Tentative View of Democratization of Business Enterprises' in which the ideology of *shusei shihon shugi*, or 'revised capitalism', was prominent. Its aims were threefold. First, it promoted the separation of ownership and control of a business concern stating that a corporation's assets, and thus its control, belonged equally to three parties: the shareholders, the management and labour. Representatives from each of the three sectors were to comprise a board that would be the corporations's ultimate policy-making and governing body. Profit was to be shared equally among the three groups. In this way the *Doyukai* rejected the traditionally dominant ownership rights of shareholders. Second, the proposal called for both labour and management to be guaranteed a minimum wage. Third, it pointed out that these principles would affect the character and role of the labour union. Instead of functioning as an external agent, the union would become an integral part of the organization's decision-making body entrusted with the task of promoting the welfare of workers through its contribution to increased efficiency and productivity.

When the 'Tentative View of Democratization of Business Enterprises' was made public, reaction on the part of business leaders was divided and ranged from strong approval through scepticism to violent opposition. Nevertheless, it provided food for thought for executives who were looking desperately for an ideological foundation suitable for the new era.

Soon after the *Doyukai*'s proposal was publicized, the worsening economic conditions in Japan caused a revision in the Occupation's economic policy and, with the subsequent deterioration in American–Soviet relations, the United States committed itself to Japan's rapid economic recovery. It was in this managerial and socio-economic climate that Onitsuka took the first formal steps towards realizing his dream for the youth of Japan.

3 | Onitsuka Corporation

Corporate Assets

It was 1949. The New Year festivities were almost over and Onitsuka began preparations for his new venture. The office was a corner of Mr and Mrs Onitsuka's living room. He accepted the offer of his adoptive father's desk, chair and telephone. That was the extent of his tangible assets. In the intangible column there was much more: the friendship of several people—even though the full value of this was yet to be appreciated.

In Japan, an individual's connections are all important, especially at the outset of a business venture. Having an acquaintance provide an introduction to a prospective business contact is not simply a polite custom; it is an integral part of Japanese business ethics. Ideally, the shokai-sha, or introducer, is someone whose status is respected or to whom the prospective business contact is already obligated. The shokai-sha is often a close friend or relative, a former schoolmate or professor, a superior in the same company, an important supplier to the company, or an officer in the company's bank. Doors are always opened to the person carrying a letter of introduction from a mutual friend or an important business person.

Later, after the introduction has been made and business dealings initiated, the shokai-sha may assume the role of chukai-sha, or mediator, to help iron out difficulties in the negotiations. Serving as a highly esteemed business go-between, the chukai-sha often plays a crucial role in determining the outcome of the negotiations.[1]

Acting as shokai-sha, Hori helped Onitsuka obtain a delivery job. Items for delivery included children's shoes and teaching materials for schools in the area. The job was to provide a necessary source of income as Onitsuka made preparations for his new business. First, he applied for a permit to operate as a wholesale distributor. This was required in order to carry out business in the controlled economy. At this time production materials were supplied by government under a strict quota system. Hori assisted Onitsuka in obtaining the requisite permit to receive the government allowance of shoe materials. Onitsuka would take these materials to the King Rubber Factory to have them made into shoes for school-children. He would then fill the orders he had earlier received from the prefectural schools. A little later Onitsuka also became the supplier of rubber footwear to the fire department, the police department, and other government offices. In addition, he did some business in bicycle tyres and tubes.

Two men had joined Onitsuka in his business by this time. Toshiki Hagiwara had been a subordinate of Onitsuka's in the Army. A judo instructor, he left the company less than a year later to become involved in the distribution of *judo-gi*, or judo uniforms. The other employee was Yoshiji Shimonashi. When the war ended Shimonashi was stationed at the Ibusuki Air Force Base. After he returned to Kobe he worked for Amagasaki Steel Corporation for four years until the friendship between his mother and Mrs Onitsuka led to his joining Onitsuka's company.

Recalling New Year's Eve 1950, Shimonashi says:

Mr Onitsuka and I (I was then the only employee) worked until midnight. Talking afterwards about the future of the company, Mr Onitsuka said, 'This year I want to strive for five times our current monthly sales.' His dream and his fighting spirit were contagious. I shared his resolve and soon the goal was reached.

Shimonashi stayed with the company and played an important role in its development until he became ill in the early 1970s. Subsequently, he retired and went to work in his family's tobacco shop.

Onitsuka felt a great responsibiity to live up to his ideals of what an employer should be like. He recognized that it was so much easier to criticize other people than to do well oneself.

Onitsuka acknowledges 29 May 1949, his thirty-first birthday, as the date of Onitsuka Corporation's inception. On 1 September 1949 it was registered as an incorporated company, having two employees and 300,000 yen capital, money which Onitsuka had borrowed from the Kobe Bank in order to register the company. Onitsuka felt it was important to do things properly from the start. This business was not for his own profit: incorporating it reflected that firm resolution. It was from this humble beginning that ASICS Corporation, one of the world's foremost sporting goods manufacturers, evolved.

The façade had been established but the biggest concern was financing. Onitsuka was not apprehensive about the income from sales. This was more or less guaranteed since the company was dealing with rationed goods in the controlled economy. The greatest problem was working capital. He had started with borrowed money which he had subsequently returned. Now he had no choice but to negotiate with the vendors and wholesalers so that he could pay for the goods as the finished products were sold. In some cases this was not possible as the suppliers, too, needed working capital. Then sufficient money had to be collected to enable prepayment of the order. Onitsuka would sometimes seek help from his clients—the schools and the police department—and ask them for payment in advance, so that he would have enough cash to make advance payment to the materials suppliers. In one way or another, he managed to survive through many such tight spots.

Fortunately for Onitsuka, his adoptive mother had personal contacts within the police department. She had been president of the local branch of a national women's organization which, among other things, offered their services to the country by looking after the homes of police officers while they were away on active service. Through the trust that Onitsuka's clients had in his adoptive mother and in Hori, Onitsuka was able to gain their confidence and arrange to receive their money before it was due. Within the Japanese business system, so dependent upon go-betweens, this trust is never offered lightly to just anyone requesting favours.

Rising to the Challenge

Onitsuka had not forgotten his dream of manufacturing sports shoes. As well as working as a wholesale distributor, he was also learning manufacturing skills at the Yoshikawa Rubber Factory, a factory that made canvas shoes. It was essential that he learn everything properly. His dream was to make sports shoes of the very best quality. Yet even learning the basics was not easy. As he struggled to construct shoes, he felt the contemptuous glances of the female factory employees working alongside him. Was this really the president of a shoe company? Onitsuka's first shoes were clumsy specimens indeed!

What kind of sports shoes should he make? Onitsuka had not yet decided. Most of the shoes that were available were what were colloquially referred to as 'campus shoes'. They were similar to tennis shoes. Basketball shoes, however, were in demand and very hard to come by. Basketball was invented in 1891 by a Canadian, Dr James A. Naismith, while he was an instructor at the International YMCA Training School at Springfield, Mass., now Springfield College. In 1908, it was introduced to Japan by Heizo Omori, a graduate of the YMCA Training School. Immediately popular there and elsewhere in the world, by the outbreak of World War II it was played in seventy-five countries.

After the war, basketball shoes were available in Japan only as commodity items of the American Army for the soldiers of the Occupation Forces. The manufacturing of these shoes was considered to be very difficult. They required strong reinforcement against abrasion and for movement in all directions. Also, they had to provide strong ankle and lateral support and have good traction for slippery courts.

Reasoning that it would not make much difference where he started, Onitsuka settled on basketball shoes. As a complete novice, he would find everything difficult. If he started with something challenging, it would make things much easier when he went on to other efforts. Torao Yoshikawa, president of the Yoshikawa Rubber Factory, expressed some concern over his decision, pointing out the difficulty of the undertaking, but Onitsuka was not deterred.

Greater encouragement came from Yukio Matsumoto, coach of the girls' basketball team at Kobe Senior High School and chairman of the Board of Directors of the Basketball Federation of Hyogo prefecture. Matsumoto's friendship was a legacy of Onitsuka's days with the Higashida Company during the construction of the sports centre. Now, he offered to be of whatever assistance he could. Matsumoto was one of the leading figures in basketball in Japan. He had translated American books on basketball into Japanese and had even devised new strategies and formations for the game. He is another friend to whom Onitsuka is greatly indebted.

The controlled economy still presented a problem. One could not make and sell as one wished. Production materials were scarce and often of poor quality and the distribution channels and prices were controlled. Onitsuka decided, however, to make a few trial items that could be evaluated by Matsumoto.

At any time Onitsuka could have gone to the black market. Many had been successful with canvas shoes, obtaining the materials illegally and selling the finished products on the black market or obtaining the materials through regulated channels and then selling a portion of the 'adjusted' output unlawfully. Onitsuka's recollection of his experience with the Higashida Company was sufficient to rapidly dissuade him from this course. He knew that the controls would eventually be lifted. There was still a great deal of preparation to be done before that time.

Both the Japanese economy and Onitsuka's business were on the eve of a turnaround. When the controls were finally lifted in April 1950, he saw many black market profiteers fall to their ruin. If he had succumbed to the temptation of the black market, he would most likely have had to pay dearly in the long run.

The removal of the economic controls heralded the return of the free economy and the emergence of a viable mass consumer market. Onitsuka, not wasting a moment, made a bee-line for the wholesalers, sample basketball shoes that he had made at the Yoshikawa Rubber Factory in hand, hoping to obtain orders.

On arriving at the first of his potential customers in the Yodoyabashi district of Osaka, he was confronted by a young apprentice packing goods in front of the warehouse. He asked to see the head clerk but was flatly refused. No amount of coaxing would change the young man's mind. Surprised by Onitsuka's strange name (*oni* means 'ogre' or 'demon' and *tsuka* means 'marker')—a name he had never heard before—the apprentice even questioned Onitsuka's nationality.

Onitsuka was furious. To be treated like that—he who used to be a deputy regimental commander and an instructor of 1,500 men. Then he realized how ridiculous it was for him to take offence. Those things were of little consequence now, and nothing could be gained by such behaviour; he was not there to argue. Slowly he regained his composure and set off to the next wholesaler.

He went from one to another, the scene repeating itself time and again. Try as he might, he could not get beyond the apprentice to see the head clerk. Even though he was repeatedly rejected by the wholesalers, he continued his efforts day after day, believing that product sales were possible only through the established distribution channels in which wholesalers played a very important role.

At that time, the sports shoe market in Japan was dominated by major corporations such as Nihon Rubber, Tsukiboshi Rubber, Kokoku Chemicals and Sekaicho Rubber, companies with many thousands of employees. There were numerous small rubber companies as well. Their existence was facilitated by the ease with which the technology could be adopted and the necessity of small-batch production to accommodate a wide variety of consumer needs. Being one among so many companies was obstacle enough; in Onitsuka's case it was compounded by a lack of technology, money and a product with a competitive edge. His position seemed futile. Nevertheless, his resolve had in no way diminished.

In the early 1950s, Japan was still in what has been termed 'the premarketing phase'. During the period from 1946 to 1953, the emphasis was on the creation of sufficient supplies of products to meet basic consumer needs. This preceded the 'marketing awareness phase' (1953–1964) which saw the development of marketing as an academic discipline and comprehensive practice. There was not even a term for 'marketing' in the Japanese language. In 1953, Tsuyoshi Hamano, former executive vice-president of Toshiba Corporation, published the first Japanese marketing book, entitled *Marketing*; subsequently the term was adopted into the Japanese language. It was not until 1955 and 1957, respectively, that the Japan Productivity Centre and the Japan Marketing Association, organizations important to the development of marketing, were established.[2]

In 1950, Onitsuka was on his own struggling along by trial and error and determination. What, he wondered, must he do to open the door to the market potential of his product?

Strategy for the Novice

Onitsuka had every confidence in his product. His immediate problem was to get people to look at it. Then it dawned on him—the athletes themselves! They were, after all, the ones who ultimately had to wear the shoes.

Accordingly, Onitsuka decided to approach the athletes rather than the wholesale dealers. Explaining this decision, he says:

> Those who are established and well-financed approach the market from upstream; they allow their products to flow down from the wholesalers to the consumers. My mistake was that I attempted to do this without the necessary prerequisites. I had to approach the market from the other end. I was determined to design and make shoes that the athletes would demand above all others. The wholesalers would then ignore my shoes at their peril.

Once he had decided, Onitsuka and his employees set to work immediately. This was the advantage of being a small business. To begin with, Onitsuka distinguished two ways of approaching the athletes, namely the 'top strategy' and the 'base strategy'. The former involved coming into contact with prominent athletes and coaches, to whom he would offer his products and obtain advice and criticism in return. Further improvement and development of the shoes would then be based on their opinions. In the 'top strategy' approach, top athletes served as a reference group. Their influence over the purchasing behaviour of lower ranking athletes was great. In contrast, the 'base strategy' consisted of selling the products to students involved in the sport. Onitsuka would travel around the country visiting schools as well as establishing ties with the local retail stores through which the students could purchase the shoes.

Onitsuka had been making shoes and improving them, with Matsumoto's suggestions and advice, since the days of the controlled economy. Not knowing anything about basketball, he spent several afternoons visiting schools and observing student basketball games, learning the rules and the footwork involved in playing the game. He continued to make further improvements in the shoes with Matsumoto's recommendations: how the shoes could be made to stand up to the sudden stops and starts, or how the soles could be made to prevent slipping. Yet there remained so much to look into.

Whenever there was a big event, such as the National Athletic Meet, the Japanese National Championships, an Inter-College Meet, or an Inter-High School meet, Onitsuka attempted to be there. Although Onitsuka was not a well-known name in sports shoes, the athletes were generally more interested in how the product handled on the basketball court than in the corporate name. They had few reservations about using a relatively unknown brand. If athletes could be persuaded to use the footwear, others might follow suit. Sports shoes were, after all, made not for the wholesalers but for the athletes.

Onitsuka sought their help in improving the shoes: which facets of his shoes met their needs and which did not and why; and how did his shoes compare with those of his competitors? He would supply the athletes with shoes in return for their honest opinions about their quality and performance. Suggestions for improvement would be incorporated into the next shoes produced and the results delivered to the athletes with a request for further recommendations.

In the long run, Onitsuka's close contact with the consumer through personal selling was of greater benefit than immediate acceptance by the established distribution system would have been. In those days, there were no other manufacturers who approached the athletes directly as Onitsuka did. He knew that athletes were looking for good quality shoes. This was one way of providing them. His method had the additional advantage of making the customer feel like 'one in a million'—a tradition Onitsuka maintains today. In a year or so, 'Onitsuka, the shoe salesman' had become an attraction. Many athletes looked forward to his visits, wondering what he would bring and how he had solved earlier problems.

They showed considerable interest in the products of a company determined to 'market' rather than to 'sell', that is, a company focusing on the question 'What does the customer want to buy?' rather than on 'What does the company want to sell?' The fact that Onitsuka was able to ask this question and answer it correctly contributed to the corporation's growth and distinguished it from those companies dependent upon the rising tide of the economy or of the industry for their development.

The products that were developed had to be accepted and bought by the market at the 'base', however, if the business was to succeed. Here, too, Matsumoto was a great help. A letter of introduction by Matsumoto was an invaluable token of trust for an anonymous shoe salesman visiting local schools and universities. Onitsuka set out with this letter in one hand and his basketball shoes in the other. His goal was to establish contacts with high schools, universities and retailers throughout the country. Initially, in order to minimize travel time and costs, he concentrated his efforts on those cities where the semi-express trains stopped.

On the Road

Onitsuka would be away for a week at a time, visiting as many as ten cities. On his return he would fill the orders he had received, work on the suggested improvements, deal with the finances, and attend to any other matters of business that might have arisen during his absence. Then he would set off again, without a break; Sundays and holidays were working days.

The foremost problem facing him was a shortage of funds not only for investment purposes but also to maintain an adequate base of working capital for day-to-day operations. The company had negotiated a small loan from the Kobe Bank but, as it expanded and more capital was required, its assets were insufficient to serve as collateral against a larger loan. The bank requested that the company apply for a guarantee from the prefectural Credit Guarantee Association.[3] Under the auspices of the prefectural government, this association evaluated the credit strength of small and medium-sized businesses for which, without the association's guarantee, it would have been difficult to secure a bank loan. Onitsuka complied with this request and, in accordance with the specifications of the guarantee, received a second loan.

Even so, Onitsuka had little money for his trips. He would take with him barely enough for transport, food and postage. The latter was critical as he would send all orders to the office by express mail as soon as he obtained them. The office would then contact the subcontract factory and production would begin immediately.

There was no extra money available, not even for accommodation. If a trip lasted longer than a week, Onitsuka might spend one or possibly two nights in a cheap hotel; otherwise he enjoyed the comfort of a railroad station bench in the winter or on rainy days. In the summer, he had the luxury of a park. He learned to defy the incursion of mosquitoes by sleeping with a cloth over his head and gloves on his hands. Despite the stifling heat, such was his exhaustion that he had little difficulty falling asleep for three or four hours at a time. Nevertheless, asleep or awake he would worry constantly about whether the company would be able to pay today's bills and tomorrow's. Onitsuka longed for a little money.

Hiroo Kaneda, a classmate of Onitsuka's at Tottori Ichichu Middle School and presently the president of the *Shinnihonkai Shinbun* (Shinnihonkai Newspaper) in Tottori, remembers running into Onitsuka in the Hiroshima railway station. Kaneda says:

> I was so surprised at his appearance. When I had last seen Onitsuka, he was working for the Higashida Company. At that time he was very well dressed; he looked like a promising young executive. In Hiroshima, he was shabbily attired and carried a rucksack filled with shoes. He told me he intended to spend the night in the station. I thought that times were very hard for him.

When it was hard, Onitsuka thought of his days in the Army. Compared to those days the present was far better. The fighting spirit he had acquired through his military training was a resource upon which he could capitalize. He had learned to set a goal, achieve it and then, no matter how small the results, to build on those results—to set a new objective and achieve it. No price was too high to pay to bring to fruition his dream of becoming a manufacturer of quality sports shoes. Besides, he was not alone on the railway benches or in the parks. All over Japan people were in dire straits, toiling relentlessly to eke out a meagre existence. The outbreak of the Korean War in 1950 brought about a gradual improvement in the Japanese economy—especially in military related industries—but the sports shoe industry felt no direct benefits.

Onitsuka would buy return or 'rover' tickets for travel to and from Kobe. This meant that, no matter what happened, he was always able to return home. To save time, he used the night trains. They were always overloaded in those days. Many among the vast number of passengers carried large bundles of luggage with them. Frequently, a traveller had to climb in through a window, and was suspended among peoples' heads for the entire night. Onitsuka, however, found a way to overcome this problem. Having become an experienced train traveller, he had learnt a few tricks. One was his discovery of a secret sleeping place in the crowded trains. At that time, there were two conductor's compartments on the trains—one at the rear, the other in the mid-section. He found that the latter was rarely used and had an excellent shelf sufficient for one person to stretch out on.

One evening, on the way to Kyushu, Onitsuka got on a crowded night train as usual. Seeing that his sleeping place was unoccupied, he quickly climbed onto the shelf and looked at all the people below him packed like sardines; it was like travelling in a special sleeping compartment. Very pleased with himself, he fell fast asleep.

In the morning, he woke up just before Shimonoseki, the last city on Honshu before crossing the Kanmon Channel to Kyushu. Having slept well, he felt refreshed. Nevertheless, he felt that something was definitely wrong. Onitsuka looked around, and to his great surprise found the conductor beneath him. He looked behind and realized that the mid-section had now become the rear of the train. The coaches must have been dropped off somewhere, perhaps Hiroshima. Luckily, the conductor had not noticed him. Onitsuka held his breath and waited quietly until the train arrived at Shimonoseki. As the conductor stepped off onto the platform, Onitsuka scurried down from the shelf and crept into the next car.

Immediately on arriving at his destination, Onitsuka would go to the post office to look up the names and locations of local sporting goods stores in the telephone book—a time-consuming task since these retailers did not merit a separate section in the Yellow Pages. Onitsuka had to search through the large miscellaneous section of the directory to find them. He would write down several names, then go to the police box to ask directions. In this way, he was able to avoid the trouble and expense of buying maps. Also, most Japanese streets do not have names; numbers are assigned to areas and within each area several buildings may have identical numbers. Asking directions at the local police boxes which are conveniently located throughout Japanese cities and towns is therefore the most effective method of finding one's way around. Onitsuka would rent a bicycle from a shop near the station and ride off, following the little maps he had drawn for himself with police assistance.

He would find the sporting goods stores and show them his products. Typically, he was mistaken at first glance for a door-to-door shoe salesman. Even if he were able to describe his product, this did not mean very much since retailers were wary about buying from some wandering salesman who appeared out of the blue. There were some who listened to Onitsuka's explanations with interest but, on the whole, he was relatively unsuccessful.

In the afternoons, Onitsuka would visit the local schools, usually choosing the ones with strong basketball teams. He would show Matsumoto's letter of introduction, which seemed to open all doors where schools were concerned. Onitsuka presented his products to the coaches and explained how they had been made. He would ask them to try out the shoes and arranged to have samples sent from Kobe immediately. The next time he called on them he would ask for their opinions, for their suggestions for improvements. On the following visit he would bring a pair of shoes with the requested alterations.

By this method, Onitsuka was able to gain the support of many schools, but he did not sell to them directly. Instead, he asked each school to introduce him to a nearby sporting goods store and arranged to do business through them. This made it easier for both the athletes and for Onitsuka. The shoes were available for them when needed and sales and collections could be planned on a regular basis. An additional advantage was that the money could be available to the company sooner. This was a great help since the company was having a difficult time with cash flow.

Onitsuka's marketing strategy led to the gradual expansion of a network of stores carrying his products. This was eventually to lead to the 'against the flow' phenomenon: from the athletes to the retailers, from the retailers to the wholesalers, from the wholesalers to Onitsuka's company. Onitsuka could not have imagined that it would turn out this way. He had resorted to this method because it was the only option open to a novice.

Riichi Shimoda of Kinko Sports, one of the early retail stores to do business with Onitsuka, recalls:

The first time I met Mr Onitsuka was about 1950. The country was still in a highly confused state. The only sports equipment my store had was some low quality baseball gear. The basketballs and shoes came via the Occupation Forces. Such was the condition of the sporting goods industry.

In the midst of this, Mr Onitsuka appeared carrying some boxes and telling me he had developed some new basketball shoes. As far as I was concerned, at that time people only dreamed about developing new products. I was rather skeptical, to say the least. I still recall vividly the plain shoe box Mr Onitsuka, full of confidence, thrust at me. As he made his detailed presentation, it became obvious to me that this man had indeed spent much time in the development of these shoes. He further told me that he was continually improving his product through his contact with members of the Basketball Federation and with athletes and coaches. He appeared to be a man of remarkable energy, travelling around the country personally promoting his shoes. I could not help admiring him.

Since our first meeting, there have been many Onitsuka products and such is my respect for his integrity that I have never hestitated to accept them. His name on the product is sufficient for me.

Nevertheless, in 1950 Onitsuka could not have imagined his future success. His existence, especially on the road, was a spartan one with one hardship following upon another. A raw day at the end of January remains etched in his memory.

Onitsuka had been through Kyushu and Shikoku and had arrived in Onomichi, across the Inland Sea from the island of Shikoku. Many retail stores remained open until ten or eleven o'clock at night. It was almost 8.00 p.m. when he left the last shop on his fifth day on the road. The next day he planned to go to Fukuyama, Kurashiki, Okayama, Himeji and then return to Kobe by evening. However, he had only 100 yen left.

Onitsuka arrived at the railroad station intending to spend the night there, but it was bitterly cold. The prospect was unbearable: his body had absorbed all the punishment it could take from the long hours, the cold nights, and the lack of sleep. Staying at an inn was out of the question—it would cost between 200 and 300 yen, at least. Also, he had not eaten all day and he was starving. He headed for a noodle shop close to the station. The cost of a bowl of noodles was 60 yen. He stood there trying to decide whether food or hospitable accommodation was the priority for him. He determined that the latter was paramount. After searching unsuccessfully for a room for a full half hour, he noticed a red lantern glowing at the far end of a side street. This was the familiar emblem of a cheap boarding house. He hurried in out of the cold.

Most of the people already there were travelling salesmen, much like himself. There were about twenty of them, all sleeping in their clothes in a large room. Relieved at having found somewhere warm to stay, Onitsuka lay down on the floor for the night. There was no bedding. He was so famished he could not sleep. He got up and stepped out into the cold night in search of something to eat. The accommodation had cost 30 yen, leaving him 70 yen to tide him over until he returned home the following night. He was still unhappy about the prospect of spending 60 yen on the noodles: this would leave him only 10 yen, which would not get him very far. Just then, he heard the whistle of the baked sweet-potato trolley.

Japan, in the years immediately following the war, has been described as a land of sweet-potato eaters: this dietary staple kept people going as they struggled to recover from the wartime devastation.[4] Onitsuka bought three thin slices of sweet potato, for 30 yen, and ran back to the inn with his warm food wrapped in a newspaper. He asked for some hot water from the kettle on the stove, and washed down the sweet potatoes. Finally he felt satisfied; he dropped off to sleep, hugging his knees. Forty yen remained for the next day.

It was well after midnight when Onitsuka returned home on the following day, having visited the four cities. The last 40 yen was spent on the bus fare. He had had nothing all day except the tea that was served to him at the retail stores he had visited.

Marriage Arranged

Onitsuka repeated his visits to local stores and his list of clients grew steadily. Business was finally beginning to progress. It was during this period that his adoptive father, who suffered from cataracts, began to lose his sight rapidly and to worry about the future. In particular, he was concerned about when Onitsuka planned to marry. This was not the first time Onitsuka's adoptive father had broached the subject but now, with his impending loss of eyesight, he pressed Onitsuka to consider the benefits of marriage and children. Somewhat reluctantly, perhaps from a sense of obedience, Onitsuka began to consider matrimony. Aware that his future wife, in the early years at least, would live under the same roof as his adoptive parents and would shoulder the major responsibility for their physical care, Onitsuka decided that he would ask his adoptive parents to find a woman with whom they were compatible.[5] As they were not related to him by blood, perhaps a member of either of their families would be a good choice. If he liked the woman they selected, he would consider marriage. Onitsuka made it clear to his adoptive parents that they were to be responsible for creating a congenial atmosphere in which his bride would feel welcome and accepted.

Before long, Onitsuka's adoptive father had found a likely spouse for him among some distant relatives living near his home town of Fukuoka on Kyushu Island. The elderly gentleman suggested that they visit the prospective bride. Onitsuka, however, considered a special trip unnecessary. It would be sufficient to call on her the next time he travelled to the Fukuoka area on business. Reluctantly, his adoptive father agreed.

Before long Onitsuka had to visit Fukuoka and the *o-miai*, or marriage meeting, was arranged. As this was going to be their first meeting, Onitsuka felt he should be dressed appropriately. A good pair of shoes would help. The man at the local shoe store showed him a pair that had been specially ordered for an American, but never purchased. They were red and white and of the very best quality. This American must have been a small man, however, since the shoes fitted Onitsuka's feet perfectly. The retailer offered to let Onitsuka have the shoes at cost—5,000 yen, reduced from 7,000. Given that Onitsuka's monthly pay at that time was under 10,000 yen, they were rather an expensive luxury for him. But they would last a lifetime. He made the purchase and embarked on his trip to Kyushu.

It was past eleven o'clock when he left the last store in Kurume city and it was raining. Onitsuka was planning to take the first train to Kumamoto in the morning. As usual, he decided to sleep on a bench in the station. After eating at the cafeteria near the station, he went to find a bench. He lay down with his shoes on. Although he was hesitant to take them off, he realized that they might interfere with other people using the bench. Accordingly, he removed them and chose to push them far under the bench instead of putting them in his carrying bag.

Onitsuka woke up at about one o'clock. Worried about his shoes, he looked under the bench. The shoes were there. Relieved, he went back to sleep. At half past four the ticketing for the first train started. Onitsuka was woken by voices. He got up and went to put his shoes on. They were not there. His new shoes had disappeared—they had been stolen.

Onitsuka had lost a pair of shoes worth 5,000 yen in order to save 200 or 300 yen on an inn or a hotel. He did not know whether to weep or rage. Outside it was still dark. It was too early for the stores to be open, so he could not buy another pair of shoes. He still had to travel to Kumamoto, Oita, Miyazaki and Kagoshima; he could hardly go barefoot. Thinking he could perhaps borrow an old pair of slippers from the station master, he picked up his bags and started for the office. Suddenly it dawned on him— he was a shoe salesman and his bags contained the wares of his business: shoes. In his consternation he had completely forgotten.

The bags were full of basketball shoes, newly developed volleyball shoes, and training shoes. In order to avoid excess weight, he invariably carried only one shoe out of a pair. When a prospective customer expressed interest in particular shoes, Onitsuka would arrange for sample pairs to be sent for trial. Consequently, he had to wear an attacker volleyball shoe on his right foot and a training shoe on his left. Suitably shod, happy at the usefulness of being a shoe salesman, and now feeling positive about life, he climbed aboard the train.

It was about eight o'clock in the morning when the train pulled into Kumamoto station. Onitsuka made his way to the Taiikudo sporting goods store. Introducing himself, he explained that his company had recently developed a new volleyball shoe.

Various functions are required of volleyball shoes. In Japan at that time, nine-man play was the norm, as opposed to six-man play today. Therefore, the shoes were designed according to the player's positions. For those in the front row, the attackers, the shoes had to withstand the shock of jumping and landing. For those in the back, the defence, it was important that the shoes allowed agility in lateral movement.

When the retailer asked to see the shoes, Onitsuka pointed to his feet. He was too embarrassed to say that he had had his shoes stolen the night before while sleeping on a bench in order to economize. Instead he said that he found the volleyball shoes very comfortable.

The retailer was impressed. He had encountered many salesmen but Onitsuka was the first to come wearing the samples. Not knowing what to say when the retailer praised his dedication, Onitsuka remained silent as he showed him the shoes, putting out each foot alternately. When the retailer ordered a dozen pairs of shoes Onitsuka was astonished. He could barely suppress his excitement. Losing his shoes was proving to be a lucky disaster.

Having succeeded so well, Onitsuka continued with the same method in Oita, Miyazaki and Kagoshima. Everywhere he went the reaction was favourable. Retailer after retailer expressed the desire to do business with him. Things were going well.

Onitsuka bought a pair of leather shoes for 2,000 yen in Hakata, and went to meet his prospective bride, Tsune Tominaga. His adoptive parents were present for the occasion. The meeting place was Susenji village in Fukuoka prefecture. This village was located next to the village where Onitsuka's adoptive father had grown up. Tsune's father owned the general store there. That store carried grocery staples, wooden clogs, umbrellas, brooms, agricultural tools and so on.

Eleven years his junior, Tsune had a sturdy build, looked healthy, and was quite beautiful. Onitsuka was pleased. He could see no reason not to proceed with the marriage plans. Not only had his business gone well, but also, this lovely woman was going to be his wife   He was very happy.

Onitsuka and Tsune took the bus to the Shinto shrine at Hakozaki in Hakata, prayed, and then sat on the nearby beach and talked. Looking out at the Sea of Genkai, she confided that her preference was for someone who had his own business. This was because she was familiar with business ownership through assisting her father in the family store. It was easier for her to identify with such an individual. Onitsuka was delighted. Tsune, he was sure, would understand and support his dedication to his business. Recalls Onitsuka, 'I felt as wonderful as the blue sky of April that stretched over our heads'.

4 | Corporate and Personal Survival

Work is Everything

In October 1951, Kihachiro Onitsuka married Tsune Tominaga in Hakata. They went to Beppu on a combined honeymoon/business trip and then crossed the Inland Sea on the *Sumire-maru* to return to Kobe. Remnants of Japan's wartime defeat were everywhere; against such a background, the overnight boat trip seemed luxurious. Notwithstanding the fact that it was their honeymoon, they had little privacy on the ferry. The only sleeping accommodation was on the floor in one large room shared by all the passengers. 'I remember', recalls Tsune Onitsuka, 'that from our spot on the floor all we could see was a stairway'.

When they arrived in Kobe, Onitsuka led the way through the narrow streets to his adoptive parents' house, which also served as an office. Located in a downtown, prewar residential district, the house was inaccessible by car and the area unsuitable for business activities. Mrs Onitsuka recalls:

> It was so different from what I had imagined it would be like. So much smaller. It was nothing like the homes and offices of the wholesalers in Hakata with whom I had done quite a bit of business on behalf of my father. I really thought I had been tricked. I had to remind myself that I would much rather be married to a man with his own business than to a company employee.

Marriage did not change Onitsuka's way of life. His work pattern did not alter. He would be away two weeks out of four, expanding his sales network. When at home, he would spend many late nights with Yoshikawa, president of the subcontract factory, reviewing the suggestions made during his most recent trip. They would examine various ways of designing and constructing their products. Usually, Onitsuka continued working at home.

In almost every Japanese home there is a *butsudan*, a Buddhist family altar, and/or a *kamidana*, or a family Shinto shrine, in front of which family members pray daily for good luck and divine protection. The *butsudan* houses a photograph of each deceased relative and his *ihai*, or memorial tablet, upon which is inscribed his *kaimyo*, the Buddhist name given to the deceased at the time of death by the priest of the temple that looks after the family cemetery. Many families burn incense and candles daily in the *butsudan*. Onitsuka would melt the wax of the candles from the Buddhist altar onto a wooden last and shape it. Then, scrutinizing his own feet and using them as a model, he would carve and reshape the last, working into the early hours of the morning.

It is the last which gives the shoe its shape and size. Today, lasts are made from wood, aluminium or, most often, high-density polyethylene. Every shoe is constructed over a last, a sized form shaped like the shoe to be made on it. The fit and durability of the shoe are determined by both the shape of the last and the methods used for constructing the shoe around it. Traditionally, lasts have been either straight or curved.

Whether he realized it or not at the time, Onitsuka was attempting, with the candle wax, to design a semi-curved last. This kind of last has recently gained popularity with a number of sports shoe manufacturers because it allows for a good blend of stability and performance.

Packing and shipping the orders was not as simple as it might seem. The goods, on being delivered to the company office from the sub-contractor, would be sorted according to customer requirement. Then they were packaged into apple crates purchased from a nearby fruit store. This packing operation usually took place at night, often until one or two o'clock in the morning so that the shoes could be shipped to the customers on the first train of the day. The neighbours often complained about the noise of hammering. In order to muffle the noise, the hammering was done under pieces of cloth or blankets.

Inevitably, Onitsuka would ask the dozen or so people whom he employed at the time to stay and finish the work. They would agree, but as the evening drew on they would begin to get restless. Although Onitsuka would come close to telling them that they could go home, he could never bring himself to do so as long as there was work to be completed. He simply could not tell them to leave and, for their part, the employees would never ask. This would go on until nearly eleven o'clock when finally someone would remind Onitsuka that they had to leave or they would miss the last train.

Shimonashi and Onitsuka would continue working after the others had left until Shimonashi had to leave for home which was a kilometre's walk away. Once everyone had gone, Onitsuka would lie down on the sofa in the one-roomed building that served as both office and warehouse. About 70 square metres, this building was built on the empty lot next to his adoptive parents' house.

The employees remember their early days with the company. Shozo

Isohata who joined the company in 1953 and is now manager of administrative affairs recalls:

> I saw a 'wanted ad' which included among its requirements 'interested in sports.' I played table tennis. My Japanese literature teacher who was responsible for the high school basketball club was a close friend of Mr Onitsuka. He told me that it was a company with prospects and recommended that I apply. I was hired and began work immediately. I found myself working late every day. Everyone would stay until the last train, and then only just make it in time. The staff had to run from the office to the station to catch the train. I lived fairly close so I would be given the task of clearing up after they had left. We were a lively bunch in those days and strangely enough I do not remember finding it particularly hard.

Hideo Takemoto who joined the company a year earlier and is now senior executive and general manager of factory operations at Kohaku Rubber Company, a subcontract factory of ASICS, remembers:

> My teacher was a friend of Mr Onitsuka from their army days and suggested I apply. I was interviewed and was told to start the following morning. On the first day, I was allowed to leave at the official time of five o'clock. That was the first and last time that happened. From then on I worked until the last train.

Tokio Sakaguchi who joined the company in 1954 and now heads product development says:

> I had just come to Kobe from Tottori. On my first day, at about five o'clock, we were served noodles for supper. I assumed that the day's work was over. I was astonished, however, by the long hours of work after supper. When the company acquired its own production facilities, even those working at the factory would come to the office in the evening and help with packaging until after midnight. Then we'd return home, visit the public bath, and do the laundry to be ready to start work again at eight o'clock in the morning. I soon learned that conditions were no worse at Onitsuka Corporation than anywhere else. Everyone worked extremely hard, to the point where some succumbed to tuberculosis, the dreaded killer of the time.

Masaru Yato, acting head of ASICS' Overseas Operation Division, recalls:

> We used to complain among ourselves about working conditions but rarely would our griping go beyond the company's walls. Japan had new postwar labour laws but there was scant evidence of their

application in the early days of Onitsuka Corporation. We were a very young company and there was no one but us to do the work. But we were young too and energetic. Sometimes, after we finished work at one or two in the morning, we would go out drinking until four or five (Kobe was an 'all night' city in those days) and report for the next day's work having never been to sleep. I think almost all of ASICS' executives who started out with Onitsuka Corporation experienced this kind of life. It wasn't just the hard work alone that caused some of us to succumb to tuberculosis. I contracted the disease but was one of the fortunate ones who recovered after six months at home.

Onitsuka wore all hats in the company. As well as being in charge of research and development, production, sales and shipping, he was also responsible for all the other facets of the business, including personnel, tax and cash flow planning, and accounting. Accounting gave him considerable cause for concern. He could not find a suitable person to assist with the bookkeeping. He could have asked his wife to look after the books, but he had decided that his family was not to be involved in the financial end of the business. The lack of clear demarcation between family and business had been a factor in his resignation from the Higashida Company. He was determined that he would define the difference clearly and adhere to it as a matter of principle. He has done so consistently. It was for this reason that he had incorporated the business into a limited company as early as 1949.

Onitsuka had also decided to ask his adoptive parents not to touch the company funds. It was a common practice at that time, existing from prewar days, for the president and his family to 'borrow' money from company funds for their private use. This was what Onitsuka's adoptive parents were used to.

Onitsuka was somewhat uncomfortable about this request because his adoptive parents had provided him with an office and a desk and therefore could technically be described as 'investors'. They could borrow from the company and not be conscious of doing anything wrong. Wanting to maintain his principles and not embarrass his adoptive parents or compromise himself, he secured the agreement of his staff to pay his adoptive father a salary of 40,000 yen a month as a nominal director of the company. This sum was four times his own salary.

He explained to his adoptive father that he would give him 40,000 yen a month to spend as he wished, and asked for his word that he would not become involved in the accounts of the company under any circumstances. The employees who handled the cash were very young—just out of school. If asked for a thousand yen or so, they would not know how to refuse. He entreated his adoptive father to respect his wishes in the matter.

The way in which a person handles his money often reflects his moral qualities. Regardless of how honourable he may be in other aspects, if he is not honest with money, he will not be respected as an ethical manager. By keeping his books clean and straight, and by drawing a clear line between his family—'the private'—and his business—'the public'—Onitsuka felt he would be able to show his employees that Onitsuka Corporation was not geared towards aggrandizing the prosperity of Onitsuka's own family.

Onitsuka and Tsune had little time to enjoy each other's company as husband and wife. Onitsuka went home to sleep only rarely. Onitsuka says:

> Thinking back on it now, it was an awful life I led. Yet, at the time, I was not able to stand back and contemplate on the quality of my life. I felt only the tremendous pressure to get the business going. I had my employees to think of and a wife and adoptive parents to support.

Fortunately, there was work to be done. Good sports shoes were not yet available in the country. Moreover, the customers must have appreciated Onitsuka's effort and dedication. These qualities shone through in his practice of incorporating the suggestions offered by the top specialists in the field and in the enthusiasm of each and every one of his employees towards their work.

Gradually the network of retail stores was expanding, and Onitsuka's shoes were becoming more widely known. His brand name was 'Tiger', a name that, like most things in his early business life, had only been acquired with difficulty.

Tiger Brand

Onitsuka first noticed the Tiger trademark about 1950 at the factory where he was learning the craft of shoemaking. It consisted of a drawing of a tiger with the word *katsudo* inscribed beneath it. *Katsudo* means 'action'.

Inquiring as to whether the trademark belonged to the factory owner, he learned that Yoshikawa had no idea, in the confusion that prevailed in the aftermath of the war, who owned it. He had simply found it appropriate to use since his first name was Torao. *Tora* is the Japanese word for tiger and it has considerable significance.

In Asia, tigers are found in Eastern Siberia, China, Korea, India, Persia and Indonesia. Archaeological evidence suggests that there may have been tigers in Japan in prehistoric times, but records of their existence do not appear in written history until relatively recently. The earliest existing picture of a tiger in Japan is found on the side of the altar in the Buddhist temple, Horyu-ji, founded in AD 607 near Nara. The picture is believed to have been drawn by a painter who migrated from Korea. The first living tiger is believed to have been brought to Japan in 890 from China. Much later, in the sixteenth century, Hideyoshi Toyotomi (1536–1598), the Japanese warrior who attempted to conquer China but was only able to subdue Korea, had a tiger brought from the Asian mainland.

Traditionally the tiger, rather than the lion, was considered to be king of the beasts in the Orient. The tiger became very popular among the Japanese during the Edo period (1603–1868) and legends grew up around it. The tiger, it was said, could run 1,000 *ri* (4,000 kilometres) overnight. Thus, 'tiger' was an ideal name for sports shoes, Onitsuka thought. Yoshikawa had no objection to him using it.

As Yoshizo Yoshikawa, director of the Hyogo prefecture Office of Inventions explains, 'In the early 1950s, with the increased postwar economic activity in Japan, imitating brands and designs was the norm. Everything was in such turmoil. I have no recollection of legal action ever being taken against anyone involved in such activity.'

Onitsuka attempted to have 'Tiger' registered as his trademark but was refused. It had been registered in 1919 by Kumakichi Akamatsu of Osaka although his whereabouts of late were not known. Under the Japanese trademark system the first person to register a trademark is granted a monopoly trademark right. Somewhat disappointed, Onitsuka changed the name to 'Onitsuka's Tiger'. This was accepted and duly registered.

Sometime later, with Onitsuka Corporation's product line steadily expanding, Onitsuka felt that the Tiger trademark would give him considerably more options than Onitsuka's Tiger. Rights to the trademark would allow him to use the Japanese characters for *tora*, pictures of the animal, and the English word 'tiger'.

Onitsuka set out to search for the man who had registered the Tiger mark in 1919 and finally succeeded in locating him. Akamatsu had been in business before the war in Osaka but had since retired and was living in Kyoto. Onitsuka sent a representative to try to negotiate an assignment of the rights to the trademark.

The owner, having already retired and having no further interest in his business, was prepared to assign the trademark. Thus, the brand name 'Tiger' came to adorn the Onitsuka Company product line. Onitsuka hoped that his products would be as strong as the animal itself. In addition, he had learned much about patent and copyright law from the venture, thereby expanding his business knowledge.

A Brush with Death

The difficulties that Onitsuka encountered were being overcome one after another and the business was improving steadily. Finally, it seemed that things were beginning to go more smoothly. Unfortunately this was not the case: Onitsuka was shortly to suffer a personal setback.

Onitsuka had been driving himself hard for years. Perhaps because of his strenuous workload, he came down with a fever and chest infection during one of his trips about five months after his wedding. His illness was severe enough to force him to return home immediately and his condition did not improve.

Although he was ill, he continued to work as best he could out of his sense of loyalty to his business and responsibility to his wife and aging adoptive parents. Yet his condition was deteriorating steadily. The illness was much more serious than he had initially suspected. He had tuberculosis. His doctor ordered immediate hospitalization, but Onitsuka refused.

His employees and clients were increasing in number. If he were hospitalized what would become of the business? He had been running the company almost single-handedly. If the company were to go bankrupt because of his illness, what would happen to all the employees?

The doctor did not waver. Onitsuka's health was his responsibility. Onitsuka explained that a manager sometimes had to put the health of the company before his own health. He could not afford to be admitted to hospital. Realizing that he could not force Onitsuka to follow his advice, the doctor promised to do what he could for him.

At that time, the common treatment for tuberculosis was complete bed-rest, a nutritious diet, fresh air, and a prolonged spell of medication. The disease was the major cause of death in Japan, the mortality rate from the disease being three times higher than in England and five times higher than in the United States.[1]

The doctor visited Onitsuka daily and made every effort to obtain the latest drugs for him. A drug called PAS (para-aminosalicylic acid) had recently been proved effective in the treatment of tuberculosis. In 1946, a Swedish researcher, Lehmann, proposed the drug as a chemotherapeutic agent for tuberculosis after it had been shown in 1941 that benzoic and salicylic acids increased the oxygen uptake of virulent tubercle bacilli. The doctor managed to obtain PAS for Onitsuka through the American Occupation Forces. This new drug proved to be effective. Onitsuka's fever abated, along with his coughing. After eighteen months, Onitsuka and his doctor thought that he was finally on the road to recovery.

Throughout this time, Onitsuka had been confined to bed. Fortunately, the office was next door, so that he could call the employees to his room and give them instructions. The primary concern was the conduct of the company's out-of-town business. Onitsuka had been personally responsible for this, travelling constantly from city to city in order to meet with the athletes and the retailers.

Now he had no choice but to send others in his place. In addition to Shimonashi, Onitsuka selected a handful of young employees, all about twenty years of age, who were recent high school graduates. He started their training immediately. They learned how to greet the clients, how to introduce themselves, how to present and explain the product, where to stay, where to eat, and the like. Onitsuka gave them all his tips and sent them off to their target clients in eastern and western Japan. He also taught them the importance of collecting outstanding bills. Hideo Takemoto recalls that sometimes he would have to call on a retailer several times before recovering the amount owing. Occasionally, the expenses incurred in collection approximated to the amount owing. 'Even so', says Takemoto, 'Mr Onitsuka insisted that we persevere.'

Maintaining his business was not enough. Even though he was ill, Onitsuka was continually thinking of ways to improve and expand operations. Until this time, all production had been carried out in subcontract factories. A company factory would more readily facilitate research, product development and production innovation. While Onitsuka was contemplating how to actualize this plan, given the company's limited financial resources, in May 1953, he was informed by the president of Tenma Rubber, a subcontract factory, of the factory's impending bankruptcy.

Negotiations with the creditors led to an agreement whereby Onitsuka Corporation took over the factory, purchasing the manufacturing equipment and continuing to employ its thirty-six workers. This new company, named the Tiger Rubber Company, remained independent from Onitsuka Corporation until 1958 and was headed by Yoshiji Shimonashi.

By September 1953, Onitsuka was back on his feet. Slowly he resumed his business trips. The company had flourished during his illness. Hardworking employees had more than filled the void caused by his absence. The upsurge in the company continued to such an extent that by June 1954 it was able to purchase a building with 230 square metres of floor space, located near the Sannomiya station. This new office was sufficiently large to accommodate the company's expanding workforce which now numbered eighty individuals, thirty of whom worked in the new business office and fifty in the factory. In this fifth year of operation, company sales totalled 80 million yen, four hundred times what they had been in the first year.

Business appeared to be progressing well, but once again fate was to intervene. Onitsuka's cough recurred, this time with the expectoration of blood. The high fever returned and his coughing became incessant. X-rays of his chest revealed four holes in his lungs. He was told that this kind of infection was resistant to PAS.

Hospitalization was required; this time there was no alternative. But Onitsuka would not agree; he was adamant that he would remain at home. The doctor knew that despite his best efforts he would not succeed in changing his patient's mind. Onitsuka admits that this time he was frightened; he knew that his illness was much worse than before. He became acutely aware of the possibility of death. Yet he was in a catch-22 position: if he went to hospital there was a real possibility that the business and his personal dreams might dissolve; if he remained at home close to his business he might shortly die.

There was little doubt in Onitsuka's mind. Even if he should survive and recover, he felt that his life would be without a focus if his business were no longer to exist. True, if profit had been his only aim, he could always start again. But Onitsuka felt that the purpose of his business was much more than this: he believed there were many young people who needed and relied on Tiger shoes. Then there was his young staff. They had all worked so hard; Onitsuka felt he could not desert them. He would remain in his bed in the small room adjacent to the office. He was sure this was the right decision even if it cost him his recovery. Apologizing to the doctor for his refusal to enter the hospital, he implored the physician to continue to treat him daily at home.

So began another fight against the dreaded tuberculosis. Onitsuka's first daughter, Emiko, had been born in 1952 and his wife was expecting their second child. Having to nurse her husband, Tsune left Emiko in the care of her grandparents. Ordinarily, taking care of a very sick husband in her pregnant condition would have been more than enough work for Tsune. She shouldered the additional responsibility, however, of providing meals for several young persons whom Onitsuka had hired from his home-town of Tottori and who were lodging with the family. Also living with them during this period were the sons of Onitsuka's former teachers, Tokichi Fukuda and Harue Yasuda. The young men were attending university in the Osaka area and Onitsuka had seized the opportunity to repay his debts to his mentors.

Onitsuka's illness worsened. The tuberculosis spread from his lungs to his intestines, causing severe diarrhoea. He was even forced to wear diapers. His throat and vocal chords became infected and he lost his voice. None the less, he persisted in directing the business by scribbling instructions to his subordinates, answering their questions about the daily conduct of the company.

Onitsuka's employees were doing their best and he himself helped all he could. Yet, with the tuberculosis spreading to his intestines and throat, he felt that death must be close. His cousin had died of laryngeal tuberculosis, and lung tuberculosis was the most common killer in Japan at that time. Death was considered inevitable should the primary infection spread. As he lay in his bed alone at night, he could not fight back the tears of frustration.

The Saviour

Onitsuka realized that he needed someone to take his place. He thought of Minoru Ishibashi. Ishibashi had been assigned to Onitsuka's regiment as a student soldier from the Kobe High School of Commerce, presently Kobe University. He had achieved the top grade in the Second Company of which Onitsuka was an instructor. He went on to the Military Academy for Reserve Officers and won an award for his performance, being presented with a silver watch. After the war, he graduated from Kobe University and joined Kanematsu Gosho, established in 1889, and presently Japan's eighth largest trading company. Thus, Ishibashi was one of the elite.

Since the war, Ishibashi had periodically visited Onitsuka. Onitsuka wondered what he was doing now. He was sure Ishibashi would be ideal to manage the company and guide the young employees. Convinced that he should approach Ishibashi, he asked Tsune to visit Ishibashi's home in Suma at the first opportunity. But the trip was not necessary. A few days later who should appear but Ishibashi himself! It was his first visit since the new office had been built. Ishibashi had been unaware of Onitsuka's condition. Onitsuka described the seriousness of his illness, explaining that it was for this reason that he had been thinking about Ishibashi, wondering what he was doing.

Ishibashi had resigned from Kanematsu Gosho after a serious disagreement with his superior. He had gone to work for his father-in-law who owned a silk wholesaling company but again his inability to acquiesce to his superior—this time his wife's father—had led to his resignation. Ishibashi's third employer was Igeta Securities Company Limited and he had been made manager of the company's Kyoto branch. But the family-owned company had gone into receivership and Ishibashi found himself unemployed. He had thought of Onitsuka and had decided to pay a visit, to see how he was getting along. This was indeed a remarkable coincidence.

Onitsuka described the progress of the business to Ishibashi. His dream of contributing to the betterment of the nation's youth through sport was beginning to come to fruition and his belief that a company should exist for its employees, and not its president, was slowly becoming a reality. All of this might have to be put on hold or even collapse altogether because of his illness. He could die at any moment. Ishibashi, Onitsuka believed, could take his place and direct the company's young employees towards achieving his dream. He implored Ishibashi to accept his offer and join the company.

Ishibashi was deeply moved by Onitsuka's request. Ishibashi, however, was one of the intelligentsia, a graduate of a leading university. Onitsuka was far from confident that he would accept a position in a company whose future was still in doubt, even though it was the wish of a dying man, his former instructor, whom he respected highly.

Ishibashi promised to give the matter some thought. Days passed, a week, yet Onitsuka heard nothing. After ten days, when Onitsuka had more or less given up, Ishibashi came back, apologized for the delay and explained that it had taken time to gather his family to discuss Onitsuka's offer. They had given their consent and Ishibashi asked to be allowed to commence work immediately. Onitsuka felt greatly relieved. A heavy burden had been lifted. Matters had now been arranged. His dying would be easier, knowing that his work would continue.

Onitsuka's intention had been to appoint Ishibashi as manager. Ishibashi, however, declined the offer. He felt it would not be fair to the rest of the personnel who had been working so hard to improve the company were he to start as manager. He preferred to begin on the same level as everyone else. If and when he earned the respect of his fellow workers, he would accept the position.

This attitude pleased Onitsuka. It confirmed his belief that he had selected the right individual. Ishibashi worked hard and long from the outset, sometimes through the night. His efforts caused some concern to Onitsuka who would urge him to stop. But, determined not to let things pile up, Ishibashi refused to leave before the last order was packed. He was a saviour, truly reliable. The company flourished, in large measure because of his hard work.

Changing Fortunes

Even in the throes of his illness, misfortune continued to follow Onitsuka. In June 1955, he and his wife were woken by a telephone call at two o'clock in the morning. Mrs Onitsuka picked up the receiver and was informed that the Tiger Rubber Company was ablaze. She immediately told her husband who was shocked and horrified. They quickly woke the young men boarding at the house and hurried them to the factory, but it was too late. The plant had burned to the ground.

Onitsuka had been renting the factory space in a large building divided into rooms of about 20 square metres each. At that time, there were many such 'apartment factories', as they were called, in Kobe. Fortunately, no fault was attributed to Onitsuka because the cause of the fire was found not to be in the area rented by him. Moreover, nobody had been hurt.

The old maxim 'It's an ill wind that blows nobody any good', was particularly apt for Onitsuka Corporation at that time. Every June, which is Japan's rainy season, the company had difficulty selling sports shoes. Furthermore, inventory was very high that year and it was going to be difficult to reduce the level. The fire was therefore opportune, all stock being destroyed and fully insured. That was not to be the end of Onitsuka's good fortune. When the clean-up began it was discovered that many items were salvageable. The fire had started on the first floor and had caused the second floor to collapse, thereby covering many items that were only partially burned. Indeed, metal moulds and whole machines were found intact. As much as 50 per cent of the equipment did not need repairing. Thus the fire was a blessing in disguise, enabling Onitsuka Corporation to improve production processes in new rented premises.

At about the same time, Onitsuka began to respond to the drugs the doctor had administered. Streptomycin was available in Japan at that time, and isonicotinic acid hydrazide (INAH) had just come on the market. Treatment with these drugs began to reduce the fever, the diarrhoea stopped at the end of four months and then his voice returned.

Onitsuka's doctor was amazed; it appeared to be nothing short of a miracle. Awed by the improvement in Onitsuka's condition, he pronounced him out of danger and congratulated him on his astounding recovery. Onitsuka's recovery was as much a surprise to him as to his doctor. By November 1955, after having been confined to bed for almost two years, he was able to resume a normal working life. He had been victorious against the terrible enemy, tuberculosis. Yet the disease had taken its toll. 'I remember when Mr Onitsuka visited me in Tottori shortly after his recovery', recalls Harue Yasuda. 'I hardly recognized him, his facial features were so changed. The ravages of hard work and disease had made him so gaunt and worn looking.'

Unfortunate as Onitsuka's illness was at the time, it no doubt broadened his adaptive capacity. The adaptability of the typical entrepreneur, as de Vries concludes, is limited.

> He is very much a prisoner of his past history and usually not even aware of the nature of his actions and, moreover, not really interested in changing his behaviour. Only in situations of extreme stress (such as, for instance, incidents like a coronary attack, death of a person close to him, and divorce), when his defences are lowered might we occasionally encounter a certain degree of readiness to arrive at a greater level of self-awareness and re-evaluation of actions.[2]

Onitsuka's brush with death increased his awareness of the value and competence of his employees and the fact that the success of the corporation rested on the co-operation of its members. Too often this realization comes too late in life of the entrepreneur. For Onitsuka it happened just six years after the company was founded and it influenced his decisions and actions thereafter. Two decades later, when Onitsuka Corporation entered a tripartite amalgamation to form ASICS Corporation, Onitsuka's ability to adapt to the changing environment enabled him to fully delegate the daily running of the company to the two new vice-presidents.

5 | Solidarity

Retailer Support

Until his first illness, Onitsuka had devoted countless hours to visiting local retail stores and customers in order to discover their needs. The fruit of his labour was a loyal cadre of customers. There had developed a feeling of solidarity between Onitsuka Corporation and its clients, a feeling that they were all in the same boat. Throughout Onitsuka's illness, the clients had felt a responsibility to look after the company. This attitude on the part of the retail stores was in part responsible for the corporation continuing and even prospering while Onitsuka was ill in bed.

Shiro Tachibana, president of Asahi Sporting Goods Stores Limited, recalls his feelings on learning of Onitsuka's illness:

> I started doing business with Mr Onitsuka in 1950. Then, in 1952, a young man selling sports shoes came to my store instead of Mr Onitsuka himself. I asked him about Mr Onitsuka and was told that he was ill. When I went to Kobe, I visited him. He seemed very pleased to see me and started to discuss his products with me. He talked for hours, without taking a break even for his meal. I was awed by his enthusiasm despite his very poor physical condition.
>
> I remember once shouting at the young man who came to my store, 'Do you want your president to die?' I could not cope with the idea of Mr Onitsuka in his sick bed, full of vexation, frustrated at not being able to work. I wanted his young employees to do a much better job, so that Mr Onitsuka could recuperate in peace, knowing that his company was in good hands.

Shortly after Onitsuka's recovery, the company began to receive regular orders from the wholesale dealers. These were people who had chosen to ignore Onitsuka in his earlier days. Some of the wholesalers had started to approach the company in 1952, but Onitsuka had refused all orders. He and his employees had worked hard to establish a strong and extensive network of retail stores which carried their products, and the company shipped directly to them. They had done well in spite of the wholesalers. Onitsuka Corporation would continue to do business without them.

The 'against the flow' phenomenon alluded to earlier, whereby the athletes placed orders with the retailers, the retailers with the wholesalers, and finally the wholesalers with the company itself, was becoming more pronounced every day. The demand for Tiger shoes or Onitsuka's shoes was generally increasing to a point where the wholesalers were prepared to handle the products without any profit margin whatsoever.

In response to Onitsuka's inquiry as to why the wholesalers would consider handling his products if they did not make a profit, the wholesalers explained that retail customers had begun to refuse to deal with them unless they could supply Tiger shoes. Even one or two of Onitsuka's Corporation's main lines would suffice.

Onitsuka felt vindicated. He recalled the days when he had visited wholesalers with basketball shoes he had made himself. All of them had turned him away at the door. Mortified, he promised himself at the time that he would some day make such popular shoes that the wholesale dealers would have to come to him to ask for his product. Now this had come true. He had won! There was no longer any reason why the company should continue to refuse to do business with them. At first, Onitsuka dealt only with a few wholesalers who were prepared to operate without any margin of profit. Eventually, as this method of business became more prevalent, Onitsuka arranged for some profits to flow to the wholesalers. Nevertheless, some of the small retailers were opposed to the idea of Onitsuka Corporation doing business with wholesalers, arguing that it was they who had made Onitsuka Corporation prosper, and objecting to the intervention of the wholesale dealers.

The issue was not merely one of profits. The company had guaranteed that the retail stores would continue to receive the same margins as before. Rather, the retailers' attitude sprang from their feeling of solidarity with Onitsuka. They felt that they had worked together with Onitsuka Corporation from the beginning to enable it to become successful. It seemed unfair to the retailers that the wholesalers should now profit from their previous efforts.

Onitsuka explained the situation to the wholesalers and obtained their consent to continue to deal directly with the retail stores. By the early 1970s, Onitsuka Corporation was supplying forty-five wholesalers who in turn distributed the shoes to nearly six thousand retailers throughout Japan. At the same time the company continued to deal directly with about 150 retailers. The number of such stores has gradually decreased, however, as shop owners retire and are succeeded by the next generation. The initial objection of the retailers to the wholesalers' intervention made Onitsuka appreciate the strength of the bond that had been forged between him and the store owners.

Employee Dedication

The young employees had worked tremendously hard during Onitsuka's illness. New to the company and inexperienced, they were still in their early twenties or younger. What they lacked in business knowledge, they made up for in dedication and hard work. Following Onitsuka's example of travelling to distant parts of the country to visit local retailers was not easy. For many it was their first experience of travelling alone. Some were scolded by the store owners for their ineptness.

Despite the hardships, the young employees did not lose their enthusiasm and continued to learn. They were, on the other hand, looked after much better than Onitsuka might have been because they were so young. Frequently, they were offered meals and invited to stay the night with the retailers they visited, with whom they would talk at length about the company and its products.

Onitsuka remembers after his recovery when he had begun making trips again the owner of a store in Saga prefecture saying to him:

Mr Onitsuka, your Mr Shimonashi is a very fine man, always dependable. If he does not have something, or if he cannot arrange for something to arrive on time, he will be honest and admit it. If he says that something will arrive by a certain day, it will. He is a man of his word. Don't worry about your company, Mr Onitsuka. It will be fine with good employees like him.

Others shared this view. Takemi Tanaka, Toshihiko Niki, Hideo Takemoto, and the rest of the workforce were trying very hard, doing a much better job than Onitsuka had expected. Because of his illness, he had had to delegate authority. The employees had no choice but to work hard. They matured noticeably through the experience. As a result, instead of business coming to a halt during Onitsuka's absence, it flourished.

It was at that time, in the spring of 1955, that Tokyo Onitsuka Corporation was established to serve as a sales base for eastern Japan. Hideo Takemoto was responsible for the initial preparation. He was joined in Tokyo by Shozo Isohata. They purchased what had formerly been a hat shop in the city's Asakusabashi wholesale district. Against the advice of his doctor, a fragile Onitsuka flew to Tokyo for the opening ceremonies at the new office. The building served as both office and residence for the men. Gradually the number of employees increased. The men contributed equally to housekeeping expenses and took turns preparing meals until it was decided that Ishohata's cooking was more palatable than anyone else's.

After Onitsuka recovered from his illness, he would take the night train to Tokyo at least once a month and stay at the office/residence for two or three days. Reminiscing about this time, Isohota says, 'We all looked forward to Mr Onitsuka's visits. He would bring us treats and take us out for dinner. We were like one happy family.'

Tokyo Onitsuka Corporation, like Tiger Rubber Company established two years before, remained autonomous until 1958 when both of these merged with Onitsuka Corporation under the corporate banner, Onitsuka Company Limited. By the early 1960s, the Tokyo office had expanded to twelve employees, including Kuramitsu Nakayama, today an executive managing director and head of ASICS' Eastern Sales Division. The company purchased the building next door to accommodate the growing business.

Looking back, Onitsuka says, 'If I had not become ill, the young employees probably would not have learned as much. In this sense my illness ultimately benefited the company.' Also, it made Onitsuka aware that the success of a company depends on the co-operation of its employees. He realized that he had tried to do too much on his own. He had not been sufficiently aware of the importance of releasing the potential in each individual who worked for the company. He had learned another important lesson, this time in the delegation of authority and responsibility.

Until his illness, Onitsuka had handled all employee recruitment himself. With the educational level of young people gradually rising, it was becoming increasingly difficult for a small, little-known company like Onitsuka Corporation to attract employees, especially for factory work. Following his recovery, Onitsuka delegated the responsibility for employee recruitment to Kazunori Kanzaki, today the director of ASICS' Personnel Department.

Kanzaki sought employees throughout rural Japan, visiting prefectural employment offices, junior high and high schools. He would discuss in detail with teachers and guidance counsellers salary levels, fringe benefits and future opportunities, and school personnel would advise students accordingly. For more than a decade following Onitsuka's illness, employee recruitment remained a challenge.

Since the early years of industrialization in Japan, the concept that 'an enterprise is people' has always been considered to be of prime import-ance and personnel development has been emphasized. As Onitsuka became increasingly aware of this principle within his own company, he determined to focus his attention on staff development.

Where the number of personnel is small in a company, communication between the top management and employees is direct, without any interceding layers of middle and lower management, so that problems can be solved expeditiously. As a company expands, however, it typically increases its lower and middle level management and direct communication becomes more difficult. Careful training of managers becomes crucial in such circumstances for the transmission of company ideology.

Onitsuka Corporation's personnel complement numbered close to a hundred by the mid-1950s. The fundamental mission of the company was becoming remote for some employees. Also, Onitsuka wished to hire university graduates. Except for Ishibashi, he had not employed any university graduates thus far. He felt that this shift in personnel blend and numbers could create communication difficulties if he left matters as they were. A training programme was therefore essential.

Personnel Training

Onitsuka Corporation's head office at Sannomiya was a one-storeyed building of about 230 square metres which had previously been owned by the salt monopoly corporation, Kôbe Engyo. Onitsuka decided to rebuild this into a three-storeyed building. The third floor was designed to provide boarding facilities where employee training could take place. The idea of providing boarding was simple: Onitsuka did not want to interfere with the daytime hours of work, hence training would begin in the evening after regular work had ended.

All staff, including Onitsuka, would stay together for a period at the dormitory. They would eat from the same pot, share the same bath, and bare their souls to each other. Communal living would provide Onitsuka with the opportunity to share with his employees his views on life and his reasons for establishing the company in the first place. He wanted them to understand the philosophy of Onitsuka Corporation. Ultimately, he wanted them not only to be efficient businessmen, but also to be great men in society.

He felt this could only be achieved by obtaining a place where they could live together periodically, hopefully in harmony. Onitsuka's military experience influenced this decision. Communal living had contributed to the development of group cohesiveness, shared objectives, and mutual trust. Historically too, there was the renowned Shoka Sonjuku residential school of the late Edo period founded by Shoin Yoshida which had produced an inordinately large proportion of innovative thinkers, including Shinsaku Takasugi, Genzui Kusaka, Hirobumi Ito and Aritomo Yamagata who, with the Meji Restoration, led Japan into the modern era.

Requiring financial assistance to realize his objective, Onitsuka went to see the manager of the Yamate branch of the Kangyo Bank and told him about his plan to build a dormitory. The manager failed to understand why boarding facilities were required when the majority of employees were from Kôbe. He could have justified a loan for a factory but not for a dormitory. Realizing that clarification of his ideas was required, Onitsuka met with the bank manager again and again. He explained that the young people who joined Onitsuka Corporation were like unpolished stones. By polishing them skilfully, in other words by providing them with the proper training and guidance, they would turn into gems. They would become great 'Onitsuka men' as well as worthy members of society. This result could only be achieved by providing the opportunity for everyone to live together. This would give them an opportunity to learn through discussion; they would learn more about business, learn to learn from one another, and learn more about one another.

The manager had suggested that Onitsuka invest in a factory instead of a dormitory. The assumption was that simply by providing the goose with a golden cage, Onitsuka could make it lay golden eggs. Onitsuka rejected this assumption, explaining that the quality of an enterprise lies in its people, the employees. He had to at least provide the nest for the geese who had the potential to lay the golden eggs. He would worry about the factory after the boarding facilities.

Finally the manager understood the wisdom of Onitsuka's proposal. Recognizing how important dormitory facilities were to Onitsuka's plan for the development of company personnel, he agreed to provide the necessary funding. It had taken Onitsuka six months to obtain the manager's consent.

Renovations to the head office, including the addition of boarding facilities, were completed in September 1956. The first floor contained the warehouse and floor space for packing and shipping. The second housed the office and the cafeteria. The boarding facilities were on the third floor. In the coming years, many talented individuals would stay in the Tiger Dormitory and pass through the training programme. Several would become key managers who would guide the company through the major crises that lay ahead.

Through the training programme, company employees were expected to become familiar, through personal experience, with the managerial ethos and the corporate philosophy of the Onitsuka Corporation; to experience communal life by living together; and to master the skills and knowledge required to perform their duties. Onitsuka was the superintendent of training and the dormitory and Ishibashi and three others acted as dormitory inspectors and instructors. Once the dormitory was completed all male employees with the company were required to undergo a three-month training course.

The company held a meeting for the families of employees in order to explain the purpose of the programme and to obtain their consent. There were a few men who were already married. The men would be allowed to go home on Sundays only. Onitsuka asked for the families' understanding. The training programme would make the employees into great 'Onitsuka-men', Onitsuka promised. Reaction from family members was favourable.

The programme required employees to rise by six o'clock every morning, take attendance, exercise, and then go for a two-kilometre run. Those in charge of cleaning the dormitory and the cooking were excused from the run. They took turns with the housekeeping duties. After breakfast shortly after seven o'clock, each person would head for his place of work. At night, for three hours, there were lectures and discussions on management ideology, products, sales, manufacturing technology, and so forth.

Everyone—the president, executives and employees—took all this very seriously. In order to release the pressure that is sure to build up among a group of individuals in a relatively confined space taking intensive training, parties would be arranged periodically. These parties fostered the development of close bonds. While most of the employees who participated in the initial dormitory programme saw its merits, there was at least one dissenting voice.

Shortly after the programme began, Onitsuka was surprised to receive a phone call from the *Kobe Shinbun* (Kobe Newspaper) asking him to come in and discuss a personal matter. The newspaper had received a letter that concerned Onitsuka and they wanted to verify its contents. The letter read in part:

> We are awakened at five-thirty each morning, and made to assist with cleaning the dormitory as well as with the cooking. We also run around the town each morning. In the evenings, we are confined to the dormitory for the president's lectures. This man was a former instructor in the army and a fascist. Something like this should not be allowed in a democratic and humanistic society.

Onitsuka confirmed that, apart from the personal slurs, the contents of the letter were correct. He added, however, that the employee's consent had to be given before taking part in the training which was ultimately for the employee's benefit.

Suddenly the reporter with whom he was speaking, Ryoichi Miki, recognized Onitsuka as his former Army instructor, Sakaguchi. He had not recognized the name Onitsuka nor associated Sakaguchi with Onitsuka Corporation. A student at Kyoto University, Miki had been assigned to Onitsuka's regiment when conscription was extended to university students. After the war he had become the local news editor of the newspaper. He later became president of the *Kobe Shinbun*.

Onitsuka explained what he was trying to do. He had no intention of using these young people for his personal gain. On the contrary, he was concerned about the next generation. He had begun his business with their well-being in mind, and the training programme at the dormitory was designed to enable them to understand these ideas better.

Miki laughed. Having known Onitsuka as Instructor Sakaguchi, he was not surprised at his idea. But he warned Onitsuka that countless people held views that differed considerably from his. At that time, public opinion was leaning heavily in favour of a democratic society and was very sensitive to anything that suggested militarism. He advised Onitsuka to take these matters into consideration.

Onitsuka acknowledged that Miki was right. Some of his actions could have been construed as 'un-humanitarian' at first glance. It was possible that he had acted like an army instructor although this had never been his intention. Perhaps he had been carried away with the idea of training his personnel.

The author of the letter, which was never published, was soon identified as an apprentice pattern cutter. A graduate of the same Tottori middle school as Onitsuka, he had come to Onitsuka Corporation looking for any kind of work when he lost his job as a contract carpenter in Kobe. Onitsuka thought that the man's skill with a chisel could be applied to cutting the layers of shoe material. He had been apprenticed for some months by the time the dormitory programme was instigated and had agreed to participate in the programme which had begun about two weeks before he wrote the letter. Onitsuka took him aside and explained that he was not running the dormitory programme as a fascist. He regretted that the man had not come to him directly with his concerns instead of writing to the newspaper. This incident was resolved by the pattern cutter resigning from the main company. Onitsuka helped him to become established as a subcontract pattern cutter supplying Onitsuka Corporation. He continued in this job for about a year.

In the spring of 1957, Onitsuka Corporation offered employment to its first six university graduates as well as over forty high school graduates. It was a surprise to some that such a small corporation held formal entrance examinations. Entrance exams for Onitsuka Corporation, as for most other Japanese corporations at the time, were held on one or two designated days for all applicants together. They consisted of a written test of general knowledge and an oral interview with Onitsuka and senior executives and were preceded by a talk in which Onitsuka explained corporate philosophy and aspirations. Applicants were inspired by listening to Onitsuka and took the commitments they made to the corporation in their subsequent interviews very seriously.

Financial constraints prevented Masaaki Uetsuki from attending university. Instead he applied to Onitsuka Corporation for employment, one of two graduates from Tottori East High School to do so in 1957.

'When I heard Mr Onitsuka speak,' says Uetsuki, 'I desperately wanted to work for him. I remember Mr Onitsuka saying that the company belonged to its employees.' Uetsuki was overjoyed when informed by telegram that he had been hired. 'I had a burning desire to make Onitsuka Corporation number one and Tiger brand known world-wide.' As general manager of ASICS' Sales Promotion Division, Uetsuki has done much to actualize this desire.

Onitsuka questioned Kazunori Kanzaki about his family responsibilities when he applied for a job. He was the eldest son in a farming family and might have been responsible for carrying on the family's agricultural tradition. Onitsuka asked him how long he would be able to work for the corporation. 'I remember telling him', says Kanzaki, 'that I would stay with the company all my working life. That is the promise I made and I feel I must fulfil it, no matter what.'

Like new employees in all Japanese corporations, those at Onitsuka Corporation commenced work on 1 April, immediately after graduation from their respective institutions. All forty or so of the new male employees moved into the Tiger Dormitory. For three months, they worked during the day and took part in the orientation and socialization programme in the evenings.

The programme was strenuous for all participants, including Onitsuka. He felt much was to be gained by common hardship. The success of the programme was to be revealed in the subsequent achievements of those who completed it. Onitsuka is convinced that almost everyone benefited from it in some way.

Yoshiyuki Takahashi, a senior executive managing director with ASICS, joined the company in 1958 after graduating from Doshisha University. Takahashi has vivid memories of dormitory life:

Often after work Mr Onitsuka would join us in what we affectionately called the 'takobeya' or 'bond labourers' pen'. He would bring the sake and we would drink together while he expounded on his philosophy of life and delivered admonitory lectures. There was a melodramatic tone to dormitory life which, to some extent, still persists in the company.

A dormitory song, Onitsuka thought, would help to bind the employees together and foster the growth of a corporate spirit. All who wished were asked to contribute ideas for the song. The resulting composition consisted of verses written by Onitsuka and two of the early trainees, Shigeaki Tanaka and Kazunori Kanzaki. A third trainee, Shoji Kitami, and his friend, Nobuhito Sasaki, both of whom had been active in the glee club during their years at Kwansei Gakuin University, composed the melody. The song, below, is still used occasionally at dormitory related events.

> Yet higher,
> We hold our pride and ideals.
> Gathered are we full of youth,
> At our sanctuary of joy.
> Our Tiger Dormitory.
>
> East of our home,
> Lies a pure spring.
> We will seek this water,
> Together at the time of strife.
>
> Under the great blue sky,
> Mount Rokko stands solid.
> And at its base is our Tiger Dormitory,
> Fresh and green as a young plant.

Onitsuka maintains that while formal education can teach the individual a great deal, many essential business skills can best be learned through experience. He takes the view that his company's dormitory living experience enhances communications between new employees and corporate executives. It provides an opportunity for executives to instil in new employees an appreciation of corporate philosophy and aims and, in return, executives discover what the new employees' needs and expectations are and how they might best be assimilated into the enterprise.

Onitsuka holds the view that to try to negate what exists is not only wrong, it cannot be done. One must acknowledge the presence of unpleasant phenomena and search for ways to improve the situation. This idea has influenced problem recognition and resolution in the corporation. With regard to employees who lack sufficient ability, Toshihiko Niki, presently one of ASICS' executive managing directors, says:

> You cannot burn, or cast into the sea, or fire such people. They will continue to exist within the corporation so it is necessary to seek out their attributes and consider how to capitalize on their strengths. If you view such individuals in a positive, rather than a negative, light, workable solutions will emerge.

The dormitory experience provided management with insight into the attributes of each new employee, and familiarized them with the strengths and weaknesses of the corporation's human resources. In addition, dormitory life quickly broadened the perceptive capacity of new employees through shared experience, short but intensive, and honed the ability of managers to communicate with their subordinates.

The way Onitsuka treated his employees ultimately paid dividends in the form of loyalty, trust and support. Many of the employees who took part in this orientation course in the first two years subsequently became managing directors with the company. Toshihiko Niki, Takemi Tanaka, Yoshiyuki Takahashi, Kuramitsu Nakayama, Shoji Kitami and Kazunori Kanzaki presently hold that rank.

Kanzaki, a graduate of Tottori University who joined the company in 1957, recalls:

At that time, I was ready for anything. I did not find the evening training programme particularly strenuous. On the contrary, I was very interested in Mr Onitsuka's views on management and found the communal life rather enjoyable. A training programme requiring full board was rare in those days. The experience of living together and forming close ties as a result of the communal life was indeed a valuable one.

Nakayama and Niki echo Kanzaki's sentiments about the dormitory programme. 'We were used to working late into the evening anyway,' recalls Nakayama. 'Working 'till midnight was the norm, not just at our company but in any small company in Japan.'

'It was a time', says Niki, 'when companies advertising job openings would promise two Sundays off a month or even every Sunday, but in reality employees would very seldom take any time off.' In the frenzy to rebuild Japan after the war labour laws were nominal. Everyone seemed to be committed to growth at all costs.

Onitsuka Corporation's new employee training programme was among the earliest of its type; today, initial managerial education is the foundation of human resource development in Japanese industry, where the practice of lifelong employment persists. A formalized programme of collective orientation and socialization is given to new employees with most companies immediately after they begin work.

The aims of these programmes typically include the following: the education of new graduates as members of the company with emphasis on self-discipline and the transition from student life to company life; the acquisition of a professional attitude and an understanding of the significance and meaning of work; the provision of background information about the company, its products, and its market standing; the familiarization of employees with basic company procedures, fundamental business rules and etiquette, and corporate philosophy; and the cultivation of a spirit of harmony and teamwork among employees.

Today, ASICS offers its new employees, both male and female—but excluding those hired to work in the factories—a live-in training programme lasting ten days. The employees stay in one of ASICS' several dormitories in the Kobe area and attend lectures at head office. Six months later these same employees are given a three-day training programme. At this time, lectures related to concrete business issues are given by top executives, including Onitsuka. The focus is on such things as corporate policy on research and development, product development, marketing strategy, and employee benefits. Once again they live together, sometimes in the dormitories and sometimes at resort facilities.

New employees at ASICS' subsidiary factories are given a two-week training programme, more 'practical' in nature than that given at head office. Following a brief introduction to corporate history and ideology, new employees receive lectures on products, production process, quality control, safety and on-the-job training in garment or shoe assembly.

The reduction in the length of the new employee training programme is in accord with a nation-wide trend brought about in part by the aversion of the 'modern generation' to lengthy live-in training and the lack of dormitory facilities to accommodate the large numbers of employees.

Onitsuka's concern for his employees extends much beyond their performance in the workplace. Many times over the years he has assumed the role of 'go-between' for an employee's marriage. Kazunori Kanzaki and his wife were the seventh couple on whose behalf Onitsuka acted as go-between when they were married in the late 1950s.

Kanzaki remembers that Onitsuka offered to introduce him, then a young man of twenty-four, to a prospective bride. But Kanzaki asked Onitsuka to wait. There was a young woman in Tottori whom Kanzaki had dated during his high school and university years. If she was still single, he wanted to marry her. Onitsuka agreed with Kanzaki's preference for *renai kekkon*, or love marriage, and urged him to confirm her availability. Kanzaki returned to Tottori immediately. The young woman was indeed waiting for him and she accepted his proposal of marriage. Her father, however—the owner of a resort hotel at Misasa hot springs—would not agree to give his daughter in marriage to a company employee, especially one who had come from a farming background.

Certain that Kanzaki and the young woman wanted to marry, Onitsuka made up his mind to assist them. With Kanzaki, he visited the woman's father in Tottori and persuaded him to agree to the marriage. 'Since then', says Kanzaki, 'I feel my bond with Mr Onitsuka has been very strong, stronger than my bond with my own father.'

6 | Growth and Greed

Olympic Involvement Begins

Melbourne, Australia was the site of the first Olympic Games to be held in the southern hemisphere. Japan had not been invited to the first postwar Olympic Games in 1948 held in London. In 1952, at Helsinki, although Japan was allowed to attend, it was able to send only some seventy-two athletes and officials. The Melbourne Games of 1956 were the first where the size of the Japanese group more accurately reflected its athletic dimension. At the time of the Helsinki Games, Onitsuka Corporation, formed only three years previously, was not in a position to serve as official supplier to the athletes. By the time of the Melbourne Games, the company had grown to a size where it could become involved in a substantial way.

Tetsuo Hamuro, a gold medallist at the 1936 Berlin Olympics in the 200 metre breaststroke, was now a sports reporter for the *Mainichi Shinbun* (Mainichi Newspaper). Onitsuka knew him because he was in charge of basketball coverage. In the early 1950s, he had introduced Onitsuka to another journalist with the *Mainichi*, Kohei Murakoso. Murakoso had been a runner in the Berlin Olympics, finishing fourth in both the 5,000 metre and the 10,000 metre race. Since their introduction, Onitsuka has been filled with respect and admiration for this man, so much so that when he retired from the *Mainichi* in 1967, Onitsuka asked him to become an adviser to the company.

Murakoso was chosen as coach to the Japanese track team which was to compete in the Melbourne Games. Subsequently, Onitsuka Corporation was asked to supply the track shoes for the team. Onitsuka jumped at the opportunity. What an honour it would be to have Tiger shoes at the Olympics!

Onitsuka's training shoes had acquired an excellent reputation as a result of the development of a sole that incorporated both natural and synthetic rubbers. Natural rubber by itself was too springy and wore out too quickly. Synthetic rubber alone was too hard. The combination of the two substances provided the correct balance of elasticity and strength, Onitsuka had discovered.

Having been appointed as supplier to the Japanese runners competing in the greatest sports event in the world, Onitsuka felt that his dream of making the best shoes in Japan was now realized: the cream of the nation's athletes would be wearing Tiger shoes. This recognition caused the morale of Onitsuka and his team of young employees to soar.

Although his corporation was just getting on its feet financially, Onitsuka none the less found the money to help Kiyoshi Nakamura attend the Melbourne Olympics to observe coaching strategy and the athletes' performance. Twenty years earlier, Nakamura had represented Japan in the 1,500 metre race in the Berlin Olympics. From 1947 until his sudden death in 1985, Nakamura was track and field coach at his alma mater, Waseda University in Tokyo, except for the period when he was a director of the Japanese Association of Track and Field. Nakamura observed how coach and athletes come to share a common sporting destiny, a destiny that Onitsuka's company also became part of through its efforts to develop the best possible athletic footwear. For his part, Onitsuka says that he and his staff find it exciting to share this destiny and to realize that their efforts may help win gold medals.

Shortly after the Olympics, Onitsuka Corporation received another honour. The Company was asked to supply winter boots for the Emperor and Empress to wear to the Winter National Athletic Meet to be held in Nikko, north of Tokyo. Three decades later, Emperor Hirohito would pay Onitsuka the honour of a personal visit to the company's Sanin factory in Tottori prefecture.

Just as Tiger shoes were gaining the recognition Onitsuka had dreamed of for his footwear, however, the integrity of the company itself was challenged.

Accused of Tax Evasion

Onitsuka was woken one morning in June of 1957 by an employee who had arrived early to clean the office. The night before, there had been a Board meeting to discuss bonuses. As the meeting had continued beyond the departure time of the last train, everyone had stayed, sleeping in the night watchman's room next to the office.[1]

The woman reported that, as she was about to start tidying up, investigators from the tax office had arrived and had seized the company's books. They were investigating possible tax evasion. Onitsuka was taken aback. Tax evasion was not an activity in which the corporation indulged—at least not directly. Occasionally, however, a wholesaler would request that a transaction be recorded in Onitsuka Corporation's 'other' account book.

When this happened, Onitsuka felt that he could not refuse. The company did not want to lose these clients. Accordingly, they kept two sets of books, the official one and the 'other' one. Unfortunately, one of the wholesalers had been under investigation by the tax office. The wholesaler's wrongdoing had been discovered and, in the investigation, Onitsuka Corporation's involvement had been identified.

Even though Onitsuka Corporation had not deliberately set out to engage in tax evasion, the company had benefited by co-operating and had undoubtedly broken the law. Put simply, the company had not reported part of its income from sales. Onitsuka's fetish for accuracy meant that there was a record of all transactions and this was seized as evidence.

At the tax office, Onitsuka attempted to demonstrate to the officials that he had not 'skimmed off' corporate income for his own personal gain, nor had he intended to commit tax evasion. Had he done so there would have been a deliberate effort to hide any evidence, not a second set of books accurate to the last yen. Nevertheless, Onitsuka's explanations could not excuse the company from its unlawful conduct. Heavy penalty taxes, he was informed, would be levied against the corporation.

Onitsuka feared bankruptcy. Hoping to reduce the penalty, he requested that the situation be considered as a case of failure to report all sales rather than deliberate tax evasion. The tax officials seemed truly impressed by the meticulous bookkeeping, yet the company still had to pay a further 20 million yen in taxes. Had this occurred a few years earlier, it is unlikely that the company would have been able to pay such a sum. Over the years, however, Onitsuka Corporation had become financially sound, and it managed to pay the entire sum within three years. At that point Onitsuka felt as though a load had been taken off his shoulders: both he and the company were able to start anew.

Some clients persisted in asking for separate accounts, but Onitsuka was able to decline respectfully, explaining that since the difficulties with the tax office the company policy was to maintain only one set of books. The customers accepted this explanation.

The following year, Onitsuka Corporation received the Ministry of International Trade and Industry Small Business Agency's 'Model Small Enterprise' award. With this official recognition, Onitsuka and his employees felt that the company's honour had been fully restored following the accusation of tax evasion.

The incident with the tax office is a classic illustration of the Japanese saying *ame futte chi katamaru*, 'rain hardens the ground'. It was one of the many obstacles that had to be faced as the fledgling corporation grew bigger. It is also significant in the light of Onitsuka's commitment to a policy of open management and his later decision to offer the company shares for public subscription. This was not a decision he arrived at easily.

An Obligation Fulfilled

In the same year that Onitsuka encountered problems with the tax officials, another misfortune struck. His adoptive mother died in her sleep of a stroke. There had been no warning that death was imminent—she was only fifty-nine. With Onitsuka's business on a sound financial footing, she had been enjoying life, going to the theatre frequently, travelling, and, during Onitsuka's second illness, caring for Emiko, her eldest granddaughter.

Onitsuka arranged an elaborate funeral for his adoptive mother, attended by company employees and many friends. In accordance with Japanese custom, the body was cremated. Since there was no Onitsuka family grave, Onitsuka arranged for the ashes to be temporarily placed in Shofuku-ji Zen Buddhist temple in Kobe.

'My adoptive father was well satisfied with these arrangements', recalls Onitsuka. 'He felt that as the adopted son I had lived up to my promise to my mother to attend to her on her death bed.' Soon after the funeral Onitsuka's adoptive father moved in with Onitsuka and Tsune and their two little girls, the younger of whom, Takako, had been born during Onitsuka's second illness.

Search for Happiness

Japan's postwar economic recovery, slow at first, accelerated in the early 1950s and by the middle of the decade her per capita production levels of the prewar years had been regained. People were now able to think beyond immediate subsistance.

With the company prospering, Onitsuka had time to reflect on the past and he realized for the first time how hard he had struggled to attain his goal. He looked at his contemporaries and observed how many of Kobe's rubber industry entrepreneurs lived lavishly, having expensive foreign cars, villas, and even mistresses and second homes. The point was made especially forcefully to him one evening when he was invited to dinner by a business associate, the president of a prosperous company. Dinner at one of the 'better' restaurants in Kobe was followed by a visit to a cocktail lounge complete with charming hostesses. Later the president drove Onitsuka, in his imported car, to what Onitsuka perceived to be a palatial residence.

The life of a company president could be very comfortable. Onitsuka began to realize how he might enjoy such luxury. After his illness, and on the advice of his employooes, he had replaced his old bicycle with a used motor scooter. He longed for his own car. By this time, he had purchased the small house which he had previously rented; however, he, his wife and two daughters occupied only one six mat room (12 square metres) in the house. The rest of the space served as a boarding house for single young men from Tottori. His wife acted as matron of the boarding facilities, purchasing food and preparing meals for the many employees who lived there. Onitsuka was beginning to question his way of life; he was, after all, only human.

For sometime he vacillated between, on the one hand, his desire to experience more of 'the good life' and, on the other, his dedication to his employees and the youth of Japan. In the evening he would often think about all the 'good' things he was missing. When morning came, however, he would see things in a different light. Watching his young employees hard at work, he would ask himself: if he were to pursue his personal cravings, what would become of these young people who had worked so diligently during the years of his illness. They continued to apply themselves in the interests of the company. It was their dedication that had made the company prosper.

Yet the onset of the evening would see his other self—the one that longed to satisfy his personal desires—come to the fore. Onitsuka recognized this inherent dilemma for human beings and struggled continuously with his problem. As the business expanded, so did Onitsuka's responsibilities: there were new products and new marketing strategies to be developed; accounting and the training of staff had to be maintained; and, most importantly, Onitsuka believed it essential that he continued to be worthy of the respect of his employees.

He brooded over all these matters and concluded that he was not doing a good enough job in any area. His broodings created a sense of inadequacy. Questioning his suitability for the job at hand, he would toy with the idea that he might as well enjoy himself—he would only live once—he was working like a dog for nothing. Then his mood would shift as the realization dawned that this was a crucial time in the company's development and it was he who had to pull everyone else along.

Initially, Onitsuka's desire to enjoy the good life was only a fancy. Yet it gradually took hold and grew stronger until eventually his psyche was being torn in two. He continued to face the dilemma alone, confiding in no one, constantly reviewing the pros and cons of whether or not he should indulge himself more. His employees and his family remained unaware of his turmoil.

In the 1950s and 1960s, Japanese managers were eager to become familiar with American and European management styles. For example, Peter Drucker's book *The Practice of Management* [*Gendai no Keiei*] became very popular and sold more than two and a half million copies in Japan during those decades.[2] Having lost the war, the Japanese regarded economic success as the only possible way of guaranteeing the nation's peaceful survival. So they turned to America, the leading power economically and politically, to try to learn the secrets of success. By examining the American experience, rejecting some of it, adopting the other parts wholesale or with modifications, the present-day Japanese management style evolved.

In the late 1950s, Onitsuka read the Japanese translation of *Motivation and Personality* written by an American professor, Abraham H. Maslow, the originator of the humanist psychology school of human behaviour. According to Maslow's theory of the 'hierarchy of needs', people are motivated by five distinct types of need: physiological, safety, love, esteem, and self-actualization or self-fulfilment. These needs are arranged in a hierarchy, from physiological at the base to self-fulfilment at the highest level, in order of their potency in motivating people's behaviour. According to Maslow, people attempt to satisfy their lowest-level—physiological—needs first. For as long as these needs remain unsatisfied, they are a motivating force. As they become satisfied, however, they lose their motivational power and the next level of needs, security needs, becomes the dominant motivating force. This process continues on up the need hierarchy: as each level of needs becomes satisfied, the next level down becomes dominant. Maslow's theory revealed to Onitsuka the importance of recognizing that people have many needs and that, once satisfied, a need is no longer a motivator.

Nevertheless, Onitsuka felt that Maslow's theory failed to provide him with an answer to his own inner struggle. True, the theory dealt with needs and satisfaction, but it failed to show how an individual could resolve the problem of meeting his own personal needs while at the same time assuring the happiness of his associates.

Sometime later, while browsing through a management magazine, Onitsuka noticed an article about the aforementioned Konosuke Matsushita, of Matsushita Electric Industrial. Onitsuka summarized the article in this way:

> Mr Matsushita offered the shares of his company to his employees on the tenth anniversary of its founding. The motive for this act originated from a visit to the headquarters of a religious sect. He had been greatly impressed by the dedication and application of the followers. He marvelled at these followers so enjoying the pursuit of something beyond the satisfaction of their immediate desires. Matsushita wondered if something of this nature were possible at Matsushita Electric. It would indeed be wonderful if all the employees could work on their own initiative without being given orders from the top. The question was, 'How could this be done?' Having

given the matter much thought, he decided to offer his shares to the employees. Moreover, he developed a so-called 'water system' philosophy of management. By providing 'good' for society, as continuously and abundantly as water gushing from the tap, everyone would benefit, including Matsushita Electric.

Here was something that struck a chord in Onitsuka. He realized that even Konosuke Matsushita had been burdened with the same dilemma as he. Matsushita's solution had been derived from a 'religious viewpoint'. Onitsuka decided to study Buddhist philosophy and eventually it provided him with a solution to his dilemma.

Onitsuka read books, met people and listened to others. Mrs Omote, owner of the beauty salon frequented by Onitsuka's adoptive mother, praised Onitsuka for what he had done for his adoptive parents. But she counselled that, if the company were to progress, he must have a sound ideology. She encouraged him to vitalize his life—to undergo a human revolution.

The term *ningen kakumei*, or human revolution, has been popularized through the writings of Daisaku Ikeda, since 1960 leader of Soka Gakkai— Value Creation Society—an evangelical, action-oriented new Buddhist sect. Initiated in 1930 by Tsunesaburo Makiguchi, and propagated by his follower, Jyosei Toda, the Soka Gakkai is an offshoot of the Nichiren sect of Buddhism. It ran its first political candidates in 1955 and by 1964 had organized its own political party, Komeito, or Clean Government Party. Today the Soka Gakkai claims a membership of nearly 17 million within Japan and one million in 115 other countries.[3] When Mrs Omote first exposed Onitsuka to the idea of a human revolution in the mid-1950s, howver, this religious movement was still recovering from its wartime banishment and its activities were confined to seminars and prayer meetings in private homes.

Onitsuka sought out the local Soka Gakkai leaders and became familiar with the idea of a human revolution. Human existence, he came to understand, is fraught with craving and suffering. These can only be overcome by confronting each one head-on and finding a solution. In this way, the individual changes his own destiny and thus creates a human revolution within himself.

The idea of human revolution is rooted in the teachings of Nichiren, a thirteenth-century Buddhist priest. The source of Nichiren's inspiration for living and the consolation that sustained him throughout his life was the *Lotus Sutra*. By whom and when this sutra was compiled is not known, although it is believed to have been in existence by the beginning of the Christian era. The version that formed the basic text of the T'ien-t'ai

School in China and Japan, the one with which Nichiren was familiar, was perhaps the one prepared by Kumarajiva in AD 406.

The *Lotus Sutra* promises universal salvation, teaching that the Buddha is the manifestation of eternal truth, showing to all the way to enlightenment. Like rain, the Buddha's power of salvation is uniform in essence but nurtures the growth of all kinds of plants. The *Lotus Sutra* teaches that the Buddha is eternal and that this eternity is held by everyone who has faith and devotion.[4] Nichiren's values, Keigo Okonogi points out:

> demand more than just a believing heart: one must continually be acting out one's faith in society and *vis-à-vis* the state. This is the *shakubuku* spirit. It is also the bodhisattva spirit, whereby one puts the good of all members of society ahead of one's own success or benefit.[5]

Gradually Onitsuka came to understand more clearly the 'essence' of human happiness. Everyone wants to be happy; yet at times this necessitates depriving others of their happiness. It became clear to him that the Buddha does not suffer this problem, because happiness for the Buddha is the happiness of others. The term Buddha refers to the mental state of those who have attained happiness in being at one with others, that is, those who have attained enlightenment.

Juryo-hon, the sixteenth chaper of the *Lotus Sutra*, teaches that, 'We should not seek happiness outside ourselves, but within our own lives. Moreover, we can change this world into an enlightened place by dedicating our entire being to helping others find their own happiness.'[6] Onitsuka became aware of his own self-centredness. Happiness could never be attained in this way; rather, this path would lead to his own ruin.

Further inquiry led Onitsuka to the Buddhist concept of the Ten Worlds (*jikkai*), corresponding to the 'ten life-conditions which a single entity of life manifests in the course of the flow of time. The major factor in the postulation of the Ten Worlds is the subjective sensation experienced by the "self" in the depths of an individual life.'[7] The Ten Worlds, as briefly described by Yasuji Kirimura are:

1. The state of Hell (*jigoku*): the condition in which one is swayed by the impulse of rage to destroy and bring ruin upon oneself and others. This life-condition is represented by extreme suffering and despair.
2. The state of Hunger (*gaki*): this life-condition is dominated by endless selfish desires for wealth, fame or pleasure, in which one is never truly satisfied.
3. The state of Animality (*chikusho*): in this life-condition one follows

the pull of desires and instincts, lacking the wisdom to control oneself.

4. The state of Anger (*shura*): conscious of one's self but egotistic, one cannot grasp things as they are, and disregards and violates the dignity of others.

5. The state of Humanity or Tranquillity (*nin*): this is the life-condition in which one can temporarily control one's desires and impulses with reason. One lives a peaceful life in harmony with one's surroundings and other people.

6. The state of Heaven or Rapture (*ten*): this is a condition of contentment and joy which one feels when released from suffering or upon satisfaction of some desire.

7. The state of Learning (*shomon*): the six conditions, from Hell through Heaven, are brought about by impulses or desires, but they are completely controlled by the restrictions placed on them by one's surroundings and are extremely vulnerable to changing circumstances. Learning, on the other hand, is a condition experienced when one strives towards a lasting state of contentment and stability through self-reformation and development. Concretely, *shomon* is the state in which one dedicates oneself to creating a better life by learning from the ideas, knowledge and experiences of predecessors and contemporaries.

8. The state of Realization (*engaku*): this life-condition is similar to Learning in that both indicate striving for self-reformation. However, what distinguishes Realization from Learning is that, instead of trying to learn from the achievements of one's predecessors, one tries to learn the way to self-reformation through direct observation of phenomena.

9. The state of Bodhisattva (*bosatsu*): this is a state of compassion in which an individual devotes himself to the happiness of others even if he must make sacrifices. People in the states of Learning or Realization tend to lack compassion, going to extremes in pursuit of their own self-perfection. A bodhisattva, in contrast, finds that the way to self-perfection lies only in the act of compassion—saving other people from their suffering.

10. The state of Buddhahood (*butsu*): this life-condition is reached when one gains the wisdom to realize the ultimate reality of one's own life, the infinite compassion to direct one's activities constantly towards benevolent goals, a perfected eternal self, and total purity of life that nothing can corrupt. Buddhahood is an ideal life-condition which one can attain through Buddhist practice. Since no life-condition is static, Buddhahood cannot be thought of as a final goal; rather, it is a condition that one experiences in the depths of one's being as one

continues to act with benevolence in everyday life. In other words, Buddhahood appears in everyday life as the actions of bodhisattva—good deeds and compassionate acts.[8]

Onitsuka perceived himself to be vacillating within the lower worlds. This confusion within began to resolve itself. He began to see clearly what his problem was and finally was able to end his internal conflict.

He had started his business with three aims: first, to cater to the well-being of youth by providing them with sports shoes, thereby enabling them to take part in sport; second, to establish a company where honesty and diligence were considered valuable assets; and third to respect the dignity of each and every employee.

His ideal was to secure the happiness of the individual and the prosperity of the company by carrying on an enterprise that would benefit mankind as a whole. His studies had begun to clarify the criteria required to understand how human beings should live, how self-development could occur, and where one could find the ultimate principle of human values by which to live. Onitsuka came to realize that the essence of proper existence lies in respect for human beings. In corporate society, especially, this is important.

Onitsuka needed to actualize his 'enlightenment'. With business going well, he had become preoccupied with the external trappings of life, forgetting that the company was succeeding only because all the employees had worked so hard during his illness, remaining loyal to him and never criticizing his extreme expectations. The profit therefore belonged to them: by analogy, the company could be said to be holding their profits in trust for them. Onitsuka felt that he must be morally accountable to his employees and that he must manifest this by his activities.

At that time the company had a capital of 8.3 million yen, with net assets of 30 million yen. All of this, however, was in the name of Onitsuka: the shares belonged exclusively to Onitsuka and his adoptive father. The employees were all being paid a fair wage as well as receiving semi-annual bonuses.[9]

That he and his father were the exclusive shareholders troubled Onitsuka. He felt compelled to distribute a large portion of the shares to his employees but, with the exception of Matsushita, he could find no models for this course of action. For a year he searched for a solution but he could find no other way to make himself morally accountable to his employees.

Finally, on the tenth anniversary of the company, he offered 70 per cent of the shares to the employees. The shares were distributed to the employees according to their contribution to the company. Onitsuka gave

50 per cent of the total shares to his employees as an outright gift and sold an additional 15 per cent to them at fair market value. A further 5 per cent were set aside for future employees. Thirty per cent of the shares remained with the Onitsuka family.

Onitsuka's friends and his adoptive father strongly opposed the distribution of shares. The latter, being from the 'old school', was outraged. Onitsuka had built the company with his sweat and blood. Twice he had nearly died for it. He paid his employees good salaries and bonuses. His adoptive father could not comprehend why he would give away the shares. His friends were similarly mystified. Distribution of 30 per cent of the shares and retention of 70 per cent might have been acceptable. The reverse was perceived as lunacy. Warned that people were not as good as he wished to believe, he was advised to let go of his idealism before his employees turned on him and kicked him out.

No one congratulated him on his decision. As far as Onitsuka could tell, he was the first company owner in Japanese history to distribute more than half the shares to his workforce: not even his model, Matsushita, had gone this far. Onitsuka says:

> But the young employees preserved the company through my illness. I felt that if I did not put into practice what I had been saying—that the corporation belongs to everyone—their work motivation would decrease and they might even leave the corporation. If this happened, my managerial ideology would disintegrate. I decided to act according to my own judgement and distribute the company shares.

The company had been Onitsuka's entire life and he was resolved that it would continue to be so. Yet, being human, he knew that he might, at some future time, be tempted again to use the company for his own benefit. If he was considered unworthy to be its president, he would be removed. This was fair. Being the corporation's founder did not justify a greater say in the running of the company. But he was not unduly worried about losing his job. According to Onitsuka:

> The theory of group dynamics holds that in a group, 30 per cent will always be for, 30 per cent against and the remaining 40 per cent will be undecided on a given policy. With my planned ratio of the distribution of shares, it was still possible for me to have the support of the majority of the company. I might lose 30 per cent, but I could keep the 70 per cent according to my abilities as a manager. This is definitely what democracy is all about.

Onitsuka's tenure would stand or fall on his own managerial abilities and the trust his employees had in him. He did not doubt that his decision was correct.

'The leader who prepares an escape route for himself is without lasting appeal', says Onitsuka. 'When the leader perceives his destiny to be inextricably bound to that of his employees then the employees will support him fully.'

Onitsuka recalls vividly the company's tenth anniversary celebration. He told his employees:

> From this moment on, if I should attempt to inflict unreasonable 'one-man' management on this company on the rationale that I am its founder, then you have my permission to call a meeting of the shareholders. Should you decide at that meeting that I am unworthy of being your president, remember, you have the legal right to oust me from my position. Onitsuka Corporation belongs to you more than it does to me or my family. We shall all work together, the 'labour', the 'capital', and the 'management'.

Onitsuka's wife and daughters were invited to the anniversary celebration. For Mrs Onitsuka, it would be the last occasion of official contact with the employees, many of whom she had cared for in her home over several years. In particular she would miss the young men from Tottori. From that point on Onitsuka would keep the affairs of his family separate from those of the company and, in keeping with the trend of the time, employees would board in a company dormitory rather than in his home. It was becoming common then for Japanese companies to provide boarding facilities not only for employees from out of town but for all those young, single workers, male and female, who wished to live away from home. Customarily, four employees would share a room similar in size to the one in which Onitsuka had lived as a student with the Fukudas.

At the ceremony, the employees presented Onitsuka with a tiger skin. They told him that it was to express their sense of gratitude. The unexpected gift caused tears to well up in Onitsuka's eyes. Finally he felt confident as a manager. He knew they could work together, all of them, to build the corporation. Ten years earlier he would not have dreamed that he would come so far. Onitsuka felt overwhelmed as he sang the company song, composed for this occasion:

> Yet higher, yet stronger, yet deeper,
> Seek eternally.
> Yet higher, yet stronger, yet deeper.
> Seek eternally.
> We Onitsuka!

This song, an expression of Onitsuka's corporate ideology, puts forward the belief that if people hold high ideals and goals, if the bonds that unite them are strengthened through deep friendship, and if they search eternally for the road to co-prosperity (among employees, shareholders and management), each individual will contribute to the benefit of Japan and the world as an industrial man. At the same time, individual happiness will be attained and the prosperity of the corporation guaranteed.

Onitsuka's resolution to his internal conflict has come to be well-known among leading Japanese executives, particularly those in the sports industry. Tosaku Nishida, president of Goldwin Corporation and Onitsuka's long-time business associate, points out that Konosuke Matsushita, Tadao Yoshida of YKK—a leading zipper manufacturer—and Kihachiro Onitsuka, have much in common when it comes to management philosophy.[10] Having been involved in management himself for many years, however, Nishida finds it hard to imagine that these men held their lofty ideals from the outset of their business ventures. Nishida cites his own experience.

> When I started my company, I wanted to make a great deal of money, to live in a magnificent house, to feast routinely on all sorts of delicacies, and to be fawned over by beautiful women. I think most managers, just like any other people, have such material ambitions. But the harder you work to satisfy these desires and the more you experience the 'good life', the more you become aware of the triviality of these pursuits.

By its tenth anniversary, Onitsuka Corporation had come a long way since the early days when it had nothing but a borrowed desk, a chair, a telephone and two employees. Now the company was reasonably well-known, its base was well established, and its reputation as a quality sports shoe manufacturer was spreading. Its performance continued to improve.

The distribution of shares generated a new energy within the company and acted as a catalyst for the transformation of the initial struggle associated with the establishment of the corporation into concentration on future development.

A Fair System of Merit

One of Onitsuka's earnest desires was to avoid all taint of nepotism, class and the old school tie in the operation of the company. He avoided nepotism despite the possible advantages in terms of maintaining unity and trust based on blood relations. He was concerned that the employment of relatives might result in favouritism which would undermine staff relations; he did not want a 'they/we' attitude to develop.

He was also determined to avoid 'one-man management'. The president who allows himself to practise one-man management is often supported by a few relatives who flatter his ego. This ultimately breeds nepotism and those employees who could be really helpful to the organization begin to disengage themselves from the situation, to the long-term detriment of the corporation. Onitsuka remains convinced today that a company built on shared ideology is much stronger than one held together by blood relations.

Nevertheless, there was one exception to the rule, namely Tokio Sakaguchi, his nephew, who had joined the company in 1954. He was the son of Onitsuka's eldest brother who had nine children. Onitsuka's brother had written to Onitsuka asking him to take care of one of his sons. Onitsuka replied that ordinarily he would be happy to do so, but that it was against company policy to employ blood relations.

Shortly thereafter, Onitsuka was to hear from one of his business associates, Masato Osaka, the owner of the oldest and largest sporting goods store in Tottori city and a man for whom he had great respect. Though five years Onitsuka's senior, both men had attended Tottori Ichichu Middle School. Osaka was also a member of the Tottori city council and later became vice-chairman of the Japan Association of Retail Stores. An irate Osaka chided Onitsuka, as the employer of close to a hundred young people, for refusing to give a job to a nephew. He threatened to take his business elsewhere if Onitsuka persisted in this heartless course of action.

The employees, too, suggested that Onitsuka should allow his nephew to join the company. Shimonashi, who was then factory manager, recommended that Onitsuka employ him as he would any other young man and treat him the same as everyone else. Onitsuka finally conceded that they were right. Nevertheless, he cautioned his nephew when he arrived that if he showed any signs of behaving as though he were his nephew, he would dismiss him immediately. Sakaguchi was forbidden to see Onitsuka in private under any circumstances whatsoever.

Despite this, Sakaguchi says, 'Initially my fellow workers avoided discussing any important business matters with me. They were afraid I would report everything to my uncle. When he would reprimand someone they suspected that I had squealed on a co-worker.'

When the time came for promotion Onitsuka ensured that his nephew was always a year behind the others. When he made mistakes he was treated more harshly than anyone else. Eventually the other employees realized they had nothing to fear. They began to ask if Onitsuka was perhaps being too hard on Sakaguchi and to urge that he be treated normally, like anyone else.

This pleased Onitsuka. He felt that everyone now understood that he meant what he had said about not showing favouritism to blood relations. Thereafter, Onitsuka treated his nephew the same as any other employee.

Onitsuka's treatment of his nephew emphasized to the employees that their advancement within the company depended not on who they were but rather on ability and hard work. Looking back, Onitsuka says, 'The young executives grew and blossomed after this. ASICS is still reaping the benefits today of a well nurtured management group.' Several years later he welcomed his niece, Takako Sakaguchi, to his staff. She now manages ASICS' Sports Gallery in the Portopia Hotel in Kobe. Also on staff in ASICS Tiger Corporation, ASICS' American subsidiary, is Motoi Oyama, Onitsuka's son-in-law.

Managerial Training and Advancement

In order to equip his managers effectively to instruct and develop their subordinates, in 1959 Onitsuka asked Kazunori Kanzaki to enrol in the month-long Management Training Programme (MTP) offered by the Japan Industrial Training Association. MTP had been introduced to Japan by the United States Far Eastern Air Force and it focused on the middle manager as educator/instructor. On his return to the company, Kanzaki first gave a four-day immmersion session to Onitsuka and the senior executives and then twice repeated the session, first with one half of the corporation's department heads and section managers and then with the other half. Included in these four-day sessions were such topics as managerial planning, control, how to give orders and instruction, techniques for chairing meetings, and human relations.

Kanzaki next instructed personnel at the supervisory level. In a ten-hour session he focused on job instruction, worksite improvement, and treatment of subordinates. Kanzaki recalls:

> I was very excited by the idea that our corporation was going to introduce systematic managerial techniques and that I was going to be instrumental in its introduction. But after working with the programme for about a year, I came to realize that it is very difficult to narrow the gap between reality and the ideal state that the management training programme was seeking. Human resource development cannot be reduced to theory. The educational training I provided may not have been a total success but I feel it did prepare the ground for managerial modernization.

Onitsuka has always been aware of the need to treat all employees equitably. He maintains that the manner in which the human resources of a small or medium-sized corporation are nurtured has a critical bearing on the success or failure of the organization. From the outset, Onitsuka attached more importance to merit than to academic qualifications. He says:

It never made sense to me that academic qualifications would automatically determine employment level and promotion. Why should university graduates necessarily be given preferential treatment over high school graduates and high school graduates over middle school graduates, before they have proved themselves?

Prior to joining the Army, Onitsuka had briefly tried to secure a job and had experienced at first hand the severe discrimination against people with little education. After the war, the idea of the equality of individuals was strongly promoted during the Occupation, reinforcing the feelings that Onitsuka himself had long held. In the early 1960s, Onitsuka's strong belief in equal opportunities for all his employees found expression in the introduction of an examination system for managerial positions.

The examination was first held in March 1963 and thereafter has been repeated annually. Regardless of the employee's educational background, passing this test is mandatory if he is to move into a managerial position. To be eligible to write the examination, employees who are junior high school graduates must have been with the company five years, night high school graduates four years, day high school graduates three years, junior college graduates two years, and university graduates one year.

The examination focuses on an understanding of the corporation and its functions rather than on academic knowledge. The first four-hour exam in 1963 included such topics as corporate objectives, strategic planning, corporate history, organizational structure, products and production processes, accounting and finance, salary, benefits, allowances and employee rights. Fifty-nine employees took this test and forty-five passed. The success rate was highest among high school graduates (86 per cent), followed by university graduates (67 per cent), then junior high graduates (45 per cent). Although data concerning the candidates' years of service, position in the company, etc. are not available, the fact that more high school graduates passed the test than did university graduates perhaps suggests that, so far as Onitsuka Corporation was concerned, academic training was not as important as on-the-job training.

Promotion was not decided on the basis of the examination alone. The workers' everyday performance was also a factor. Today, employee evaluation is done on a point system incorporating a written test and personnel merit rating.

Not all of those who meet the standards for promotion can necessarily be accommodated in managerial posts. Irrespective of whether an individual joins the managerial ranks, however, he receives an annual managerial supplement. This incentive induces many employees to attempt the examination for promotion. In recent years about a hundred employees have been evaluated annually and the pass rate is about 35 per cent.

Some have sat the general written examination more than once—highly skilled technical workers being a common example—but have not quite managed to pass. Onitsuka has established a 'specialist system' for these workers. When a candidate is recommended for promotion by his department manager and the recommendation is approved by the executive committee, he is classified as a 'specialist', a category that corresponds closely to a managerial position and is paid accordingly. Today the specialist category also includes many who have successfully passed the examination but whose high level of technical competence renders them more valuable in their specialized areas than in 'general' administration.

The merit system of promotion was reflected in Onitsuka Corporation's senior executive circle before the amalgamation. As few as one half of the fourteen top executives were university graduates; the rest were junior and senior high school graduates who had worked their way up through the company. Onitsuka Corporation was not the only company to introduce written examinations as a prerequisite for promotion but it was certainly in the forefront of innovative enterprises to move in this direction in the early 1960s.

A Promise Fulfilled

With the business going well and his children growing up, Onitsuka had been toying with the idea of building a family home in Ashiya, a residential district midway between Osaka and Kobe. In 1964, however, his adoptive father became ill and died suddenly at the age of eighty-three. With this turn of events, Onitsuka began to have second thoughts about his plans for a new house. He says now:

> The more I thought about it the more I realized that my living in Kobe and being engaged in a business I so enjoyed was my *karma*. It was through the Onitsukas that this was actualized. I felt I could not live comfortably myself without first properly caring for my adoptive parents. I had to enshrine their remains in a family grave.

City cemetery plots in Japan are very expensive, especially in Kobe where the mountains rise out of the sea and the only inhabitable land is a narrow coastal plain. The plot Onitsuka wanted would cost 6 million yen—close to the cost of the house he wished to build. This was a high price to pay, yet he realized that if he neglected to prepare a family grave at this time the responsibility and expense would fall on his children at his death. Onitsuka talked with his wife and she agreed. It was important that he proceed now to prepare a place where his adoptive parents' remains could rest in peace for eternity.[11] New living quarters for the family could wait. And wait they did—it was not until 1974 that Onitsuka was finally able to purchase a lot in Ashiya and build a family home.

When the grave site was ready and the appropriate rituals completed, Onitsuka's adoptive mother's ashes were moved from Shofuku-ji temple and placed beside those of his adoptive father in the Onitsuka family grave. This done, Onitsuka felt that he had finally fulfilled his promise to his friend and war comrade, Lieutenant Ueda.

Travelling Abroad

In August 1960, Onitsuka flew to Europe for the Rome Olympics. He wanted to see his company's products in action, as well as the athletes from eighty-six countries. It was also his first trip overseas, and his first opportunity to see the foreign market. At this time travelling abroad was not common; nearly five hundred people came to Kobe's Sannomiya Station to wish Onitsuka well and see him off on the train to Tokyo, on the first lap of his journey. Onitsuka was attending the Rome Olympics in anticipation of the Olympic Games to be held in Tokyo in four years time.

Prior to the Games, he toured Europe with a group of Japanese sporting goods manufacturers. The experience was both exhausting and exhilarating. Weighed down by the three cameras he carried and the sample shoes he purchased, Onitsuka tried to absorb as much as he possibly could in the short time available. The itinerary was hectic. Within two weeks the group visited London, Brussels, Paris, Cologne, Frankfurt am Main, Zurich and Geneva. The final stop was Rome and the Olympics.

By this time, Onitsuka Corporation's product line had expanded so that in Rome five Japanese teams—basketball, track and field, wrestling, gymnastics and fencing—were using Tiger shoes. The Japanese teams, with Onitsuka's shoes, performed well in the Rome Games. In particular, the men's gymnastic team won the gold medal for overall performance: Onitsuka was overjoyed at seeing Tiger shoes dancing in the air as the gymnasts performed.

In the marathon, Abebe Bikila won the gold medal, becoming the first to do so from Black Africa. Unknown outside his own country until these Olympics, this was only the third marathon ever run by this member of the Imperial Guard of Haile Selassie of Ethiopia. It was not only the unexpected victory by an Ethiopian that surprised the world, but the fact that he had run the entire race barefoot. As Onitsuka watched him during the race, he felt a strong urge to have Bikila run in Tiger shoes. A year later, this wish was to become reality.

During his European tour and the Olympics, Onitsuka saw many different foreign brands of shoes. They were all very colourful, and most were made of leather. Japanese shoes, including Tiger shoes, were made of canvas. Both have their advantages, but it was obvious that there was still much room for improvement in Tiger shoes.

After the Games, Onitsuka travelled to the United States to get a first-hand look at the country and its market conditions. This was the country that Japan had fought against; the Japanese had been told a great deal about the nation. Onitsuka was curious to see what it was really like. What he found there was a modern civilized nation. Japan, still in the midst of her recovery, could not be compared to the United States in terms of economic success. Onitsuka was very impressed by the quality of American sporting goods and sports facilities. Onitsuka Corporation still lagged far behind the huge American sporting goods manufacturers such as Wilson and MacGregor. These observations made Onitsuka realize that he was just a little fish in a big pond.

This first trip abroad gave Onitsuka a new perspective, inspiring him to expand into the international sphere. He was determined that Onitsuka Corporation should not rest on its laurels of being the best in Japan: they should strive to be the best in the world. As Tsune Onitsuka recalls:

> My husband was overwhelmed by what he saw in Europe and in the States; he made up his mind that Onitsuka Corporation would not be left behind. After that first trip abroad his life became even busier than before. He seemed to be running in all directions at once.

Now, more than ever, Onitsuka paid heed to the teaching of Sun Tzu, a sixth century BC Chinese general and military theorist. Sun Tzu's *The Art of War*, a sophisticated treatise on strategy, tactics, logistics and espionage,

> had had a profound influence throughout Chinese history and on Japanese military thought; it is the source of Mao Tse-tung's strategic theories and of the tactical doctrine of the Chinese armies. Through the Mongol-Tartars, Sun Tzu's ideas were transmitted to Russia and became a substantial part of her oriental heritage.[1]

The Art of War has been, and continues to be, widely read by Japanese businessmen.

In 'Offensive Strategy', the third chapter of the *Art of War*, Sun Tzu states:

> those skilled in war subdue the enemy's army without battle. They capture his cities without assaulting them and overthrow his estate without protracted operations ... Know the enemy and know yourself; in a hundred battles you will never be in peril. When you are ignorant of the enemy but know yourself, your chances of winning or

losing are equal. If ignorant both of your enemy and of yourself, you are certain in every battle to be in peril.[2]

Onitsuka determined to arm himself with as much knowledge as possible about the international market. He set the Tokyo Olympics as the company's goal and planned the development of new products for the occasion. These Olympics would provide the setting for the debut of 'Onitsuka of the World'.

Product Innovation

From the company's inception, the development of new products had always been an important feature of corporate policy. The firm's small size was a definite advantage in planning for innovation. Onitsuka Corporation was close enough to the market to know quickly what improvements and new products were needed. Knowing that they could not do everything themselves, Onitsuka and his employees were always on the lookout for any ideas and developments outside that could possibly be used to improve their products. Some ideas came from the most unlikely sources. For instance, the early basketball shoes required a non-slip sole to prevent sliding on sudden starts and stops on slippery gymnasium floors. The idea for the solution to the problem came from the pickled cucumber and octopus that Onitsuka had for dinner one day. The suction cups on the octopus tentacles were the answer.

He applied the same principle to the soles of basketball shoes. Onitsuka still remembers the expressions of joy and amazement on the faces of high school students who tried the shoes for the first time. Eventually these shoes became so popular as to secure 60 per cent of the domestic market.

The constant improvement in the skill of players meant continuous product innovation. Onitsuka continued to keep a watchful eye for new ideas. Says Emiko, Onitsuka's eldest daughter, 'My father has microscopic powers of observation. He is interested in everything. Very little escapes his notice.'

Another inspiration came to Onitsuka in the late 1950s when he was being driven to work in a taxi. A child ran out in front of the vehicle, causing the driver to slam on his brakes. The car screeched to a halt before reaching the child. Suddenly it dawned on Onitsuka—the tyres were designed to enable a vehicle to stop and start suddenly: the major function of basketball shoes. Could the principle and technology be applied to shoe construction, he wondered.

Onitsuka asked Tokio Sakaguchi, his nephew, who was in charge of product development, to go to the motor show that was being held in Tokyo. Sakaguchi was instructed to have a good look at the tyres—just the tyres. (The motor shows were well-known for their beautiful women as well as their flashy cars. Sakaguchi was not to forget that the purpose of his visit was to investigate tyres, not to enjoy the distractions of the elegant cars and the beautiful women.)

On his return Sakaguchi reported that he had gone round the entire hall on his hands and knees looking at the tyres (and not the beautiful legs!). Eventually he realized that there were different patterns and structures for tyres. Also, for some cars, there were slight differences in the pattern of grooves between the front and the back tyres.

Onitsuka and his researchers learned that there are three important factors in making good tyres. One function is to set the direction, another to adhere to the road surface and the last to enable the use of tractive force. It is possible, through variation in tread pattern, to adjust the combination of these factors to suit the different types of cars and driving conditions. The rib tread pattern runs in the direction of the tyres, minimizing side slipping and maximizing manœuvrability and stability. Rib treads are found on the majority of car and truck tyres intended for use on paved roads. Lug treads, which run across the tyre, excel in traction on unpaved roads and are used primarily on the tyres of dump trucks and heavy machinery. Block pattern treads give excellent control and manœuvrability in snow and mud.

The following year, the company produced two new shoe models based on their research into tyres. The first was the Silver Tiger basketball shoe for outdoor games which employed the principle of tractive force. The second shoe, the A-type shoe for indoor games, utilized the principle of adhesion. Together, these two models cornered nearly 90 per cent of the domestic market.

Recently, the link between tyres and sports shoes has grown even more marked. Some of today's running shoes have outer soles made of hard, abrasion-resistant rubber such as Vibram's Infinity Compound or Goodyear's Indy 500—a high carbon rubber which is also used in racing tyres.

Distance Running Shoes

Shoes used for long-distance running have a long history although shoes developed especially for this purpose did not appear until the mid-1930s. The earliest known footwear—sandals made of crushed sagebrush bark dating back some 10,000 years to the end of the last Ice Age and discovered under a rock mass in a cave in Oregon in the 1930s—were no doubt running shoes. Their cave-dweller owners probably spent a great many hours in the daily pursuit of food: a good hunter had to be a good runner.[3]

A vase dating from 1300 BC, found in Cyprus, provides the earliest representation of runners in art. The two men depicted are unshod and naked, except for headgear. With the birth of the Olympic Games in 776 BC, which were subsequently revealed in the art and literature of the age, our knowledge of running and running footwear increases. There is no evidence to suggest that footwear was worn. Furthermore, clothing for men was abandoned early in the Games' history. By the time the Romans abolished the Olympic Games in AD 393 the emphasis had shifted from competition to combat, reflecting the Roman preference for militarism. Participants in Roman sports wore protective clothing and armour and probably used footwear not unlike that of military *caliga*—a heavy-soled, hobnailed sandal with gartering which involved elaborate strapping and tying above the ankle.[4]

It is likely that most of the shoe fashions and basic construction techniques known today had been developed by the beginning of the Tudor period (1485). The turnshoe and welted construction, still used today, were in existence by the twelfth and fourteenth centuries respectively. In the former, the shoe is made inside-out so that the seams on the finished shoe are on the outside, allowing for a smooth surface next to the skin. Welted construction accommodates the use of heavier materials since the shoe does not have to be turned inside-out.

The name 'pump', signifying a light shoe or indoor slipper, usually of turnshoe construction, entered the English language in the sixteenth century. By the nineteenth century pumps had developed into plimsolls in England. The latter were usually made of canvas, encircled by a line of rubber where the sole and uppers met—from which they got their name. The line was suggestive of Plimsoll's mark, the loadline painted on ships which Sir Samuel Plimsoll, the English reformer and Member of Parliament, introduced through legislation in the hope of preventing overloading, thus increasing marine safety.[5] By 1900 the plimsoll had developed into the sneaker—the basic all-American sports shoe—for the next seventy years.

It should be noted that the development of the rubber-soled shoe only became possible after the discovery in 1839 by Charles Goodyear of the process of vulcanization, which is the treatment of rubber to give it strength, elasticity and resistance to solvents, and to render it impervious to moderate heat and cold. He patented this process in 1844 and paved the way for the birth of the rubber industry. He spent further years perfecting the process that would make rubber a universally used material. A major boon to running shoes, rubber shoes offered greater protection than leather against constant impact.

Eton College was in the forefront of the 'athletics' revival in nineteenth-century England, introducing track and field competitions within the school in 1837. Special clothing and footwear for running was not initially considered necessary. The advice to walkers and runners contained in *Walker's Manly Exercises* in 1839 was typical: 'the coat and all unnecessary clothes should be laid aside . . . the waistband of the trousers should not be tight, and the boots or shoes should have no iron about them.'[6]

Specialized sports footwear appeared only slowly in England. Pumps and sneakers, all-purpose recreational shoes, were used for running. The first spiked shoes were made for cricket, not running. The Spencer shoe, a close relative of the early cricket boot, was probably the earliest mass-produced, spiked running shoe. It was a low-cut, all leather, light-weight shoe with three spikes under the ball of the foot and one under the heel. A broad toe band added lateral stability. Peter Cavanagh felt that the Spencer shoe:

> pinpoints the first branch of the evolution of running shoes. From 1865 on, specialized shoes for running turn away from street shoes to form their own line of evolution. The Spencer shoe was the precursor of track spikes as we know them today. The line was to branch again in 1896 . . . The 1896 branch leads directly to our modern day training flats.[7]

By 1894, footwear was available for a variety of sports, as evidenced by the Spalding Spring and Summer Catalogue of that year. Nevertheless, the catalogue included no shoes for distance running, presumably because demand did not yet warrant their production.

Distance running established its popularity with the first modern Olympic Games, held in 1896. Professor Michel Breal, a friend of Pierre de Coubertin, suggested the inclusion of an event not found in the Greek Games, a 40 kilometre race to be called the marathon, to commemorate the legend of Pheidippides, one of Greece's most famous distance runners. According to legend, in 490 BC, Pheidippides ran from the Plains of Marathon to Athens to proclaim the victory of the Athenians over the Persians. On arriving at the Athenian legislature, he allegedly shouted 'Nike', the Greek word for victory, and then dropped dead.

The standard marathon distance of 42.195 kilometres (26 miles 385 yards) established in 1908 with some slight variations until 1924, has been maintained. Earlier marathons had covered a 40 kilometre course, but organizers of the London race of 1908 wished to start the race at Windsor Castle and finish at the Olympic stadium in White City: hence the extension.[8]

The first Olympic marathon profoundly influenced modern long-distance running shoes. The latter differ from track shoes as the race is not run in laps around a track. This difference led to the evolution of today's running flats, although little progress was made during the next thirty to forty years in their development. John A. Kelley, who ran his first Boston

Marathon in 1928, used sneakers, high-jump shoes and bowling shoes for his races. There were no shoes specifically for distance runners until 1935 when Spalding introduced a 'marathon' shoe. As recently as 1966, there were only a handful of companies manufacturing shoes for distance runners. It is not surprising that running shoes became synonymous with track spikes, tennis shoes and sneakers.

In Japan, wooden *geta* and straw *zori* are the traditional outdoor footwear. Both consist of a flat sole and a thong that passes between the big and second toe and over the instep. The wooden sole of the *geta* is raised on two parallel wooden supports. *Geta* and *zori* evolved to assist in everyday work activities such as rice cultivation. Leather shoes were introduced from Korea prior to the beginning of the Christian era but they were little used except by the upper class for ceremonial occasions. Straw boots were developed for use in the snow country. None of this footwear was adaptable for distance running.

With the introduction of cotton to Japan in the Muromachi period (1333–1573), the Japanese began to wear *tabi* on their feet, especially indoors. Fastening at the back of the ankle, *tabi* resembled socks with a separate division for the big toe, required to accommodate the thong when worn with *geta* or *zori*.

Early marathon runners in Japan ran barefoot, but concern with the transmission of bubonic plague led to the use of *tabi*. *Tabi* for this purpose were made more durable with the addition of two or three layers of canvas to the sole. Eventually, to strengthen the *tabi* even further and prevent slipping, corrugated rubber soles were added. For a better fit, the *tabi*'s ankle-wrapping top and fasteners were eliminated, and laces and vertical support bands added to the uppers. Except for the separate division for the big toe, *tabi* now functionally and in appearance bore a close resemblance to contemporary running shoes.

In the fifth Olympic Games held at Stockholm in 1912, Japan's first marathoner, Shizo Kanaguri, wore a pair of *tabi* with reinforced rubber soles. These 'Kanaguri *tabi*', as they came to be known, were most commonly used by Japanese runners prior to World War II. Kitei Son, the Korean who represented Japan in the 1936 Berlin Olympics (Korea was under Japanese rule from 1910 to 1945), wore laced *tabi* in the marathon, which he won to become Japan's first marathon medallist. Marathon *tabi* were marketed in Japan until the mid-1950s. They were replaced first by canvas rubber-soled shoes and later by a lighter, stronger type of shoe with a synthetic rubber sole.[9]

Early Research

The improvement in shoes did little to alleviate the persistent problem of blisters among marathoners. After his victory in a 1908 New York race, Matt Maloney was quoted as saying:

> Regarding running shoes, I like to have the soles of my shoes fairly stiff so as to keep the foot steady: if too pliable the foot bends on the inside and the result will be a blister on the foot and very soon it will begin to hurt, with the result that you are forced to stop and change your shoes—then you are through.[10]

Jock Semple, associated with the Boston Marathon since 1923, remembers soaking his feet in brine nightly to harden them and rubbing his shoes with neatsfoot oil to protect himself against blisters.[11]

Were blisters inevitable in long distance running? Onitsuka was determined to overcome the problem. Having neither sufficient funding nor personnel for this specific research, Onitsuka turned to the research and professional expertise of associates outside the company. During the course of his investigations he discussed the problem with many people, including the leading Japanese marathoner, Kurao Hiroshima, who had won the Mainichi Marathon at Beppu, and who was a member of the Japanese Olympic team for Rome. He was suffering from the perennial problem of blisters. But he assured Onitsuka that when the blisters stopped bothering the runner he knew that he had become a first-class athlete.

Onitsuka questioned him about the possibility of making shoes that prevented blisters. A wonderful idea, Hiroshima agreed, but probably a dream. Onitsuka decided that he would attempt to fulfil this dream. His principle in developing new products has always been to find out why the athletes are dissatisfied with what they have and to make improvements. Onitsuka started by investigating how blisters are formed. He followed the runners on his bicycle. At 10 kilometres and 15 kilometres no problems had developed with their feet. By about 20 kilometres, the soles of their feet had turned red. At 30 kilometres, they reported engorgement and pain. By 35 kilometres, most runners had blisters.

Onitsuka went to visit Professor Yotaro Mizuno of the Department of Medicine at Osaka University, seeking an explanation as to why blisters are formed by running. Professor Mizuno explained that it was based on the same principle as a burn or scald. When a scald occurs, caused by hot water, for example, blisters are formed by lymphatic fluid flowing to the source of heat. The liquid 'soaks up' the heat and protects the muscles from experiencing a rise in temperature.

When a person runs for a long time, heat is generated by the continuous impact of the feet against the ground. Similarly, continuous clapping will produce heat in the palms. When running long distances, the sole is being slapped against the ground thousands of times. The blisters are formed because of this impact heat.

From the point of view of sports dynamics, a person who weighs 60 kilograms has precisely that amount of pressure on the soles of his feet when he stands. When he walks, this pressure increases to between one and a half and two times his own weight. When he runs, it increases to between two and a half and three times his own weight. A runner, weighing 60 kilograms and running with a stride of 1.6 metres, slaps his feet against the concrete surface a total of 26,000 times during the course of the marathon. The heat generated is substantial and blisters form accordingly.

Onitsuka now understood. Also, he recalled that when, as soldiers, they had walked for long distances, they would take off their shoes during the rest breaks. This cooled the feet and helped prevent blisters.

Would it be possible to cool the feet without stopping? With this question in mind, Onitsuka looked to automotive engines. Automobile engines, he knew, could be cooled without stopping the car. Cold water was used for this. For motorcycles, however, cool air was used, since it had the advantage of being virtually weightless.

That was the answer. The shoes had to be constructed so that the sole of the foot could be continuously air cooled. This was how the 'Magic Runner', the marathon shoe with an air-cooling system, was developed.

The principle behind it was simple, similar to that of the bellows. Small holes were made in the toe and sides of the shoe and an air pocket was built into the instep. As the foot was lifted, cool air entered through the holes. As it hit the ground, the air was pushed out. In this way, cool air was being constantly pumped to the sole of the foot. The aeration on the top of the feet was also improved through the use of a special material with increased ventilation in the uppers.

The Magic Runner was introduced in 1960. Within three to four years it had become so popular that it captured about 80 per cent of the entire Japanese running shoe market.

It was around this time that Onitsuka Corporation developed a code by which various locations on the last could be readily identified. This facilitated communication among those involved in shoe research and development.

In June 1961, Abebe Bikila, the gold medallist at Rome, was to arrive in Japan. He had been invited to run in the Mainichi Marathon. This was the opportunity that Onitsuka had been dreaming of: he longed to see Bikila run in Tiger shoes. Accordingly, he approached the sponsors, the *Mainichi* newspaper and the Japan Amateur Athletic Federation. They were concerned about Bikila running barefoot, too, but for a different reason; namely that he might hurt his feet on pieces of glass on the Japanese roads. Therefore, it was arranged that Onitsuka Corporation would provide his shoes. Onitsuka's wish was about to come true.

Onitsuka met Bikila at his hotel in Osaka, in order to get his measurements for the shoes. His feet were soft, except for the soles, which seemed hard enough to replace shoes. Three days later Bikila's two pairs of shoes, one for training and the other for the race, were ready.

On the day of the race, Onitsuka followed Bikila for the entire course by car just to watch him run in Tiger shoes. He won the race, as expected, and very easily. Afterwards, Onitsuka asked him about the shoes. Bikila admitted that they were very comfortable, very good. The quality of Tiger shoes had been acknowledged by the world's top runner.

Only three years remained before the Tokyo Olympics, three years in which to come up with a range of new products. Onitsuka had learned from his experience with the Magic Runner that it would not suffice to focus attention exclusively on superficial features such as materials and design. There was a limit to the improvements that could be made in those areas. In order to make the very best shoes it was necessary to investigate the workings of human anatomy, especially the feet. Consequently, in 1961, Onitsuka commenced his research in human engineering, and in particular foot morphology, that is, the study of the shape and dimensions of the foot.

Professor Yaichiro Hirasawa of Shizuoka University had obtained his doctorate in medicine by studying the footprints of over 200,000 people. Onitsuka went to visit him to learn more about feet. Professor Hirasawa had developed the 'pedoscope', which was used to photograph feet. The camera was placed under a glass sheet on which the individual stood. Continuous shots were taken to record how the point of gravity shifted with movement. Onitsuka intended to apply these data in making better lasts. In order to collect more data on foot morphology, he dispatched a group of employees to collect the footprints of a few thousand athletes from a cross-section of sports, including track and field, volleyball and basketball. In addition, they were able to obtain footprints of a few hundred visiting foreign athletes.

Efforts to further improve Onitsuka's products proceeded by asking such fundamental questions as: 'What facets of shoe construction affect the suitability of a shoe for an athlete?' 'How can we develop a shoe that meets all those requirements, even though some have not yet been recognized by the athlete?'

In the area of sports dynamics, Onitsuka sought the assistance of a mathematics professor, Katsuji Ono of the University of Nagoya. His research was concerned with the quantitative analysis of the various track and field events. He was interested in how the form, angle and weight of the athletes affected the distance, height and speed of their movement. From him, Onitsuka learned more about the relationship between speed and weight. This knowledge was applied to the development of new materials which maximized speed and bounce while, at the same time, being resistant to shock.

Kazutoshi Kobayashi, a physics professor at Juntendo University in Tokyo, provided advice on the relationship between the texture of the track and the shoe soles. This was an important factor that affected the efficiency of each step. The knowledge was used in making further improvements to the shape and the materials of spikes.

Research co-operation between academics and Onitsuka Corporation had an important effect on the quality of Tiger shoes and the range of product lines. By the early 1960s, Onitsuka's focus had begun to broaden to include, in addition to basketball, volleyball, and marathon shoes, experimentation with footware for hiking, climbing, baseball, gymnastics, ballet, badminton, golf, wrestling, discus and javelin throwing, table tennis, and skiing. The preparations for the Tokyo Olympics were well under way. Onitsuka Corporation would be prepared to demonstrate to the world its achievement after barely fifteen years in operation. It was to be a great event. Some of the aforementioned new products were already doing well in the market.

Marketing Strategy

One of the factors to which the company attributes its rapid success is the application of what Onitsuka calls 'top strategy'. This is an approach to marketing that recognizes consumer preference and market dynamics. The 'top', says Onitsuka, refers exclusively to a small portion, 2 or 3 per cent, of the population who are actively involved in a particular sport. This small group are regarded as the 'trend setters'. The next set is known as the 'innovator class'. This comprises about 18 per cent of participants in the sport. This group is characterized by its willingness to try those things adopted by the 'top'. Next down is the so-called 'middle group'. This constitutes 30 to 40 per cent of the entire population engaged in the sport.

The consequences of successfully deploying such an approach are astonishing. New equipment adopted by the 'top' and 'innovator' classes will eventually filter down to the middle class as well. Therefore, by securing the 'top' 2 to 3 per cent, it is possible ultimately to secure as much as 60 per cent of the entire population. This is a very powerful marketing strategy.

This strategy had been recognized in the United States for some time and was subsequently utilized in Japan. Onitsuka's 'top strategy' had developed from this and he has used it consistently.

Viewed within the context of 'top strategy', the Olympics are considered an extremely important event among sporting goods manufacturers. Leading athletes from all over the world gather together to compete on this occasion. Not all Olympic events, however, lend themselves readily to the 'top strategy'. Events such as wrestling, fencing, and walking are relatively limited in terms of participants. Here the investment in development cannot be expected to return a profit. Onitsuka, because of his personal philosophy regarding youth and involvement, has no hesitation about committing himself to such an investment. Whether or not a sport is popular is not of paramount importance to him. What matters most is that participants are doing their best. As long as young people are involved in a sport, regardless of its popularity, the corporation strives to provide them with the appropriate shoes; it is a social commitment. 'This is our ultimate objective', says Onitsuka. 'When we fail to strive to meet this goal we will be in danger of losing sight of our corporate mission.'

In 1957, rising to the challenge provided by the proposed Japanese–Chilean Patagonian Expedition, Onitsuka Corporation, in conjunction with Toray Industries, one of Japan's leading manufacturers of synthetic fibres, undertook production of snow boots. Thirty-seven pairs of these boots were used by expedition members.

In the early 1960s, the leader of the wintering party of the Japanese Antarctic Observation Team, Dr Tetsuya Torii, suggested that Onitsuka Corporation develop arctic boots. Onitsuka accepted the challenge and arranged to work on this venture in conjunction with Teijin Limited, presently the largest polyester maker in Japan and a leading manufacturer of synthetic fibres. With help from the low temperature laboratories at Hokkaido University, they developed boots made of synthetic fibre which were tested at temperatures as low as $-85°C$ ($-121°F$). These boots were adopted not only by the Japanese team, but are used by a further eleven countries today with observation teams in Antarctica.

Arctic boots are even less profitable than footwear for the less popular sports. The cost of their development is enormous and the demand is strictly limited, although they are also used on board fishing vessels in the Arctic and Antarctic waters and for work inside refrigerated storage rooms. Naoki Uemura, the Japanese explorer who conquered the highest peak on each continent and crossed Antarctica alone, wore ASICS Polar Boots on his solo trip across the Arctic early in 1978. The members of the Nihon University Arctic Expedition who competed against Uemura to reach the North Pole also used the boots.

Members of the British Transglobe Expedition have used Onitsuka

Polar boots since the outset of their Arctic training journey in 1976. The following is an excerpt from a 1980 radio message sent to ASICS by Sir Ranulph Fiennes, the expedition leader:

> I am sending this radio message to you from our winter camp at 6,500 feet above sea level on the edge of the Antarctic ice plateau. We have been using two types of Onitsuka Polar Boot since 1976 when our Arctic training journey began. We have learned that they are undoubtedly the best polar boots available anywhere in the world . . .
>
> The wind chill factor, as I write, is −131°F (−90.5°C), at which temperature any exposed flesh freezes in less than 25 seconds. Fingers and toes are the first to get cold unless they are protected by the best possible gloves and socks. Our Onitsuka boots have lasted us five years and they are still wonderfully warm and strong despite the fuel and oil which has stained them and the sharp ice which they have been in contact with for so long.

Onitsuka and his personnel remain constantly vigilant for new ideas and are quick to apply new technology to develop new products. Occasionally a new product may not be commercially successful but its development through the application of state of the art technology will have provided new knowledge that can frequently be used to bring about improvements in other areas through technological transfer within the corporation.

The Onitsuka Circle

One of the major difficulties facing manufacturers is the accommodation of frequent changes in production of a large variety of products produced in small quantities. The high production costs incurred have been the downfall of many manufacturers. Sports shoe manufacturing is a classic example of the ineffectiveness of one-product mass-production and the necessity for multi-product, small-batch production.

Until 1953, when Onitsuka established his company's first self-managed factory in rented space, the company had been completely dependent on subcontract factories. In September 1960, the company moved its head office to newly constructed facilities in the Suma district of Kobe which accommodated a second factory operation as well. The main thrust of production, however, remained centred in subcontract factories. This was primarily because it is more or less impossible to take on the production of small quantities of a large variety of products in one or two factories only. Both money and time costs are prohibitive.

A major drawback of subcontract production is that the quality of the product is not directly controlled by the issuing company. How does one maintain the high quality required? Onitsuka decided that the best approach would be to establish a research and development centre at head office. This would make it possible to co-ordinate production supervision and technical training for employees at the affiliated factories. The company's Suma factory would concentrate on producing those items that required special skills or equipment, and frequently included the greater volume items. Even today, as Cavanagh points out, 'The footwear industry is not known for its research and development. One veteran shoe manufacturer describes how, until recently, walking into a shoe factory with a tape measure was considered research.'[12] Onitsuka was certainly ahead of his time in his efforts to standardize quality among his subcontractors.

Onitsuka Corporation was virtually dependent on the subcontract factories, and vice versa. There were sixty or so of these factories at the time, all fairly small, employing between ten and fifty workers each. Some made the entire product, while other more specialized factories performed one particular manufacturing process such as cutting, pressing, stitching or moulding.

The use of *shitauke keiretsu gaisha*, or affiliated subcontractors, was, and continues to be, widespread throughout Japan. Large enterprises, in particular, had a great deal to gain from this practice. Immediately after the war the substantial wage disparity between large and small enterprises, which resulted primarily from a seemingly inexhaustible labour supply, made possible the realization of substantial savings in the production costs of large manufacturers when the labour-intensive portions of the production processes were assigned to subcontractors. Throughout the 1950s, exploitation of the weak bargaining position of small subcontractors was not uncommon. Large manufacturers' primary interest in the subcontractors was the maximization of short-run gains and the reduction of risk through their extensive use.

The subcontracting firms served as a buffer against economic fluctuations. The lifelong employment practice of the large corporations rendered them unable to respond to downturns in the economy with layoffs of personnel. Instead they held the number of permanent employees to a minimum and depended on subcontractors and temporary workers to absorb excess volumes of work. For large and small parent corporations alike, subcontract firms assumed much of the risk associated with capital investment, inventory storage, and so on. Onitsuka had never considered his affiliated subcontracting firms as mere contracted producers. Rather, they were integrated into the system as part of the team coordinated by the parent company and, as such, constituted a vital part of Onitsuka Corporation, responsible for 70 per cent of the total production.[13]

Subsequent to the offer of shares to all employees on the occasion of the tenth anniversary of Onitsuka Corporation in 1959, a similar offer was made to members of the *Onitsuka-kai*, or Onitsuka Circle, in 1961. The *Onitsuka-kai* had been established some five months before the offer was made. It consisted of about a hundred affiliated factories and suppliers who were actively involved with Onitsuka Corporation.

Onitsuka viewed the company not solely as a composite of his own employees. His concept of the corporation included the affiliated factories without whose involvement the company would not have succeeded. The company's essential multi-product, small-batch production system was made possible through the co-operation of the affiliated factories. The corporation and the factories were one entity, one being. Therefore, it seemed only right that they should have access to the management of the company and participate in decision making. Only then would mutual enhancement be possible.

Onitsuka's attempt to formalize the close relationship between his company and its affiliated firms through the formation of an association was not unique. Many manufacturers were moving in this direction. In the automobile industry, for example, each major manufacturer organized an association for its subcontractors. Such associations foster co-operation among the subcontractors themselves as well as promoting close ties between the large corporation and its affiliates.

Association members regularly meet with the management of the parent corporation to exchange views and be kept up to date on plans and developments. The association often offers educational activities such as management seminars and technical training and provides for the exchange of technical information. It is through the association that financial, managerial and technical aid is provided to the affiliated firms by the parent corporations.

Such associations generally contribute markedly to the development of a feeling of solidarity and loyalty among the affiliated firms and between the affiliated firms and the parent company. Since the establishment of the Onitsuka Circle in the early 1960s, the extent of its involvement in the running of the company has increased concurrently with the increase in capital. The dedication and the loyalty that grew as a result of such participation were to play an important role in helping Onitsuka Corporation during subsequent times of crises.

When Onitsuka's father, Dentaro Sakaguchi, died in 1963 at the age of eighty-three, the presidents of thirty Onitsuka Circle companies accompanied Onitsuka to Tottori for the funeral.

The Tokyo Olympics were fast approaching and, though the company's strength was ever increasing, an unexpected dark cloud was looming on the horizon.

8 | Diversification Disaster

Stock Exchange Listing

Onitsuka's wish, and one of his aims in enforcing 'glass pane' management, was to have his company listed on the Stock Exchange. Distributing the shares on the company's tenth anniversary was one of the steps towards achieving open management. Although, at the time, listing seemed but a dream, it was to become reality sooner than he had expected. The capital increased slowly but steadily. In 1963, wholesalers and retailers joined Onitsuka Circle members as shareholders, together owning 50 per cent of Onitsuka Corporation stock. The remainder was owned by Onitsuka and his employees. When Onitsuka felt that the company was ready, he went to the Ministry of Finance.

His request was refused, however, on the grounds that it was premature, although the company met the minimum capital requirement of 100 million yen, and the length of establishment requirement of two years. With a capital of approximately 110 million yen and 530 employees, the company would have been the smallest firm ever listed.

Onitsuka was not deterred, however, and some months later, with the support of the company's major investment banking house, Yamaichi Securities, presently one of Japan's 'Big 4' securities firms, his request was granted. In February 1964, fifteen years after the company's inception, it was listed on the Stock Exchange in Kobe. Two months later it was due to be listed in the Second Section of the Osaka Stock Exchange.

This was a momentous occasion for Onitsuka. His dream had come true. His joy should have been shared by all, but it was not. Some senior executives had been against the idea from the beginning. Curiously, they were all personnel recruited from other companies. Onitsuka took note of this but failed to give it much attention. Yet it was an undercurrent, the significance of which was to manifest itself later.

The vice-president, Minoru Ishibashi, Mamoru Okitsu, the head of the finance department, and Toshiaki Takashima, a senior executive, were of the opinion that Onitsuka Corporation was too small to be listed. Someone could easily take it over if they tried. While agreeing with Onitsuka's idea that an enterprise should not be privatized, they felt he was being too idealistic in trying to achieve this aim at this time. The company had done reasonably well so far. They wanted to carry on as they had been doing and see how things would develop.

Onitsuka did not deny the possibility of a takeover. He argued that if someone tried to buy the company out, he and those among his employees who supported him would let their stock go. With the earnings from the sale, they would establish a new corporation with more modern facilities. What the buyer would get would be only the shell of Onitsuka Corporation. The corporation could not be run by money alone. Human intelligence, wisdom and dedication were required to manufacture the product. The employees/shareholders were the central pillar of the corporation. So long as they remained united, even in the face of a takeover, they could still actualize their dreams.

The real objection of Onitsuka's opponents, however, lay not with the possible prematurity of the decision or with the fear of a takeover. Their real fear lay in their dislike of the concept of open management. As executives with considerable business experience, Onitsuka felt they should have realized that listing was the logical step to follow the distribution of shares on the tenth anniversary. He was disappointed that they had not felt comfortable in expressing their concerns to him earlier.

He was strongly opposed to any maintenance of the status quo and felt that one must always seek better ways of doing things. Often companies sit back and bask in their current success, thinking it will persist indefinitely. Management, however, must be dynamic not passive: creativity and risk-taking must be constantly encouraged, never stifled, or success will be short-lived.

Onitsuka argued his points, and eventually convinced the sceptics that listing was desirable. Nevertheless, the problem was far from solved. This incident was the tip of an iceberg that was to undermine Onitsuka Corporation management.

Diversification Out of Control

In the early 1960s, the Japanese economy was racing ahead with annual growth-rates of around 10 per cent. Industries were flourishing. The output of chemical and petrochemical products quadrupled during the decade ending in 1966. The number of factories with thirty or more employees grew from 30,868 to 52,499 and the number of workers they employed increased from 3.7 million to over 6.6 million.[1]

Prime Minister Hayato Ikeda, in office from 1960 through 1964 (the last year when the Japanese–American balance of payments was in favour of the United States), envisaged a doubling of national income by the end of the decade and embarked on a bold programme of economic expansion encompassing both the manufacturing and agricultural sectors. Now, for the first time since the Meiji period, the Japanese populace recognized the pursuit of money and personal happiness as virtues. Consumer commodities such as televisions, cameras, transistor radios and automobiles found a market beyond a handful of wealthy urbanites. So rapid was the economic growth that Ikeda's income doubling goal was reached in seven years, not ten.

The trend at the time among manufacturers was to expand through diversification, capitalizing on expanding consumer purchasing power. Onitsuka had been considering doing this with his company as well. He conferred with an external management consultant about the prospects of diversification. From the corporate management diagnosis, the consultant concluded that diversification would assure future development.

In 1962, Onitsuka sent the vice-president, Ishibashi, to the United States for two months with the intention that he would bring back new management ideas. During this time, Ishibashi visited various sport and leisure industries, as well as conducting a marketing survey. Onitsuka had felt such a trip was of prime importance to the development of Ishibashi, his heir apparent. Ishibashi, on his return, informed Onitsuka that he had benefited greatly from his trip and was full of new ideas for the company.

Onitsuka could not have been more pleased. The subsequent activities of Ishibashi, however, were to become a matter of serious concern. At times, Ishibashi appeared to be satiated with adrenalin: he would rush from one point to the next, one issue to another. He appeared to have been highly charged by the immense energy of the American economy. His zeal did not seem to abate, rather it was accelerating. His behaviour was out of character. Initially, Onitsuka had put Ishibashi's conduct down to over-enthusiasm, but now he had become a little alarmed.

Ishibashi was responsible for the sales department and whereas in the past he would consult with Onitsuka frequently, seeking his advice on important decisions, he no longer did so. Now on those odd occasions when Onitsuka gave advice, it would be ignored. Ishibashi began to sign all manner of contracts without consultation with Onitsuka.

He ventured first into bowling equipment—bowling was becoming increasingly popular at the time—then into golf equipment, sleeping bags, bamboo skis, and a myriad other things. Eventually he became involved in the sale of miniature tape recorders and even diamond jewellery.

As time progressed, Ishibashi began to show signs of depression. He would withdraw into himself for long periods and speak to no one. Recalling this period, Kuramitsu Nakayama, currently an executive managing director with ASICS says, 'Ishibashi would become frighteningly quiet. We would avoid approaching him at these times if possible'.

Ishibashi was a very able businessman who had acquired his early training with a trading company. Onitsuka knew him to be more interested in money management and the movement of goods than in actual production. He preferred to involve himself strictly in selling as opposed to product development and marketing. In addition to this preference and Ishibashi's stimulating experience in the United States, there was a general business trend towards diversification. Onitsuka thought that perhaps these factors together had led Ishibashi to push diversification too far too fast.

Onitsuka was not really opposed to diversification in principle. Yet he preferred to expand the business in a planned and deliberate way, never over-extending the capacity of the company. Some vertical integration had occurred with the establishment of Taigon Chemical Industries in 1959 for the purpose of manufacturing sneakers for export to the American market and winter boots, using chemicals. Within a short time, though, the American market had virtually disappeared as buyers turned to Taiwan and Korea where shoes made with synthetic materials, particularly nylon and vinyl, were being produced much more cheaply.

Onitsuka encountered problems with the synthetic winter boots as well. The largest market for these was in Hokkaido. They sold well the first year but the second year the market was flooded with cheaper imitations produced by other Kobe footwear manufacturers.

Three years after its inception, Taigon Chemical Industries was absorbed by Onitsuka Corporation. Seeing other synthetic footwear manufacturers go bankrupt in the interval, Onitsuka made the decision to concentrate on the manufacture of high-quality sports shoes and leave the synthetic, cheap footwear market to others for the time being.

While Taigon Chemical Industries existed, Onitsuka had devoted himself to his new venture, placing Ishibashi in charge of Onitsuka Corporation. This first-hand experience with diversification heightened Onitsuka's awareness of its hidden dangers. Because of this, Onitsuka's idea of diversification differed from the dominant view which favoured rapid expansion on many fronts simultaneously and without proper coordination. He believed that one should not risk spreading oneself too thin through expansion into too many avenues at once. He counselled Ishibashi to be cautious and take things one at a time.

Ishibashi disagreed with Onitsuka's view, accusing him of being unable to appreciate his plans for diversification. He went so far as to suggest that if Onitsuka could not realize that what he was doing was very important for Onitsuka Corporation's future, he was not worthy of being its president.

Ishibashi had formed a little clique of followers. They were mostly the personnel who had been recruited from other corporations. He would take his group out in the evening for drinks in Sannomiya to voice his opinions about the incompetence of the president.

Ishibashi had commenced visiting local retail stores in a newly acquired imported car, taking a young company secretary with him, and peddling a wide variety of products. Word of this quickly reached Onitsuka who began receiving complaints from the dealers who wanted to know what the vice-president was up to. He would arrive with a carload of merchandise totally unrelated to sports and try to sell these things to the retailers. The retailers were demanding sports shoes, not tape recorders.

Ishibashi had also visited the company's external adviser, Masato Osaka, of Osaka Taishodo in Tottori. Realizing that something was amiss with Ishibashi, Osaka immediately contacted Onitsuka. Not only had Ishibashi criticized Onitsuka and his management practices, he had rambled on about being of noble origin. Things had definitely gone too far. Onitsuka decided it was time to put an end to this turbulence.

Ishibashi had simply been diversifying for the sake of it and his endeavours had failed totally. His attempts were based neither on market unity nor on unified technology. The products did not share a common 'identity' or 'personality'. Most of Ishibashi's ventures did not even break even. As if this was not enough, the economy was starting to slow down.

While overall economic gains were still healthy, individual business failures were at an all-time high. In 1963, when Japan was enjoying a favourable economic climate, 1,738 companies with debts exceeding 10 million yen went bankrupt. In 1964, as the recession set in, this figure jumped to 4,212 and, in 1965, a total of 6,141 such companies failed.[2] The seemingly insatiable consumer demand at the outset of the decade had tapered off. Industries were confronted with a serious labour shortage and rapidly rising labour costs. From the latter half of 1963, the money market had been gradually tightened in order to control inflation. Together these factors brought on a recession which lasted through 1965.

At this time Onitsuka Corporation was like a rabbit among a pack of wolves. The situation was serious. There was an increasing amount of reject merchandise in inventory, sales revenue was decreasing, and financing was becoming difficult. Onitsuka was alarmed by the possibility that the effort of the past fifteen years would come to nothing. Something had to be done quickly. His response was to return to his company's roots, that is, to specializing in sports shoes.

Unfortunately this was complicated by the company having been listed on the Kobe Stock Exchange in February 1964 and being at the point of listing at Osaka in April. A strategy of withdrawing from several areas would now occasion an inevitable deficit for the year end. To have a deficit in the first year of listing was unheard of. Onitsuka was concerned about the subsequent severe criticism should he proceed with retrenchment. Furthermore, the Olympics were only months away and the company had earmarked considerable funds for the event. All these matters caused Onitsuka to hesitate.

Hesitation would not improve matters. The more he delayed the worse the situation would become. He was convinced that diversification carried out at a hectic pace was the cause of the present difficulties and by removing the cause it would be possible to re-establish Onitsuka Corporation in the field of sports shoe manufacturing.

Onitsuka decided that it was time for the president to show courage. He felt that he could not view the problem in terms of short-term losses, including loss of face and personal criticism. It was a gamble and marked an important turning-point for Onitsuka Corporation.

First, something had to be done about Ishibashi. During this period of decision, the head of the finance department, Okitsu, came to see Onitsuka complaining that he could no longer cope with Ishibashi. He felt that Ishibashi was not of sound mind. Okitsu had been one of Ishibashi's foremost supporters but it seemed that he, too, had begun to have doubts about the man.

Onitsuka was having similar thoughts. Ishibashi was no longer the sincere and humble man he had once known. A personal friend of Ishibashi, Motoki Sakata, who, through his friendship with Ishibashi had become a technical adviser to Onitsuka Corporation, was extremely concerned about the apparent changes in Ishibashi's personality and arranged for him to see a psychiatrist. He was diagnosed as a psychotic manic-depressive.

The doctor suggested that he be hospitalized for treatment. This was arranged immediately. There was a Board of Directors meeting and it was decided to relieve Ishibashi of the vice-presidency. The Board demoted him to a managing director, choosing to wait and observe the course of his illness before taking further action. Onitsuka also took this opportunity to explain to the Board his decision to embark on the retrenchment course that was to decide the future of Onitsuka Corporation.

The Circle Stands Firm

Onitsuka had been caught up in the widely-held belief that the road to success is through growth. Many businessmen see growth of sales as the solution to all problems and diversification as the route to achieve growth. Yet now the error in this strategy became clear to Onitsuka. Shrinking the number of products and product lines seemed to be the surest route to recovery.

Onitsuka set his course. It was one of immediate retrenchment, commencing in May 1964, only a month after the listing on the Osaka Stock Exchange. First, all purchasing in those sections earmarked for elimination ceased. This applied generally to the sections established through the diversification programme. He next asked for voluntary resignations from those sections, of which he obtained about a hundred.

Still more jobs had to be eliminated and Kazunori Kanzaki was given the task of selecting and firing eight employees. 'It was an extremely difficult thing to do', recalls Kanzaki, 'We had come through a lot together, I couldn't stomach firing more than one person a week so the process dragged on for two months.'

Heizo Tanaka had to fire four of the employees he had so carefully nurtured as production managers. 'I couldn't sleep for several nights, I was so upset', recalls Tanaka. 'When I was faced with a similar demand ten years later, my memories of the first experience were so vivid and so distasteful, I couldn't comply. Instead, I found other ways of reducing costs.'

Ultimately the workforce was reduced from 530 to 413. All stock in the newly established sections was to be sold off. In order to expedite the liquidation, Onitsuka resorted to total group mobilization. Almost all employees, even those in accounting and production, were allocated to the project. They were sent out as temporary salespeople to government offices and various companies with instructions to sell at cost or even less, if necessary. The company was short of cash and the retention of now redundant stock was nothing more than a burden.

One recognized strength of the Japanese corporation is the ease with which a leader can effectively mobilize employees when required, made possible by group solidarity, supported by strong vertical interpersonal relationships. Onitsuka Corporation's employees rose to the occasion and threw themselves whole-heartedly into their assigned task. Onitsuka took a substantial salary cut, and sold the recently purchased car which had replaced his motor scooter.

Inevitably, it was not long before the rumour machine got into full gear. The company had anticipated the possibility but was hardly in a position to pay much attention at the time: 'Onitsuka Corporation was only recently listed, but now it has started to cut back. What is the company up to?' 'Onitsuka Corporation is only a short step away from bankruptcy.'

The rumours were beginning to paint a very black picture, and exaggeration was rampant. Onitsuka became concerned for the well-being of his suppliers and subcontract factories who could not help but be affected by these rumours. Sadao Suzuki, president of Shinwa Corporation, an Onitsuka Circle member, recalls that some companies were reluctant to do business with Onitsuka Corporation. As a result, Shinwa was receiving a great many Onitsuka orders. 'I promised Mr Onitsuka I would fill his orders', says Suzuki, 'even though the banks and material suppliers were threatening to terminate relations with Shinwa if I persisted.'

At a meeting of the eighty or so members of the Onitsuka Circle called to apprise them of the company's situation, Onitsuka explained that the company was suffering from its rash attempt at diversification. The decision had been made to put an end to this scheme before it was too late, and return to specializing in shoes. The company would most likely be in the red for some time and might possibly run short of capital. Confident that together they could pull through, Onitsuka asked for the co-operation of the Circle members.

The Circle members had suspected that there were some things wrong at Onitsuka Corporation and they had heard the rumours relating to the company's possible bankruptcy. Now they understood the problem. They were pleased, however, that Onitsuka had sought their confidence and had explained the background to and reasons for his decision. Because Onitsuka had been honest in his dealings with them in the past they believed his explanation and they pledged their confidence and understanding.

Overwhelmed by this response, Onitsuka was unable to express his gratitude. Only two of the Circle members failed to pledge full support—dealers in raw materials who had joined the Circle only shortly before. They insisted that their future dealings with the company would have to be on a cash basis. Later they declined to do any business with the company. Onitsuka did not try to dissuade them. Some years later, when Onitsuka Corporation had fully recovered and was prospering once more, the two companies attempted, through the intercession of the banks, to re-establish business relations with the company. No longer needing their services, it was Onitsuka's turn to decline, and he felt justified.

Dealing with the Banks

The most serious problem facing the company during the period of retrenchment was that of cash flow. Returns on products sold for less than cost barely sufficed to sustain the company. It was necesary to approach the Kangyo Bank, the main bank that the company had dealt with for some fifteen years. Onitsuka expected that it would provide the financing his company so desperately needed. He discovered, however, that the bank was not sympathetic. He was turned down. The bank viewed the company critically, claiming that many of the sales credits were long overdue and many stock items were worthless. It mortgaged the inventory as well as Onitsuka's private assets and made daily checks on the company finances. The stranglehold the bank had on the company nearly immobilized it.

There may have been some justification for the bank's approach. More than four thousand businesses went bankrupt in 1964. In the Kobe rubber footwear industry, such corporations as Chuo Chemical and Chiyoda Rubber and even the giant Shibata Rubber Industries filed for bankruptcy. Compared to Shibata Rubber, Onitsuka Corporation's financial basis, as well as its corporate scale, was inferior. Many banks endured a considerable loss of prestige when evidence of carelessly made loans surfaced during this period. In accordance with the trend of the time of growth for growth's sake, many companies had over-extended themselves. To counteract this, interest rates were raised and loans for facility investment severely curtailed.

Justified or not within the economic climate, Onitsuka resented the bank's treatment of a long and faithful customer. Slowly the shortage of funds began to tell on the company as notes issued were being rejected by the banks. The bank suggested that the company approach its suppliers for payment extensions. The company was being put to the test. If the suppliers agreed to the extension the bank would lend the company more funds. Onitsuka had little choice but to approach his suppliers and explain the situation. They were most responsive despite their own difficulties. Although he was deeply touched by their trust, Onitsuka was embarrassed at having to ask favours of them.

The position did not appear to be improving even though the retrenchment operation was proceeding smoothly. The financial headache persisted. Now the rumours seemed to have substance: bankruptcy was a real possibility.

At that time, Kenichi Kashiwai, president of Kashiwai Paper Company, was chairman of the Kobe Junior Chamber of Commerce. As part of its leadership training programme, the JCC compiled a case study book. Well-known and highly respected for its marketing strategy and personnel management, Onitsuka Corporation was included in the text. When Kashiwai heard of Onitsuka Corporation's predicament and its rejection on the part of the banks he determined to do what he could to help.

Says Kashiwai:

I felt that the banks had an obligation to help a fine company like Onitsuka Corporation through its financial crisis. If the company had gone bankrupt, repercussions would have been felt throughout the Kobe rubber footwear industry. I didn't know Mr Onitsuka personally at that time and I couldn't directly influence the banks but I enlisted the aid of a former Junior Chamber of Commerce member, Hisashige Hirose, manager of the Kobe branch of the Bank of Japan.

Although the Bank of Japan, in its role as the bank of issue, the bankers' bank, and the government's bank, could not provide concrete financial assistance, Hirose could, through his position, exert considerable influence over the lending banks. A meeting was arranged between Onitsuka and Hirose. Onitsuka was by now totally deflated and exhausted from the business going so badly. He will never forget Hirose's words of encouragement:

> Mr Onitsuka, don't lose your spirit. Have you forgotten that your ways of management won you and your company the prize as the ideal small-sized enterprise? I won't try to deny that the company's diversification plan was a mistake, and as president, you are responsible. However, you are willing to admit your mistake and are doing your best to remedy the situation. This is brave and admirable, especially as the timing was so bad, with your company having just been listed. There are many companies that will collapse because they are unable to admit that they have made mistakes. I am counting on you to set a good example for all the other small businesses, as you have done in the past. I am sure that you will pull through successfully from this recession. I will support you as much as I can.

It was reassuring, in these difficult times, to know that there were people who appreciated Onitsuka's efforts and ideas. How encouraging Hirose's words were! They helped Onitsuka to carry on. Hirose was later killed in a Japan Airlines crash in 1972. Says Onitsuka, 'I will be forever indebted to him for his encouragement and his efforts on my behalf'.

Hirose acted on his promise to support Onitsuka and threw his weight behind Onitsuka's decision to approach Hideo Kusaka, a senior executive managing director at the Kobe Bank (now the Taiyo Kobe Bank). Kusaka had been one of the senior officers in the Himeji Tenth Division and the chief accountant for his regiment during the war. Onitsuka had known him from their Army days.

When Onitsuka established the company he had dealt with the Kobe Bank but as the sales network expanded throughout Japan he had found it necessary to make the Kangyo Bank the company's main bank. The Kobe Bank lacked the extensive nation-wide branch system of the Kangyo Bank, making customer payment through the bank difficult. The company had continued to have some dealings with the Kobe Bank and, when finances had become tight as a result of diversification, Onitsuka had asked the bank to examine the company's financial situation. Even before this, interested in expanding their relationship with Onitsuka Corporation, the bank had been making its own assessment of the company.

By the time Onitsuka met with Kusaka, Hirose had already spoken with him. Kusaka told Onitsuka that the bank's assessment showed that the

company's financial difficulties stemmed from its diversification programme. It had been too expansive and too rapid. Before this happened
the company had been on a sound financial footing. The bank recognized
that Onitsuka's recent course of action indicated that the problem had
been identified and that the necessary steps were being taken to rectify it.

Promotion of local Kobe industries was one of the bank's policies.
Kusaka regretted that the Kobe Bank had not been Onitsuka Corporation's
main bank much sooner. Now he pledged his bank's full support.
Onitsuka could hardly believe his ears. He felt like some weary traveller,
lost in the dark, who finally spies a light shining from a house in the
distance.

Onitsuka Corporation strengthened its relationship with the Kobe Bank.
The Fuji and Tokai banks were henceforth to be the secondary banks.
These two banks were impressed by Onitsuka's achievements in the past,
his zeal for the business, and the potential of Onitsuka Corporation.
Accordingly they concluded that the company was worth helping in these
tough times.

The retrenchment programme, begun in May 1964, was continued with
the assistance of the new banks. The speed of recovery increased, faster
than expected. By October 1964 the company was in the black. At this rate
the company could break even by February 1965 when the annual
accounts were prepared, subject to one proviso. The funds budgeted for
the Tokyo Olympics would, if taken into consideration, keep the company
in the red.

Onitsuka Corporation had set aside a budget of 30 million yen for the
Olympics. The company planned to have a service counter as well as
shops to sell its products. Several managers considered that the budget
was too high and should be reduced under the circumstances of financial
exigency. Onitsuka, however, remained adamant that the original plan
should stand. He considered the short-term sacrifice to be worth it for the
corporation in the long run.

As expected, the company had a deficit of 29 million yen in February
1965, equivalent to the budget for the Olympic Games. Thus the company
had a deficit for its first year of listing. Naturally, no dividends were paid
out. The company shares, which were valued at just under 200 yen when
the company was listed, had dropped to 35 yen. The criticism with which
Onitsuka was bombarded, especially from those in the securities
business, was severe: 'Onitsuka is a swindler!' 'He doesn't even know the
ABC of management!'

Onitsuka had no choice but to accept the rebukes that assaulted him
from all directions. He reflected on his mistakes, and considered where he
had gone wrong. He had learned a bitter lesson.

9 | Point-of-Focus Management

Parting with the Heir Apparent

Ishibashi came out of hospital in July 1964 at the height of the retrenchment programme, six months after his illness had first been diagnosed. Onitsuka had been thinking of placing him in charge of the retrenchment operations when he returned. He had intended to make Ishibashi responsible for seeing the programme through to completion. His errors were the main cause of this situation, Onitsuka reasoned. He quickly realized, however, that the man who had returned to him after half a year of hospitalization was not the same man who had once been his 'right arm'. Ishibashi seemed totally dispirited. Onitsuka saw that he could not shoulder such a responsibility.

Eventually, Ishibashi left Onitsuka Corporation, having become aware of the significance of the matter for which he was responsible. Onitsuka missed him greatly. He was the man who had come to Onitsuka's rescue eleven years earlier when he had been ill and on the verge of death. He was a very intelligent man and was respected by the young employees. Many of ASICS' present executives were trained by Ishibashi. Says Kuramitsu Nakayama, 'We learned so much from him. He was not only an exceptionally competent businessman but a gifted teacher as well.'

Ishibashi had worked his way up from manager to executive director and eventually to vice-president in 1961. Onitsuka had decided sometime before that Ishibashi would be his successor, and had made this intention known both within and outside the company. It was sad, indeed, for Onitsuka to part with someone whom he held in such high esteem. Nevertheless, Onitsuka felt that a corporation is an integrated whole where ideology plays a central role. Ishibashi's views on business differed from Onitsuka's and he had openly criticized the president's managerial philosophy. Notwithstanding that these differences were accentuated by Ishibashi's illness, Onitsuka could not appoint him as the leader of the organization now; he simply could not continue to work with him.

Says Yoshiyuki Takahashi:

The ideological differences between the president and the vice-president had become very clear. Mr Onitsuka's overriding objective at the time was to deprivatize the company and become listed on the Stock Exchanges. This, of course, entailed a policy of open management. Mr Ishibashi, on the other hand, favoured maintaining the status quo. He could not see the advantage of listing such a small corporation and feared that such a move would eventually result in a takeover. He wanted to focus the company's energy on making profits and not be concerned with the Stock Exchange. Mr Onitsuka argued that if a takeover was unavoidable, so be it. The important thing was to move out of the confines that necessarily limit the growth of a private corporation.

Onitsuka made no attempt to dissuade Ishibashi when he submitted his letter of resignation. It was difficult for Onitsuka. Thinking back on all that had happened, he could not help but sense a void which could not be filled. Upon his resignation, Ishibashi asked Onitsuka to help him set up a bowling equipment sales agency. To do this he wanted to take control of the established distribution channels for bowling shoes, taking with him the three managers from Onitsuka Corporation's bowling equipment section, the only recently created section that had not yet been closed down. At about that time, bowling was becoming very popular and bowling alleys were mushrooming all over the country.

The first bowling centre in Japan had been established in Tokyo in 1952. It had forty-six lanes. With the introduction of automatic pinsetters in 1961, the popularity of ten-pin bowling spread throughout the country. By 1965, 200 centres had been opened, with a total of 5,400 lanes and within four years these figures had increased to 970 centres with 23,000 lanes nation-wide. The bowling craze reached its peak towards the end of 1972, by which time 3,900 centres housed 125,000 lanes. The main supporters of these centres were young company employees and students. In addition to the bowling alley, bowling centres usually offered restaurant/tea room facilities and provided meeting/socializing space so much in demand by young people.[1]

Onitsuka granted Ishibashi his request. The bowling section had a credit of about 10 million yen. Onitsuka commissioned him to collect the money and allow him to use it without interest. In addition, Ishibashi had also expressed his desire to handle Dunlop bowling balls. Dunlop had said that they would sign the contract provided that Onitsuka was prepared to be his guarantor. Onitsuka agreed, assuring Dunlop that he had arranged for the capital and provided Ishibashi with able management staff. In this manner Ishibashi went his own way.

Many of Onitsuka's friends and acquaintances disapproved of how he had handled the situation. They rebuked Onitsuka for being too good to Ishibashi, too easily moved to compassion. But, in retrospect, Onitsuka's compassionate nature has stood him in good stead.

Katsuto Izuno, the president of a large wholesale company, Hiroun, with which Onitsuka has dealt since 1960, says, 'Mr Onitsuka honed his decision-making skills and conduct in the Army. Military decisions, though, are coldly rational, often involving life and death, while human compassion and warmth are a part of effective business decisions.' Izuno cites factors in Onitsuka's background, especially his extended struggle against tuberculosis, his family responsibilities, and his paternal attitude to his employees, as contributory to the humane element in Onitsuka's decisions. 'It is because of his humaneness', says Izuno, 'that not only his employees but his other business associates continue to be attracted to him and stand by him.'

Ishibashi had been the vice-president of the company and had assumed responsibility for guiding the young employees during Onitsuka's long illness. The company was indebted to his significant contribution to its development. Onitsuka felt strongly that he should not desert a man who had given so much to the company. In choosing his course of action, Onitsuka had taken into consideration the effect it might have on the employees: those who had been with the company since its early days and who appreciated Ishibashi's long-term contribution, and those who did not. Onitsuka did not feel that he was being too lenient. Ishibashi's subsequent behaviour, however, disappointed Onitsuka.

Ishibashi's new company grew rapidly with the bowling craze. It became the largest wholesale dealer for bowling equipment, with total annual sales of about 5 billion yen. He built two impressive buildings, one in Tokyo and the other in Kobe. Everything seemed to be going very well. Yet gradually, the monthly reports of accounts, which Ishibashi had promised to send Onitsuka, ceased to arrive. Finally, he convinced Onitsuka Corporation's subcontractor for bowling shoes to work for him, not for Onitsuka. Ishibashi commenced his own manufacturing and wholesaling of bowling shoes. He had acquired what he needed for his success and could sever his connections with Onitsuka Corporation. His goal was now to compete with his former employer.

Onitsuka felt that things had gone too far and refused to have any further dealings with Ishibashi. Eventually the bowling craze began to ebb as the sport lost its novelty and with it the flourishing market for bowling shoes. Within four years after its peak in the latter part of 1972, 70 per cent of the bowling centres had closed, many going bankrupt.[2] Onitsuka understands that Ishibashi's company was eventually bought out by Dunlop.

As a result of Ishibashi's resignation, many of the 'grafted' executives—those recruited from other corporations—also began to leave. The first was Toshiaki Takashima who had earlier been president of one of the affiliated factories, Takashima Rubber Manufacturers. When Taigon Chemical Industries was established in 1959, Takashima Rubber was absorbed into the new company and Takashima was made a managing director of Taigon Chemical. Three years later, when this company merged with Onitsuka Corporation, Onitsuka made him a managing director of Onitsuka Corporation.

He was an excellent manager but unfortunately the management policy and philosophy of Onitsuka Corporation were not to his liking and he eventually sided with Ishibashi in the rift. Onitsuka discussed the matter with him. It was agreed that Takashima should re-establish and head Takashima Rubber Manufacturers. It is still one of ASICS' main affiliates.

Mamoru Okitsu was another to leave. He had been a university friend of Ishibashi and joined the company on the latter's recommendation. He was a talented accountant, but again he sided with his old friend and was among his strongest supporters. Strangely enough, he was the one who had complained at an earlier point that he could no longer cope with Ishibashi. This incident led indirectly to Onitsuka appointing him as the accounts manager for the retrenchment programme.

Okitsu did not last long in the difficult circumstances facing his accounts section. Debtors were delaying making their payments for as long as they could in the hope that Onitsuka Corporation would go under in the meantime. Also, the banks were reluctant to provide financial support. Not surprisingly, perhaps, Okitsu's dedication to his job began to wane.

One day, Onitsuka called Okitsu in to discuss an urgent matter. He was not in the department. His co-workers informed Onitsuka that he was taking a driving lesson. Onitsuka was astounded! In Japan, the country of kamikaze drivers, getting a driver's licence is not easy. It requires over a month of consecutive days of lectures and practical experience at a government-approved driving school.

As Onitsuka saw the situation, getting a driver's licence was a private matter. Of course, had the company been doing well, Okitsu could have taken a few hours off each day for his lessons. But during this crisis the head of the finance department should have been devoting all working hours to company business trying to develop a strategy that would enable the company to regain financial stability. After visiting the banks together, Onitsuka wanted Okitsu, as the company's financial representative, to continue to attempt to negotiate with them on his own.

Okitsu, however, felt that he had little influence, that the chance of his being able to secure a loan on his own was very slim. Onitsuka was already making every effort in this area and Okitsu preferred to leave these negotiations entirely in his hands. Onitsuka interpreted Okitsu's actions as a loss of confidence and interest in the company. He was saddened and shocked that Okitsu had given up.

Onitsuka decided, however, that it would be unwise to dismiss him at this stage. Outsiders had little confidence left in the company's finances. Firing the head of the finance department would only fuel speculation. He appointed as Okitsu's representative Shoji Kitami who was working under Okitsu in the accounting section. Onitsuka went with Kitami to call on the banks. A talented and experienced accountant, Okitsu was later offered a job in another company and voluntarily left Onitsuka Corporation.

Ultimately, all the executive directors who had been recruited as 'grafts' left. In a situation where a business expands quickly from a small to a medium size one, there is frequently a necessity to recruit new blood. Newcomers should provide the requisite broader-based management, particularly to compensate for those areas in which the president may be lacking. Onitsuka, however, learned from bitter experience that recruitment of senior personnel has its own problems.

Onitsuka believes that the backbone of a business is its philosophy: the strength of an enterprise is determined by the extent to which the ideas of the president permeate the company so as to create a coherent 'philosophical unit'. Once the enterprise grows beyond a certain point, thereby stabilizing the structure, the management policies of the firm will not be affected by recruiting. When new staff are recruited into the management before this stability forms, the enterprise runs the risk of being undermined. Had he trained the new recruits properly, Onitsuka feels the problems could have been avoided. As it was, Onitsuka's managers favoured divergent policies, leaving the administration vulnerable at a time of crisis.

Nevertheless, Onitsuka came to appreciate the strength of those employees whom he had personally trained from their entry into the corporation. Beginning with the existing personnel in 1956, Onitsuka had been living with and training the new recruits in the company's dormitory for three months every year. The latter showed great strength and spirit during the crisis. They remained steadfast as the 'grafted' personnel fell away. Onitsuka was pleased at how well these 'nurtured' members of staff worked together and how they had matured over the seven or eight years since the training programme had been implemented. Onitsuka Corporation's crisis was eventually overcome by the strength of its middle management.

'Glass Pane' Management

Onitsuka also came to appreciate that open management is invaluable for an enterprise. Onitsuka Corporation went public in 1959, making its shares available to its employees, and subsequently, in 1961, to the members of the Onitsuka Circle and, in 1963, to its wholesalers and retailers. The company also issued business reports to its associates at six-monthly intervals. Onitsuka wanted them to know everything. He wanted them to decide for themselves, based on full knowledge of the company's operations, whether or not they wished to deal with him. Having made this choice, the affiliated factories, suppliers, wholesale dealers and retail stores could unite as one. Onitsuka did not want people to avoid his company out of ignorance of its activities. He wanted them to know and approach the company by choice. This was his ideology.

This ideology proved to be Onitsuka Corporation's lifesaver. Even as the company hit bottom, the members of the Onitsuka Circle remained unified. They often agreed to extend payment dates on bills. The recession must have been a harrowing experience for them. Yet none of them refused to co-operate. Onitsuka had been honest in his management thus far; they would continue to trust him.

Masato Fujio, president of Seiko Chemicals, one of Onitsuka Corporation's subcontract factories recalls:

About 1964, there was talk among the manufacturers of moulds that Onitsuka Corporation was going bankrupt. They were worried about the corporation's cheques bouncing. I was confident that there was nothing to worry about. We could not get money from the other companies either, unless the products were sold. So we just concentrated on making our products, as ordered. I had faith in Mr Onitsuka from our long acquaintance. He had been sending us reports, good times or bad, with information that he may have preferred to, and certainly could have, kept to himself. Instead, he was honest and forthright, telling everything. That is probably why I had such trust in him.

Shiro Tachibana, president of Asahi Sporting Goods Stores Limited, says of Onitsuka:

He is full of compassion and good will but these qualities are sometimes excessive and thus become a weakness. An example is the incident of the 'shifting of the executive directors'. As an outsider, I must say that although he showed great decisiveness in the way he handled the issue, ultimately, he was not severe enough. However, I must admit that this characteristic is what I like most about him. He is very earnest. When the company was unable to provide dividends in the first year after listing, he explained the situation to all concerned in order to obtain their understanding. He is also willing to admit his own mistakes and will make every effort to solve any problem he is faced with.

Sadao Suzuki of Shinwa Corporation reflects, 'In the end, the question is whether the president has an ideology that you can trust. I think the reason we were able to pull through under such adverse conditions was because the company had a "soul".'

Importance of Point-of-Focus Management

The crisis confronting Onitsuka Corporation in 1964 was brought about by undirected diversification carried far beyond the capacity of the company. Through it, Onitsuka was made sharply aware of the necessity of point-of-focus management. A small or middle-sized enterprise with limited capital, technology and personnel is strongest when focusing all its power into one point. It is as if one is twisting a sharp gimlet in order to penetrate a hard surface. A blunt point cannot penetrate the walls of obstacles, and thus is vulnerable at times of crisis. Onitsuka learned this lesson at great expense.

The 'concentration decision', as Peter Drucker calls it, is crucial to a company's success, regardless of its size. Drucker states:

> Archimedes, one of the great scientists of antiquity, is reported to have said: 'Give me a place to stand on, and I can lift the universe off its hinges.' The place to stand on is the area of concentration. It is the area which gives a business the leverage that lifts the universe off its hinges. The concentration decision is, therefore, a crucial one. It converts, in large measure, the definition of 'what our business is' into meaningful operational commitment. It makes possible work on one's mission and purpose. It is the foundation for effective strategy. Whenever we find a business that is outstandingly successful, we will find that it has thought through the concentration alternatives and has made a concentration decision.[3]

When Onitsuka founded the company he made the concentration decision, and he has employed point-of-focus management ever since. He started with basketball shoes and concentrated initially on one type only, aspiring to make the very best of their kind in Japan. Next he attempted volleyball shoes and then track shoes, just as if he were twisting the gimlet. He was always cautious about taking a new step, ensuring that the ground was safe and firm. This method was the only possible one at the time, although it was neither systematized nor consciously conceptual-ized into a management philosophy. He simply did not have the financial capacity to take on grand expansion schemes.

Once the business began to go well, however, it seemed that he had been deceived into believing that he could not fail. Onitsuka had lost sight of the fact that his company was still a small business. If he had had a theory of management that he was aware of, he probably would have been able to stop the vice-president before things got out of hand. He might never have considered diversification in the first place.

Onitsuka had forgotten that the company was still fragile. Even though he was anxious about the behaviour and ideas of Ishibashi, he too had had similar thoughts. He believed that diversification would be good for Onitsuka Corporation and there was so much he wanted to attempt.

As things had been going well until then, he had overestimated the company's capabilities. In the favourable market environment, Onitsuka had lost sight of the concrete demands of the market-place. He had ceased to heed his inner 'marketing sense', his intuitive feeling for the market-place that had built the corporation up.

He became aware of this mistake just as Onitsuka Corporation was about to crumble. He might not have realized the seriousness of the situation until it was too late. He was lucky to wake up to it just in time. Fortunately, he was decisive in making his moves, putting aside his pride and reputation for a while. Labouring under the twin pressures of the Stock Exchange listing and the Olympics, the company barely pulled through. Indeed, it was lucky to have survived at all. The lesson that Onitsuka learned, that point-of-focus or 'gimlet' management is essential to survival, was crucial and became the bulwark of future corporate strategy.

Yuji Nishio, Governor of Tottori prefecture, singles out Onitsuka's ability to translate what he has experienced into a concrete philosophy as the key factor in his corporate success. 'In addition', says Nishio, 'Onitsuka is patient, is an innovative thinker, and is a quick actor.'

Says Onitsuka, 'My formal education is limited; I am not familiar with the names of many scholars. But what has been helpful to me, rather than scholars' theories, are the statements and actions of those who have accomplished great things throughout history.'

Onitsuka draws a parallel between this theory of management for small and medium-sized industries and the strategy employed by Nobunaga Oda. The latter was the Japanese military commander who, in 1560, with less than 3,000 soldiers, defeated the 25,000-strong Army of Yoshimoto Imagawa which was attempting at that time to conquer Owari province, which, together with Mikawa province, constitutes the present-day Aichi prefecture.

Yoshimoto had two goals: to destroy Nobunaga's fort and to kill Nobunaga. The destruction of the fort was worth much less than the destruction of Nobunaga himself. Whereas the location of the first was certain, Nobunaga's whereabouts was not: he could have been in any of the five forts he had constructed to surround Yoshimoto's Narumi castle.

Yoshimoto anticipated that Nobunaga and his main fighting force would occupy one of the forts and use it as a headquarters to launch his defence. The danger was that, while Yoshimoto was attacking the fort, Nobunaga and his men might suddenly appear and launch a counter-attack from an altogether different direction. This is what in fact happened.

Nobunaga launched a surprise attack against Yoshimoto's troops from a direction that was geographically advantageous, the narrow Okehazama Gorge, notwithstanding that his Army was substantially outnumbered. Had the battle taken place on the open plain, 3,000 soldiers would have easily been surrounded and defeated. At the gorge, however, Yoshimoto was unable to utilize fully the 25,000 soldiers at his disposal. Nobunaga first ordered fewer than a hundred men to launch a frontal attack through the gorge. This served two purposes—to determine the placement of Yoshimoto's troops and to make them believe that a full-scale attack from the front would shortly follow.

Instead of a frontal charge, however, Nobunaga led his forces in an attack on Yoshimoto from the mountains to the side of his opponent's forces. Instead of attacking at dawn, as was customary, Nobunaga waited until early afternoon, when Yoshimoto's troops were resting. He ordered his men to aim for Yoshimoto's headquarters and, once there, to sever the head of Yoshimoto Imagawa. Nobunaga's small force was victorious. Yoshimoto's Army was defeated and Yoshimoto himself was executed.[4]

The Okehazama battle has been analysed carefully by Japanese military strategists searching for guiding principles as to how a small country like Japan could best defend herself against powerful enemies. The thrilling story of how Nobunaga's small Army skilfully defeated the mighty Yoshimoto attracted Japanese military personnel and explains in part the strategy of the surprise attack that typified Japanese military tactics in the Pacific War.

Onitsuka did not let the lessons of military history go to waste even in civilian life. Small and medium-sized companies, Onitsuka feels, do not have the strength to compete on all fronts with large corporations. One approach is to choose a suitable objective and focus all energies on it, thereby giving the employees the taste of success when it has been accomplished. Onitsuka knows from experience that this will instil confidence and help create the foundation and the energy required to aim at the next objective. Through such efforts the specific points or objectives can be expanded gradually to form a product area in which the company excels. Through this process of point-of-focus management, Onitsuka Corporation became a major sports shoe manufacturer. A contemporary expression for point-of-focus management might be laser-beam management.

The Olympics in Japan

Onitsuka Corporation had started its retrenchment programme in May 1964 with the expressed aim of resuming its specialization in shoes. By midsummer the programme was fully under way. This period coincided with the company experiencing difficulties with its main bank, alluded to earlier. The bank had refused to provide the company with a loan, making bankruptcy a menacing possibility at any time.

The support of its new bank, the Kobe Bank, and that of the Onitsuka Circle was to change all that, and the company began to show some financial improvement by the fall so that, by October 1964, the balance was in the black. October was also the month of the Olympic Games, an event long awaited by the entire country.

In 1940, in celebration of the 2,600th anniversary of the Japanese empire, Japan was to host the first Olympic Games to be held in Asia. Unfortunately the outbreak of World War II intervened and the Games had to be cancelled. For twelve years no Olympics were held, the Berlin Games of 1936 being the last. It was a period of sporting darkness, not only for Japan but also for the rest of the world. Some twenty-four years after the scheduled Olympic games at Tokyo, and nineteen years, one month and twenty-five days after the Japanese surrender in 1945, Tokyo was to host the Eighteenth Olympiad, beginning on 10 October 1964.

The facilities at Komazawa, Tokyo, the proposed site of the 1940 Olympics, had subsequently been used for baseball and other events. The entire Komazawa Olympic Park was restored, as well as the 72,000-seat Kokuritsu Kyogijo (National Events Arena). The Games held great significance for the Japanese and more money was spent on their preparation than by any other nation up to that time. In three years of preparatory construction, central Tokyo was rebuilt; hotel space tripled; and an eight-mile monorail, a new equestrian park and a swimming arena/gymnasium were built.

Since the end of World War II, the Japanese had built the world's fastest train, the Tokaido 'Bullet Train', between Tokyo and Osaka, as well as networks of highways in urban centres. There was an enormous amount of energy in the nation—which helps to explain Japan's speedy economic recovery. Dr Ryutaro Azuma, Governor of Metropolitan Tokyo and Chairman of the Olympic Organizing Committee, said that Japan deliberately used the Games to boost her standing in the industrialized world. 'Without the magic of the Olympic name we might not have gotten the investment we needed to rise as a world trade power ... It was a governmental policy to make the Olympics our announcement to the world that Japan was no longer a beaten nation.'[5] The Japanese had one other aim as well: 'to show the world that though harsh things might have been said about them as a result of World War II, they were at heart human and a friendly nation.'[6]

Some eighty thousand spectators were in attendance when Emperor Hirohito opened the Games. The final Olympic Torch bearer was Yoshinori Sakai. He had been born in Hiroshima during its devastation by the atomic bomb in 1945. For many Japanese, hosting the Olympics symbolized the revitalization and strength of the nation.

The Games also symbolized the revitalization of Onitsuka Corporation. Since the Rome Olympics four years before, the company had reviewed its range of shoes, doubling the number of products capable of competing at the international level. The large budget of 30 million yen earmarked for the Olympics was an immense sacrifice for the company. Without this expenditure the company could have avoided the embarrassment of running a deficit in the first year of its listing on the Stock Exchange. This did not dissuade Onitsuka. The budget was not reduced.

Among the events in which the Japanese team excelled, Tiger shoes were featured, for example, in wrestling, gymnastics and the marathon. In wrestling, Japan won a total of five gold medals.[7] This led to the Japanese wrestlers being invited to the United States for matches, and consequently, Tiger wrestling shoes became well-known and popular there. In gymnastics, the Japanese team also won five golds.[8]

In the marathon, Abebe Bikila was favoured to win, after his performance at Rome. Onitsuka waited for his arrival in Japan in order to offer him Tiger shoes again, but he was too late. Puma, of West Germany, had flown to Ethiopia beforehand, and signed a contract with him. Onitsuka approached the Japanese athletes, Kenji Kimihara, Kokichi Tsuburaya and Toru Terasawa. They performed excellently: Tsuburaya won the bronze and Kimihara came in eighth overall.

As anticipated, Bikila took the gold medal in the marathon, becoming the first man to win this event twice, even though he had had his appendix removed only five weeks earlier. Yet this was to be his last Olympic victory. An injured leg caused him to drop out of the 1968 Olympic marathon after ten miles, and then a car accident near Addis Ababa in 1969 left him paralysed from the waist down. He took up paraplegic sport, including archery, but what had become a bitter struggle ended with his death in 1973 at the age of forty-one.

Onitsuka went to Tokyo for the Games. He was a veritable dynamo of activity, seeing to the service corner for the athletes, overseeing the promotion campaign at the shop, and cheering for the athletes in the stadia. The Games proved to be a success for Tiger brand, establishing it as an international name.

If Tiger shoes had not been top-quality products of course their entry into the foreign market would have been more difficult and their acceptance short-lived. Onitsuka feels, however, that the ease with which his shoes entered the foreign market was due in part to the excellent reputation of the other Japanese products that had gone before. 'I am indebted', says Onitsuka, 'to the good name of many Japanese manufacturers. Their fine reputations made Japanese products in general well respected and made entry into the foreign market much easier.'

Japan is a resource-poor country. Its survival depends on its exports. Before the war Japanese export products were cheap and of poor quality. 'It was our electronics manufacturers and our automobile manufacturers who turned this around', says Onitsuka. 'I can appreciate how difficult it must have been for the early manufacturers to sell their products abroad. They paved the way for the rest of us.'

Onitsuka feels indebted to Japanese electronic and automobile manufacturers for another reason. Onitsuka says:

> Often when I'm abroad foreign buyers will say to me 'make your products as good as Honda's or as Sony's or as Yamaha's. Although they are different, I know that my products are compared to other top quality Japanese products. This serves as a constant reminder that I must always strive to produce the highest-quality goods possible.

Onitsuka makes a tangible effort to repay the debt. Not only does he use a top of the line domestic car, he takes every opportunity to advertise this fact to foreign buyers and other associates. This, despite the fact that Mercedes Benz and other expensive imports have long been status symbols in Japan. But Onitsuka won't be influenced by this. 'The best car in Japan is comparable to the best car anywhere', he insists.

For Onitsuka Corporation, 1964 was assuredly a most eventful year, including the Stock Exchange listings, the disastrous diversification programme, the 'movement' of executive directors, the retrenchment operations, and finally the Olympics. It was a year of learning for Kihachiro Onitsuka with many bitter lessons taught. As 'rain hardens the ground', so was Onitsuka Corporation made stronger by the storm of events: they were now ready, lessons learned, to recommence.

In April 1964, Japan had been admitted into the Organization for Economic Co-operation and Development (OECD). The immediate result was liberalized trade for all but a few products. The marketing arena for sports shoe manufacturers all over the world now included Japan.

Japanese manufacturers faced greater international competition in the once protected domestic market, on the one hand; on the other hand, trade liberalization provided many forward looking corporations with the incentive to expand business beyond the national boundary. Onitsuka recognized the opportunity abroad but he saw as the starting-point for international expansion the strengthening of the internal corporate constitution.

The Sakaguchi family, 1923. Seated left to right: grandfather, grandmother, eldest brother and wife, father, sister, and mother. Standing left to right: brother, sister, and Kihachiro Sakaguchi (Onitsuka).

Tokichi Fukuda (front row second from left) and grade six students. Kihachiro Sakaguchi (Onitsuka), back row second from the left.

Kihachiro Sakaguchi (Onitsuka) as a middle school student.

Sakaguchi (Onitsuka) (right front, seated) and Ueda (back row, second from left) with other officers of the Himeji Division of the Japanese Imperial Army, 1942.

Onitsuka (right) with his adoptive mother, 1947.

Onitsuka (centre front) and his employees, New Year's day, 1955.

Tenth anniversary celebration at Onitsuka Corporation, 1959.

Onitsuka at the Rome Olympic Games, 1960.

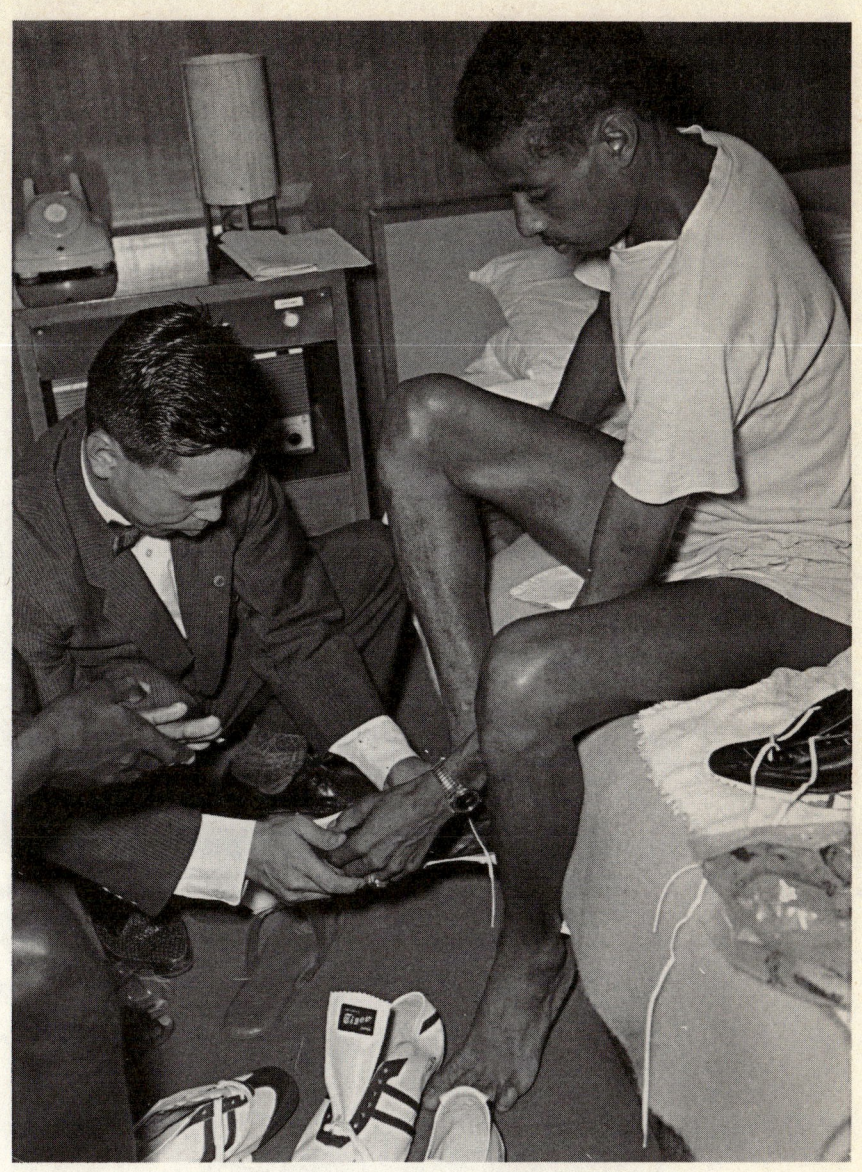

Onitsuka measuring Bikila's foot, 1961.

Onitsuka and Matsudaira toasting the gold Medal victory of Japan's men's volleyball team at the Munich Olympic Games, 1972.

A victorious Viren holding his Tiger shoes aloft in celebration of his double victory at the Montreal Olympics, 1976.

Onitsuka (centre) joins hands with Usui (left) and Teranishi (right) to celebrate the birth of ASICS, 21 July 1977.

ASICS' new head office, 1986.

Onitsuka giving Emperor Hirohito a tour of the Tottori Sanin factory, 1985.

10 | Consolidation and Expansion

Fiscal Control

It is said that hardship makes a person grow stronger. This can be said of business as well: the more severe the crisis, the greater the strength gained when it is overcome. For better or worse, small and medium-sized enterprises cannot avoid encountering such crises. The test is whether they can stay afloat on such difficult seas. Onitsuka Corporation managed to survive because the company put aside pride and reputation for a while. It was able to stay afloat only because it disposed of the extra load that was causing the business to flounder. Through point-of-focus management the company returned to specializing in shoes.

This was not a complete solution. Although a person can float to the surface by disposing of all excess weight, further measures have to be taken to ensure that he does not become exhausted and sink to the bottom again. In the business world, this necessitates making improvements to the fundamental inner strength of the company.

Improvement has two faces, one of quantity and the other of quality. Quantity is the more obvious and attracts attention. Quality attracts less attention and is directed inward. When everything is going well, the quality aspect tends to be overlooked. Business failure often begins with the neglect of quality; the structure grows bigger while the core deteriorates. Emphasizing quantity instead of quality could well have been part of Onitsuka Corporation's undoing.

Accordingly, Onitsuka sought to improve the quality of the organization by strengthening its management, particularly in regard to fiscal matters. This area had been overlooked. Without this final step, the recovery programme would not be complete.

Onitsuka Corporation worked out a five-year structure improvement plan beginning in 1964. In the early phase, the primary concern was scaling down the operation. This consisted of closing down all the diversified sections and decreasing inventory. These were merely emergency measures, whereas the ultimate aim of the plan was to establish greater fiscal control and to reduce the amount of borrowed capital.

Fiscal matters were not what Onitsuka considered to be his strength. He had tended to concern himself more with the aspects of the business that interested him, namely product development and marketing. The employees, as well, had become more involved with these same aspects. The financial side of the business had suffered badly from neglect.

Reflecting on this period, Onitsuka says:

> The weakness of a company will almost always be in those areas which lie in an opposite direction to where the president's attention is focused: those areas which are not the president's strengths, because of his reluctance to become effectively involved.

When he realized this, Onitsuka resolved to remedy the situation. He was determined to find and train a chief accountant to whom he could delegate all financial authority and responsibility.

Seiji Mihara was the man he chose. His mother had been the first matron of the Tiger Dormitory. Onitsuka thought very highly of her, which was why he had chosen her as matron. He believed that the life at the Dormitory played a vital part in the training of personnel, and that the matron played a key role. The son was a graduate of Kwansei Gakuin University, having majored in economics. It was through his mother's recommendation that he had joined Onitsuka Corporation and his initial employment was with Taigon Chemical. When Taigon was absorbed into Onitsuka Corporation, Mihara was assigned to the department of administrative affairs. He seemed to have a special skill with numbers. Now Onitsuka 'pencilled him in' at the forefront of the structure improvement plan. He was to contribute greatly to improving the quality of Onitsuka Corporation.

For the next five years Mihara made monthly trips to Tokyo to participate in corporate analysis seminars given by Kazuto Kunihiro, a nationally recognized authority on corporate analysis from Tohoku University. The seminars were organized by the financial journal publisher, Zaisei Keizai Kohosha. Participants were mainly chartered accountants and bank loan investigators, many of them former students of Professor Kunihiro. There were about twenty in all.

Onitsuka's decision to send Mihara to these seminars, even though the company could ill afford either his monthly absences or the expense incurred, paid off well. Much of what Mihara learned at the seminars was directly applicable to Onitsuka Corporation's situation. With his newly acquired knowledge he was able to guide the company successfully through its five-year structure improvement plan.

Until 1964, Onitsuka Corporation was run more on so-called 'management sense' than on concrete plans. Onitsuka, however, intended to change this. The monthly and annual plans were to be followed closely and thorough checks made on achievement. By repeating the steps 'plan', 'do', and 'see', the objectives, plans and controls were integrated.

It was only in the late 1950s that long-range planning began to receive much attention in Japan. The concept was popularized through American literature, widely read by Japanese managers, and by personal visits to the United States made by key Japanese executives. In many companies, long-range planning was introduced on a trial and error basis. Improvements followed rapidly, though, and by the mid-1960s long-range planning had become a well-honed management tool. Onitsuka Corporation was moving with the tide.

Concurrently with the introduction of long-range planning, in order to instil a sense of accountancy—that is, a feeling for numerical analysis—Onitsuka instituted a series of worksite training seminars for all employees. Mihara led these seminars, sharing much of what he was learning in Tokyo with his fellow workers. Gradually everyone was made capable of talking in numbers. This meant that the various departments now had a common code of communication, and everyone understood each other correctly. Through this common code, it was possible to coordinate the management of the different departments. The significance of this fiscal control in practice was quickly apparent to Onitsuka.

One of the main aims of this improvement plan was to increase the equity ratio. This ratio can be regarded as an index for the state of health of an enterprise. With the failure in diversification, the company learned through bitter experience the weakness of operating with a heavy reliance on borrowed capital. This was what provided the motivation to achieve their aim as quickly as they did.

Unlike corporations in the United States and Germany which rely on retaining earnings and depreciation reserves for about 70 per cent and 50 per cent, respectively, of the funds they require, Japanese corporations frequently obtain between 70 and 80 per cent of their required funds from outside sources, often in the form of loans.

Immediately after the war many Japanese firms were faced with a reconstruction task that meant replacing virtually all their physical assets. Vast sums of capital were required. Later, the rapid expansion of Japanese firms during the period of booming economic growth required the further procurement of capital. In order to bring about the industrial rebirth essential for economic recovery, and also to close the technology gap between Japan and the developed nations, corporations were motivated to invest heavily in the production infrastructure, even if it entailed extensive borrowing. Such borrowing was made more enticing by Japan's tax laws which treat interest paid on loans as an outright expense (loss), often making it more advantageous for a company to borrow funds than to increase its capital and sustain added dividends.

In the ten years prior to 1965, on average, only 40 per cent of the total fund requirements of corporations could be supplied by internal sources, the rest had to come from external sources. More than half of the funds so procured consisted of loans from financial institutions, resulting in a debt-to-net-worth ratio of major Japanese corporations in the mid-1960s of, typically, about three to one.

In 1964, Onitsuka Corporation's equity ratio was a meagre 13 per cent and Onitsuka wanted to improve this situation. By January 1969, the end of the first five-year plan, the equity ratio had increased to 40 per cent and by the end of the four-year plan that followed this figure had climbed to 52 per cent.

Seiji Mihara was the individual who taught Onitsuka the importance of fiscal control. Onitsuka had been advised by another accountant that, in his opinion, Mihara had avanced to a point where he could successfully attempt the chartered accountant examination. Onitsuka approached Mihara, suggesting that he sit the examination. His response surprised Onitsuka.

Thanking Onitsuka for the suggestion, he explained that, should he qualify, he might be tempted to seek other jobs outside Onitsuka Corporation. But he had no intention of working elsewhere. He was indebted to Onitsuka for what he had become and he intended to remain with the company. Lifelong employment at Onitsuka Corporation did not require paper qualifications. Mihara viewed their attainment as potentially undesirable as the alternatives they might offer could become a source of inner turmoil.

Onitsuka appreciated the tangible indication of the depth of Mihara's commitment to the corporation. Mihara has remained with the company and today is a senior executive managing director and ASICS' head corporate administrator.

Takemi Tanaka, presently a managing director, is another who contributed greatly to Onitsuka Corporation. In charge of production and sales, he was one of the core members, if not Onitsuka's 'right arm', and supported Onitsuka Corporation through its restructuring phase.

There is also Shoji Kitami. A commerce major, he was originally in the accounting department. Here he developed a cost accounting system that allowed shoe prices to accurately reflect production costs. Until the early sixties, definite pricing policies and procedures were lacking within the corporation. Kitami's knowledge of languages and his skill in negotiation later led to his promotion as head of the department of trade. After the Tokyo Olympics, business abroad increased and for several years Kitami travelled extensively with Onitsuka as the company sought to expand its foreign markets. Kitami, an executive managing director of ASICS, is now president of ASICS Tiger Corporation, ASICS' wholly owned subsidiary in California.

There are other notable contributions: Yoshiyuki Takahashi in charge of production, Toshihiko Niki in charge of marketing, Kazunori Kanzaki in charge of personnel, and Kuramitsu Nakayama in charge of sales.

These men were the supporting structure of Onitsuka Corporation and today are all senior executives with ASICS. They joined Onitsuka Corporation in the 1950s and were among the first- and second-year trainees of the Tiger Dormitory. In all there were seven of them. They were called Onitsuka's 'Seven Samurai', as in the title of the Kurosawa film that was popular at the time.

Domestic and Foreign Expansion

High economic growth coupled with reduced working hours precipitated an increase in public interest in hobbies and leisure activities. The number of participants in different sports was growing. Yet the majority of Onitsuka Corporation's products were intended for use in serious competition. Onitsuka recognized the need to broaden the company's focus. It is vital for suppliers to cater to demand. Onitsuka reshaped his objectives. He would specialize in competition-oriented shoes and expand into leisure-oriented shoes.

Compared to the shoes intended for athletes, leisure shoes would need to be produced on a larger scale and would be of standard quality. The materials used would differ. Synthetic rubber and fibres, which were better suited to machine production, would be more appropriate.

Onitsuka Corporation had insufficient space, however, to accommodate this new venture at the Suma factory in Kobe. Moreover, securing good labour was becoming increasingly difficult and expensive. Onitsuka decided that it would be advantageous to build a new factory in the countryside, away from the urban centres. For some years, the Tottori prefectural government had been urging Onitsuka to contribute to regional development through the construction of a rural factory. Tottori afforded several advantages. It was not too far from Kobe, and it was also Onitsuka's home prefecture. There were no large industries, so local competition for manpower would be minimal. Onitsuka was able to obtain an 8-acre lot for the sum of 120 million yen. Here there was to be built a factory of 1,320 square metres of floor space, with an initial workforce of fifty-eight and a daily output of three hundred pairs of track spikes. The construction began in November 1968. The starting date of operation was set for June of the following year.

By the end of the first year of operation, the workforce had increased to ninety and daily production output to 450 pairs of shoes, with a 0.1 per cent defect rate. A German DESMA rubber injection machine had also been installed. In the spring of 1970, a second factory was opened on the site for the production of soccer shoes and ski boots. A third factory was constructed three years later, along with a public 'golf garden', including a two-tier golf driving range and a putting green. Today, on average, two hundred members of the public use the golf garden on weekends and take advantage of the free golf lessons provided by golf pros.

Heizo Tanaka, managing director of the Tottori factory, recalls that for about the first three years of operation employee recruitment for the factory was not easy. Onitsuka Corporation's name was not well-known and the poor reputation of the rubber industry for working conditions made people hesitant to apply for jobs.

The poor working conditions did not extend to the Tottori factory, however, and in 1972 the Labour Standards Inspection Office designated Onitsuka Corporation a model for safety conditions and hygiene. In that year alone, more than six thousand workers died in Japan as the result of industrial accidents and one and a half million were injured. Onitsuka Corporation had no deaths and fewer than twenty injuries, none of them serious. In addition to internal ongoing monitoring of the work environment and constant improvement in conditions, the company employs physicians to visit its factories twice a month and check for health hazards. 'Today', says Tanaka, 'we have more applicants than we can possibly hire, so many people want to work for ASICS.'

ASICS' current popularity notwithstanding, Onitsuka foresaw that it would be only a matter of time before the problems associated with the urban labour supply spread to the countryside. Once this happened, Japanese industries would suffer from competition with the developing countries, as was already occurring in the textile industry. Something needed to be done to prevent Onitsuka Corporation from suffering the same fate.

As Onitsuka Corporation's name became established outside Japan, the company's exports increased. Therefore it was also necessary to cater to this growing market abroad. Since 1966, Onitsuka had periodically toured South East Asia with the possibility of expansion, through both licensing agreements and foreign production, in mind.

Under a licensing agreement, the licenser gives the licensee any one or more of patent rights, trademark rights, know-how on products or production processes. In exchange, the licensee agrees to manufacture those products covered by the rights; sometimes to market these products in a specific geographical area; and to pay the licencee royalties. In 1968, Onitsuka Corporation entered into a licensing agreement with Johnson Rubber Corporation in Taiwan for the production of vulcanized and non-vulcanized sports shoes.

That same year, among the many countries that he had visited, including Thailand, Singapore and Malaysia, Onitsuka decided on Taiwan as the location for the corporation's first overseas factory. There were several reasons for Onitsuka's choice. Taiwan and Japan had had close, friendly relations for many years. Among the Asian nations, its future looked stable and its potential for development was excellent. Onitsuka stresses:

> As human beings, the Taiwanese and Japanese like, respect, and trust each other. This is the most important factor in entering into a new business venture. In addition, the Taiwanese are earnest, well motivated, efficient workers. This is very important to international competition.

Taiwain offered other advantages too. Labour was abundant and labour costs were low. The government welcomed the establishment of foreign factories as part of their long-term industrialization plan for the country. Taiwan's geographical proximity to Japan and the fact that many older generation Taiwanese spoke Japanese—a legacy of the 1895–1945 Japanese occupation of the island—were also attractive features. The number of working days in a year are greater in Taiwan too: 295 (2,360 hours), as compared to 263 (1994.5 hours) in Japan. And there are very few, if any, strikes or demonstrations of any kind.[1]

Kaohsiung was selected for the site of Onitsuka Corporation's Taiwanese factory. With a population of approximately 845,000, it provided an abundant, highly literate workforce, receptive to technology education. It is southern Taiwan's leading seaport and a major industrial centre. It had been occupied by the Japanese in 1895 and they had developed the city from a small fishing village into a manufacturing centre and port. Petroleum products were among Kaohsiung's chief industrial products, an advantage in the manufacture of sports shoes which are made almost entirely from them. The company bought a 3,300 square metre lot within Taiwain's newly established Export Processing Zone in Kaohsiung on which it planned to build a factory with floor space of 886 square metres.

Locating the factory in the Export Processing Zone had many advantages. At this time it was the only area in which a foreign corporation could have a 100 per cent investment in its own operation. Low interest loans from Taiwanese banks were readily available. There was no tax on imported materials for production provided the finished products were exported, nor was a corporate tax levied during the first five years of operation. All business related to the import and export of goods could be conducted at a central government office located within the Export Processing Zone. In addition, because the products manufactured in the Export Processing Zone were to be exported, the customs officers and police closely monitored product movement in and out of the zone. Employees' departure from the area was closely watched, thus minimizing theft, a considerable problem in foreign factories located outside the zone.

For the Taiwanese there were many advantages too, including expanded employment opportunities, the acquisition of skills and technology, and five years after a company's establishment, a corporate tax of 35 per cent. In addition, payment for the exported products would be in foreign currency and much of this currency would remain within Taiwan.

The factory name had to be registered before construction could begin. Onitsuka's intention was to register the name as Onitsuka Corporation using the *kanji* (Chinese characters) which are used in both the Japanese and Chinese writing systems. The Taiwanese officials objected; the meaning of the *kanji* was inappropriate. Literally translated it read 'the place where demons congregate'.

Onitsuka's second choice was a name that would convey the idea of a co-operative endeavour between Japan and Taiwan. Taking the first *kanji* of Nippon (Japan) and of Taiwan and adding the *kanji* for sports shoes, Onitsuka devised the name which translates into English as Nichidai Sports Shoes Company Limited.

Nichidai's first manager and the man responsible for overseeing its design and construction was Akio Bessha. Having worked for Onitsuka Corporation for several years, Bessha's experience included production, research and development, and subcontract liaison. Bessha went to Taiwan in the summer of 1968. There was much to be done if the factory was to go into operation in June 1969 to coincide with the opening of the Tottori factory. Bessha recalls:

Our factory was built about a year after development in the Export Processing Zone began. There were only a few buildings—the rest of the area was a mass of parched weeds. I wondered if I would be capable of sowing the seeds for our endeavour in foreign soil, if they would take root, and if we would ever see a good harvest. After I examined my strengths and my weaknesses I thought I would be able to succeed. This job would be the challenge of my life and I was determined to do well.

Initially, Bessha's concern was to adapt himself to the new environment— to the climate, the language, and the food. There was so much to do and so little time to do it in. 'I felt like I was running in a stopped train', Bessha recalls. But gradually the pieces began to fall into place.

The first task was to select a contractor. Bessha's choice was a Taiwanese contractor who understood Japanese and who had gained his experience with the highly respected Kumagai Gumi, a forerunner among Japanese construction firms in overseas operations. Together, Bessha and the contractor designed the building. Construction proceeded as planned and Bessha ordered the required shoemaking machines from Japan. 'Now though', Bessha points out, 'all of Nichidai's shoemaking machines are manufactured in Taiwan. They are less expensive than, and superior to, their Japanese counterparts.'

Through the licensing agreement with Johnson Rubber, Onitsuka had become acquainted with the company's export manager, Peter H. Liu. Drawing on ten years exporting experience, Liu had initially agreed to help Johnson Rubber find buyers in Western Europe and the United States during its first year of operation in the mid-1960s. Within two years, the company had grown to be Taiwan's largest canvas shoe maker but ran into difficulty keeping up with the orders Liu was procuring and later with material supply, causing Liu to stay on another two years. At the end of this period, Onitsuka asked Liu to serve as an adviser to Nichidai, assisting with the establishment of the factory and with trademark and other negotiations.

With construction under way, Bessha turned his attention to employee recruitment. Peter Liu introduced Bessha to Sushin Lin, who spoke Japanese. Together Bessha and Lin conducted employee interviews and tests. In response to newspaper advertisements, over three hundred people applied for the fifty factory positions available for sewers and assemblers. The manual dexterity of each applicant was tested and his or her attitude and personal neatness evaluated in the selection process.

When the hiring was complete, two of Onitsuka Corporation's most competent production division technicians were brought over from Japan, one to train five sewers and the other to train five assemblers. These ten, under the supervision of the Japanese technicians, trained the remaining forty employees. The process took about two months.

Although Nichidai was primarily intended for the manufacture of wrestling shoes destined for the American market, the initial production was ten thousand pairs of running shoes, to be sold throughout Japan where market response to the new product could be quickly gauged. First, though, every shoe was thoroughly tested at Onitsuka Corporation's inspection department in Kobe. Onitsuka was determined to avoid introducing a poor product to the overseas market, at all costs.

Response to the new product was satisfactory, so the Nichidai factory switched to the production of wrestling shoes. Why wrestling shoes? Says Bessha, 'At first we thought perhaps we should manufacture a simpler shoe. Wrestling shoe production is highly complex, involving many different processes but it was for this very reason that we felt a factory devoted solely to their production would be advantageous.' The Taiwanese workers proved extremely well suited to the manufacture of wrestling shoes. 'Their manual dexterity', says Bessha, 'is excellent and they are patient and earnest.'

Convinced that the Nichidai factory could excel at wrestling shoe production, Bessha increased the workforce to one hundred employees by mid-1970. He attributes the factory's success, in part, to the strategy he employed with the workers. Recalls Bessha:

At first I geared myself to their pace and then very gradually increased the pace to match the Japanese standard. For example, perhaps at first we were turning out fifty units a day. Each evening I would congratulate the workers on a job well done and encourage them to do as well or even better the next day. Slowly the production increased until finally we were up to the Japanese level—100 units daily. Eventually we went beyond this and were able to turn out 120 units a day.

During this time Bessha was working hard to master the Chinese language. By the second anniversary of the founding of the factory he was able to address the workers in their own language, talking to them about the evolution of the factory from its inception to the present and about its future prospects. At the same time, the workers were picking up Japanese and there were few who did not carry a bilingual dictionary with them at all times.

By the end of the second year of operation the absolute daily output had risen to 650 pairs of shoes. Commenting on the quality of these shoes in his address to the workers on the factory's second anniversary, Onitsuka said, 'Our American agent claims that the quality of the shoes produced in our Taiwanese factory is superior to the quality of those he used to receive from Japan.'

Coexistence and co-prosperity is a concept central to ASICS' operations in Japan. The Nichidai factory also shares this philosophy as a central pillar of its management philosophy. Sports shoe manufacturers in Taiwan generally pay their production workers according to their output. Nichidai is one of the few factories that offer a fixed salary system and an annual merit bonus, thereby providing a degree of security not available from most other employers. This has contributed to a much lower turnover rate: as of 1986, 43 per cent of the employees had stayed with the company more than five years. In recognition of their dedication, since 1976, ASICS has selected three to five Nichidai factory workers annually to bring to Japan for about two weeks. Half their time is spent visiting ASICS' factories; the other half is for sightseeing. To date, thirty-four Nichidai employees have participated in these trips to Japan.

Retaining competent middle managers, however, is not easy. As Peter

Liu pointed out, opportunities for advancement at this level are extremely limited. The factory's size is more or less fixed, and, unlike Japanese companies, Nichidai has no subsidiary firms to provide opportunities for career advancement in the higher ranks. 'As a result', says Liu, 'the factory has lost competent staff in production, accounting, and material procurement.'

A second area of concern to the Taiwanese is the system of manager rotation. Every three years, the company sends a new factory head, the only 'permanent' Japanese staff member. Akio Bessha was the first head and is now back as the factory's sixth manager. Although the company tries to be consistent, individual values and managerial styles differ. This often creates confusion among Nichidai employees and, in some cases, there is a considerable gap between Nichidai's established personnel policy and current management practice. This sometimes results in resignations. 'We regret it when employees we have nurtured move to other corporations', says Liu.

To acknowledge employee dedication, in accordance with the custom prevalent in both Taiwan and Japan, the Nichidai factory holds an annual domestic company trip of two or three day's duration to coincide with the anniversary of the founding of the factory. These trips occur on company time and are considered part of the work schedule. Almost all employees participate.

Onitsuka is always present for the anniversary celebrations. He has not missed once since the company's establishment in July 1969. The anniversary is celebrated at the beginning of November each year as the scorching July heat is not conducive to celebration. Other guests at the celebration usually include ASICS executives and executives from the local firms with which Nichidai does business—about thirty in all. The Nichidai factory has done very well throughout its eighteen-year existence, showing a good profit margin annually.

Today the Nichidai Sports Shoe Corporation is one of about three hundred sports shoe manufacturers in Taiwan. Of these, four are joint ventures between the Japanese and the Taiwanese. Nichidai is the only one that is fully funded by a Japanese Corporation. It is also ASICS' only wholly owned overseas factory.

From the time Onitsuka Corporation returned to specializing in shoes, sales grew noticeably. Total sales over the five-year period from 1964 to 1968 increased from 1.06 billion yen to 2.4 billion yen. By 1973, at the end of the four-year plan, sales had increased further to 5.3 billion yen. The structural improvement, which included increasing the equity capital and efficiency in production, was accomplished at a rate that surprised even Onitsuka.

Onitsuka felt that the company had recovered completely during the preceding number of years. He also had confidence in the staff, who were at the peak of their careers. They could be depended on to keep Onitsuka Corporation going.

Onitsuka decided to leave all domestic business in their hands. He would focus his attention on the international market. The competition on this level was expected to increase with the liberalization of trade and capital.

Business Culture Differences

Onitsuka's first encounter with the foreign market had been after the 1960 Rome Olympic Games when he toured Europe and America. Between 1966 and 1970 Onitsuka and Kitami, sometimes together and sometimes separately, travelled extensively, examining the markets of Europe, North and South America, the Middle East and South East Asia. Each tour lasted about two months.

His trips abroad made Onitsuka appreciate once again the dimension of global trade. He had become accustomed to thinking only on a national scale. His dream was now to bring about 'Onitsuka of the World' by making high-quality sports shoes available world-wide. Onitsuka knew he had a long road to travel before that wish could become a reality. There were many countries where his name and Tiger shoes were neither familiar nor even heard of.

Much had to be accomplished. Onitsuka directed his efforts towards the expansion of the network of foreign agencies dealing with his company's products, increased his attendance at major sports events outside Japan, and established a base for expansion into the North American Market.

In the United States, Onitsuka's intended primary overseas market, the running phenomenon, began in the late 1960s with the publication of Dr Kenneth Cooper's book, *Aerobics*. President John Kennedy had called Americans 'soft' at the outset of the decade and urged them to leave their armchairs. Cooper's book presented a tolerable avenue to fitness. Prior to this, recreational jogging had gained attention through the work of such coaches as Bill Bowerman at the University of Oregon and Arthur Lydiard in New Zealand. In the early 1970s the flames of enthusiasm were fanned by such books as *Long Slow Distance: the Humane Way to Train*, by Joe Henderson, and Thaddeus Kostrubala's *The Joy of Running*. Frank Shorter's 1972 Olympic marathon victory glamourized the sport and provided the spark that ignited the running boom.

The timing was right. Onitsuka established the Chicago Liaison Office in 1972, primarily to collect marketing information. The office was manned by two people, Peter Tsuyoshi Sakurai and Kyoichiro Hayashi. The former had worked for Murata Pearl until the company went bankrupt and had been stationed abroad at several different locations in North America and South East Asia.

Born in Korea, Kyoichiro Hayashi graduated from Meiji University in Tokyo and worked for Moruten Rubber Corporation which had ties with Mikasa, the leading rubber ball manufacturer. He joined Onitsuka Corporation in 1972 and was posted to Chicago as head of the liaison office.

These two men found the Chicago winter unbearable. They also felt that the location was incorrect for the venture, even though the city had originally been selected as a commercial and geographic hub. Their views prevailed and, in the spring of 1973, the office was relocated in California, close to Los Angeles. John Bork Jr, an American, was hired to be in charge of sales promotion. Not only was the new location climatically better, it was also closer to Japan, and, in their view, an excellent point of introduction into the American leisure market.

In 1972, Jelenk Incorporated, the sports attire manufacturer that later merged with Onitsuka Corporation, established its first American subsidiary, Jelenk USA Incorporated, in Salt Lake City. When the companies merged to form ASICS Corporation in 1977, the Salt Lake establishment was closed since it had not been doing well.

Today ASICS Tiger Corporation (ATC), a wholly owned subsidiary of ASICS, is located in Santa Ana, California. It is one of 530 Japanese owned companies in the state of California. ATC has warehouses in both Santa Ana and Atlanta and a liaison office in New York. Shoji Kitami is the president, with a staff of ninety full-time employees, nine of whom are from Japan. Peter Sakurai is still at the California office as the liaison director while Hayashi is the sales promotion manager in ASICS' Tokyo office. Jiro Makino, a graduate of Woodbury University in Los Angeles, joined the staff of GTO Incorporated, the third company in ASICS' tripartite amalgamation, in 1976. Prior to this, he had been employed by Sumitomo Bank in the United States for two years. After the amalgamation, Makino became the director of ASICS' New York liaison office. Both Makino and Sakurai are involved in business negotiations with ASICS' licencees in the United States and Europe.

His activities abroad made Onitsuka aware of the differences between Japan and the other countries with regard to management, ideology, customs and practices in business. One example is the idea of the 'contract'. The Japanese word *keiyaku* may be translated as 'contract'. The formal, technical elements of commercial contracts in Japan and America do not differ radically because the contemporary Japanese legal structure has been largely patterned after that of the West. In Japan, however, the interpersonal relationships that make up 'honour' are the most important determinant of the behaviour of commercial parties, not the strict legal rights afforded by the language of the contract, as in America. As Anne Elizabeth Murase points out:

> Rather than imposing principles on a relationship, interpersonal dynamics may generate the principles to be applied and serve as mitigating factors if one party fails to perform. It is not unusual to have considerable modification of existing contracts although some 'basic contracts' are sufficiently ambiguous so as to allow for extremely flexible interpretation. This pliant conception of *keiyaku* may be a partial reflection of human interaction in Japan with emphasis on interpersonal understanding (frequently non-verbal), harmony and conciliation perhaps reached more intuitively than by rigorous logic. *Keiyaku* as a legal term creates the concept of rights and obligations which, however, may be more apparent than real. Rather, in keeping with traditional behavioural patterns is the notion of duty to the requisites of the established relationship. In this connection we find a marked tendency to settle disputes out of court, sometimes through direct negotiations or with the help of a mediator. To press for litigation and reject conciliation and compromise is yet considered scandalous and may be highly detrimental to one's future transactions.[2]

There are far fewer lawsuits per capita in Japan than elsewhere. According to a survey by H. Tanaka, California has more than eleven times as many lawsuits per capita as Japan, while the per capita number of lawsuits in the United Kingdom and West Germany respectively are ten and twelve times greater than that of Japan. The number of lawyers per capita in Japan is approximately one-tenth that of Canada and one-seventeenth that of the United States.[3]

In Japan, business agreements are characterized by two unique features: (1) business dealings are very often carried out either without a formal contract, or with written agreements that describe the framework for doing business only in very broad terms; (2) recourse to litigation is rare. Usually disputes are settled by discussion between parties, sometimes with the assistance of a third party mediator with expertise in the case at hand. Both these features are culturally determined preferences. If two companies have had a lengthy relationship or have been introduced by a trusted third party (a frequent occurrence), a detailed written contract is not required. The outcome of disputes, should they arise, is normally determined by the common interests of the two parties and/or by their relative strengths. Bringing a dispute to court is generally regarded as an embarrassing, time-consuming and inconvenient process.

For Japanese businessmen in the international environment, business dealings are considerably more complex, owing to such factors as linguistics, social, political and legal differences. In North America, paramountcy is accorded to the strict language of the contract: dispute resolution focuses on questions of interpretation rather than on the underlying moral expectations of the parties. Hence, great attention is given to drafting mutually acceptable contract language and lawyers are invariably retained by each side to conduct their negotiations.

This approach was totally unfamiliar to the Japanese, and surprised both Onitsuka and Kitami. Nevertheless, the extensive entrance of large Japanese corporations into the international arena has forced Japanese corporate executives to become proficient in the North American style of contract negotiation. Problems commonly arise, however, when Japanese and foreign companies relatively inexperienced in international transactions do business together. A classic example is Onitsuka Corporation's agreement with Blue Ribbon Sports, Nike's precursor.

University of Oregon professor and track coach, Bill Bowerman, acquired considerable shoemaking skill and often hand-built customized shoes for his athletes. He felt that American shoes were not well suited to runners' needs and that European shoes were too costly. Returning from a trip to Europe in 1963, Phil Knight, a former university athlete coached by Bowerman, suggested that they should find a foreign supplier to make shoes according to Bowerman's specifications.

Following through on this idea, Knight went to Japan in 1964. At this time Tiger shoes were well known within Japan and were reputed in many circles to be the number 1 sports shoes. Phil Knight met with Onitsuka and obtained exclusive sales distribution rights for Tiger shoes in the United States. Returning to Oregon, Knight, in conjunction with Bowerman, established Blue Ribbon Sports, an importing and sales company of which Knight was president.

Over the next few years, Blue Ribbon Sports contributed to the development of Tiger running shoes suitable for the American market. Thanks to the efforts of Blue Ribbon Sports in product development and sales and to the inherent superior quality of Tiger shoes, Tiger had become the most popular running shoe brand in America by the time of the 1967 *Distance Running News* survey. The agreement between Onitsuka Corporation and Blue Ribbon Sports was renewed every year until 1972.

As shoe sales increased, so did Blue Ribbon Sports' requirement for operating capital. To meet this need, the possibility of the establishment of a joint sales corporation in the United States between Onitsuka Corporation and Blue Ribbon Sports was explored. At about this time, Nissho Iwai, presently Japan's sixth largest trading firm, entered into discussion with Blue Ribbon Sports concerning the possibility of supporting the American company without the involvement of Onitsuka Corporation. Blue Ribbon Sports abandoned the idea of forming a joint sales company in conjunction with Onitsuka Corporation and Phil Knight asked the footwear manufacturer, Nihon Rubber Corporation, to produce sample running shoes. Exhibited at a national sporting equipment show held in Chicago in 1972, these were the harbinger of Blue Ribbon Sports' new line of running shoes, 'Nike', named after the Greek goddess of victory.

Says Shoji Kitami, 'The involvement of Blue Ribbon Sports with Nihon Rubber violated the exclusive distributorship agreement. I cautioned them to this effect but they did not refrain from this new course of action.'

'Whatever the reality was,' says Toshihiko Niki, 'we were hurt by what we saw. We felt we had been betrayed by those whom we trusted.' Subsequently, Onitsuka Corporation prematurely terminated its contract with Blue Ribbon Sports. A legal battle ensued, fought in both Japan and the United States.

'While the prospects of winning in Japan were high,' says Seiji Mihara, 'we realized that the trial would be prolonged. Judicial hearings proceed very much more slowly in Japan than in the United States. Our lack of familiarity with contract agreements placed Onitsuka Corporation in a disadvantageous position.' Taking this into consideration along with the high court costs, especially in the States, Onitsuka Corporation took the advice of its American legal counsel and made an out-of-court settlement in favour of Blue Ribbon Sports.

Japan is a typical example of what Edward T. Hall defines as a 'high-context culture' and the United States as a 'low-context culture'. In the former, words transmit less information than does the context of the communication, including the background, associations, and basic values of the parties involved. In low-context cultures the reverse is true and agreements are reached with much less information about the participants' values and far greater reliance on words and numbers, necessitating the careful wording of contracts and frequent legal intervention.[4]

Reminiscing about the experience with Blue Ribbon Sports, Onitsuka says, 'We believe that problems could be solved through discussion based on mutual trust. We didn't fully understand American business methods and the heavy reliance on written contracts. This incident taught us much about the reality of international business.'[5] Onitsuka says:

Another difference I observed is that individualism is more prevalent in the West, whereas in Japan, collectivism is more dominant. In the former, a company becomes but a collection of individuals and the ties between them are weak. Contracts are written out and validated by the law. This is their way of showing trust. The worker is dependent on his skill to earn his living. This is, in a sense, his only asset. Therefore, he does not 'give away' his knowledge acquired through experience, by teaching others. This is why we find so many specialists in these countries.

In Japan, it is different. The entire management is based on trust. The rule of seniority and the policy of employment for life are both based on trust: trust on behalf of the employee that the firm will look after him for life, and trust on behalf of the employer that the worker will be diligent and dedicated to the firm for his entire working life. As a result, one will find in the Japanese businessman, a strong sense of identification with his company.

As mentioned earlier, there is a saying in Japan, *kigyo wa hitonari*, 'the enterprise is people'. Chie Nakane, in *Japanese Society*, discusses the commonly held view that the ties between employer and employee are often as firm and as close as those between husband and wife. This relationship is much more than purely contractual and all members of the employee's family are included in the larger company family. It is not only a man's labour that is employed by the company, it is the total man.[6] Onitsuka observes:

As a rule, the Japanese aim is to train all-round personnel as opposed to specialists. The employees experience a variety of jobs through rotation. What is more, the ability to train and guide other people is considered essential for those in management posts. An employee is respected for his ability to train other personnel and to strengthen the unity of the company through his guidance. This is one of the aspects in which the Japanese way differs fundamentally from the Western way. In Japan, one can find schemes such as the 'suggestion system' and 'quality control circle' introduced from the United States but now having a strong Japanese flavour, where there is co-operation among the employees and between work units. Even the enterprise unions cannot think about many issues without being conscious of 'our company, our employees'.

Onitsuka has come to feel that collectivism is the major strength of the Japanese. Also, his confidence in co-operative management has been strengthened through experience. This is the principle he has followed since the beginning: it explains why his company went public. In Onitsuka's opinion, Onitsuka Corporation embodied the strengths of the Japanese way of management, being based on trust and collectivist principles.

International Rivalry

Four years after the Tokyo Games, the Olympics were held in Mexico City. Onitsuka Corporation was in the midst of its first five-year structure improvement plan, begun in 1964. These Olympic Games provided an opportunity for the company to demonstrate its achievements since the Tokyo Games.

Unfortunately there was one immediate difficulty. Onitsuka Corporation had been planning to set up its own shop on the Olympic site, its first at an Olympic Games outside Japan. But Adidas of West Germany negotiated total rights for the sale of shoes in the Olympic Village by merging with a local company. The arrangement had been approved by the Mexico Olympic Organizing Committee. Onitsuka's reaction was one of disbelief. He considered it most unfair.

In his search for an alternative, Onitsuka discovered that local retail stores could establish sales facilities within the Olympic Village. With the approval of the Organizing Committee, the local agent of Onitsuka Corporation was instructed to establish a shop and sell shoes along with other sporting goods.

On finding out about Onitsuka Corporation's store, Adidas immediately lodged a complaint with the Committee. They claimed that it was inconsistent with their agreement. The Committee sided with Adidas and, when Onitsuka Corporation refused to move, they resorted to force. The military were sent to forcibly remove the store and its personnel. Under the circumstances, Onitsuka Corporation had little choice but to leave.

They moved to a hotel in the city centre, and put up a huge sign in the Olympic Village, part of which read:

> For the above reasons, we regret that Onitsuka Corporation has been refused permission to sell Tiger shoes in the Village. In order not to create problems and for the convenience of the athletes, we have set up a shop in a hotel inside the city. We hope you will come and see us.

This sign provoked the reaction of athletes from many nations. They made their objections known to the Organizing Committee. They complained that it was unfair for one manufacturer to be granted permission to sell shoes in the Village but not others. In all, athletes from over twenty countries expressed their objections to this ruling. This response put considerable pressure on the Committee. The day before the Games were due to start, word arrived that Onitsuka Corporation would be allowed to set up shop in the Village.

This incident made Onitsuka aware of how his company had grown. Adidas, one of the world's leading brands in sporting shoes, regarded Onitsuka Corporation as its potential rival. Onitsuka products were no longer an unknown brand that did not threaten the major companies. At this juncture Onitsuka realized that he had already become involved in the highly competitive international market.

Four years later, in 1972, the Olympics were held in Munich. This time, Onitsuka Corporation made sure that the preparations and negotiations began in plenty of time. A contract was signed with the Munich Olympic Organizing Committee, which granted the company permission to set up a shop and a service counter inside the Olympic Village. Onitsuka was not notified, however, about the amount of space the company was to be allotted. Inquiries were made and on the eve of the athletes' arrival in Munich the company received notification that there was insufficient space for the shop in the Village.

Investigation by the company disclosed that Adidas and Puma had influenced the Organizing Commitee into excluding Onitsuka Corporation, but nobody else, from the Village. The West German companies' explanation was that, at the Tokyo Olympics, Onitsuka Corporation had hampered their sales. Part of their freight had been unnecessarily held up at customs and failed to arrive in time for the Games. Adidas and Puma claimed that Onitsuka Corporation was behind this incident, a claim that the company adamantly denied. However, it is well known that customs procedures in Japan are extremely complex and time-consuming. They are often considered a form of non-tariff barrier.

Onitsuka Corporation had signed a contract for the shop. They were not going to accept the excuse of 'lack of space'. Eventually the Organizing Committee relented and provided space adjacent to the entrance to the Village. The company was authorized to build a pavilion there. It transpired that this was better than having a store inside the Village. Many athletes dropped by on their way in or out of the Village, as did many reporters and tourists from all over the world. Also, Onitsuka Corporation was free to provide the Japanese team with Japanese snacks as part of their service to them. This would have been against regulations inside the Village.

For Onitsuka, the highlight of the Munich Games was the gold medal won by the Japanese men's volleyball team. The coach, Yasutaka Matsudaira, and Onitsuka had been friends since the days when the former was captain of the volleyball team at Keio University. They had worked together on improvements for volleyball shoes for many years.

In the late 1950s the number of players on the volleyball court was reduced from nine to six in Japan. Volleyball, 'invented' in America in 1895 by William G. Morgan, a student at Springfield College and director of the YMCA at Holyoke, Mass., was introduced to Japan in 1913. There it was played first by sixteen players, then twelve players, and finally nine players. Nine-man volleyball with its 'oriental rules' took hold in Asia while the original six-man game and rules spread throughout Europe and the Soviet Union. Shortly after World War II, Japan experienced its first volleyball 'boom'. The game's popularity soared since it could be enjoyed easily and cheaply. Only one ball and a net were required and, if necessary, a rope could be substituted for the latter.

The American Occupation Forces brought six-man volleyball to Japan. Both six-man and nine-man volleyball were played in the 1956 Asian Games. In 1957, both the Japanese men's and women's volleyball teams were engaged in six-man matches, the men's team in the Soviet Union and the women's team in the People's Republic of China. When, in 1961, the International Olympic Committee authorized the inclusion of men's and women's volleyball for the 1964 Tokyo Olympics, the International Volleyball Federation adopted the American plan of codifying the rules of the game and six-man volleyball became the norm in Japan.

In pointing out the differences between six-man and nine-man volleyball, Matsudaira says: 'The team of nine consists of specialists whose positions are fixed, while the six-man system has all-round players who have to rotate every change of serve. Though there is some resemblance between them, they are essentially different.'[7]

Player rotation necessitated new footwear. Volleyball shoes now had to accommodate two functions simultaneously. They had to be constructed to enhance the jumping and spiking motions of the front players and also the receiving motions of the back players. Onitsuka Corporation had developed a new type of volleyball shoe to meet this dual need in 1958 and had been working constantly to improve it.

Matsudaira had worked out a long-term plan for the team. They had trained very hard for the Tokyo Games, and won the bronze medal. Four years later, in Mexico City, they won the silver. Now, at the Munich Games, they were aiming for the gold medal. They were victorious in their match against Bulgaria. This final game decided the gold medal winner. It was a moment of overwhelming joy and excitement. On the spur of the moment it was decided to hold the victory celebrations in the Onitsuka pavilion.

The staff put away all the products on display and gathered together what food and beer they could find. There were between fifty and sixty people; the players, the training coaches, the fans who had come all the way from Japan for the occasion, and reporters from different countries. During the celebration, players and coaches from other teams came to congratulate the winners. The pavilion was crammed with happy people, congratulating one another, singing and pouring beer over each other.

As Onitsuka sang and rejoiced with the team, he thought himself fortunate in being able to share the joy of victory with these athletes. He had dedicated his life to manufacturing sports shoes for the nation's youth. He had worked tirelessly in the past and he felt that this occasion was his just reward.

The same shoes that helped the Japanese volleyball team be victorious were worn by 83 per cent of the men's volleyball teams competing in the Olympics and by 63 per cent of the women's teams. Over the years, Tiger shoes have been used by the national volleyball teams of Bahrain, Brazil, Bulgaria, Canada, Egypt, Greece, Italy, Japan, Mexico, Peru, Romania, the Soviet Union and Yugoslavia.

In wrestling and in gymnastics, 60 per cent of the participants were using Tiger shoes. In the marathon, twenty-nine out of the seventy-four participants used Tiger shoes. In basketball, however, only 10 per cent of the teams used Tiger shoes.

Following the Munich Olympics, Onitsuka felt that a wide gap still existed between himself and his competitors. He targeted several areas for improvement and expansion, including product research and development, the establishment of a databank for representative top athletes of the world and the physical setting in which they performed, continuous promotional approaches to top athletes, the establishment of a special order production system, and the development of products to accommodate totalization—the provision of co-ordinated shoes, sportswear and equipment.

11 | Strengthening the Corporation

The Oil Crisis

In May 1972, Onitsuka Corporation was listed in the Second Section of the Tokyo Stock Exchange. The business was flourishing, thanks to the growing economy.

This thriving economy, however, suddenly came to a halt. On 6 October 1973, the Egyptian forces crossed the Suez Canal and landed on the Sinai Peninsula. This sparked the fourth Middle East War. The Arab oil-producing countries quadrupled the price of oil. The result was a rapid increase in the prices of a wide variety of raw materials and primary goods. The ensuing world-wide panic was felt especially strongly in Japan because of the country's heavy dependence on imports. Raw materials for industrial use make up 90 per cent of these imports, with crude oil accounting for 30 per cent of the total.

The prices of goods produced predominantly from imported materials sky-rocketed and consumer hoarding of some items triggered further price spirals. Yesterday's prosperity was gone: nights became longer and darker as neon lights were turned off, television broadcasting time was shortened and gas stations were no longer open on Sundays and holidays.

The situation was intensified by rising public awareness of the need to control industrial pollution and of the perception of the petroleum industry as a major offender. Industrial pollution controls and reduced hours of operation were imposed on a large segment of the chemical industry, reducing output and increasing prices. Fires at a major chemical factory and an oil refinery in western Japan temporarily halted the production of secondary and tertiary petroleum by-products in numerous factories.

Onitsuka Corporation was badly affected. The materials used for sports shoes are mostly petroleum-related: the synthetic rubber for the soles and the nylon, the synthetic leather, and the glue for the uppers. Virtually the entire shoe is made of petroleum-related products. Within a year, crepe rubber had increased in price by 146 per cent, sheet rubber by 112 per cent, chemicals required for the glue by 104 per cent, nylon thread, 71 per cent, and synthetic textiles, 40 per cent. Shoe prices increased accordingly.

To reduce costs, Onitsuka looked for places where less expensive materials could be substituted without affecting product quality. In some instances, substitution was essential as manufacture of the original materials had ceased. In order to reduce material loss associated with model changes arising from fashion and seasonal preferences, Onitsuka tightened the co-ordination between research and development, production and sales.

Initially, Onitsuka had expected this to be only a passing phenomenon. As with wartime inflation, things were somehow expected to return to normal when the conflict ended. As time passed, however, Onitsuka felt differently. He sensed that this was only the beginning of a groundswell. It would get worse. He declared a 'state of emergency' for the year 1974.

As if to prove him right, the situation worsened with the advent of the new year. The level of inflation in product price greatly affected the buying patterns of the consumers. People ceased to purchase these expensive items. The sport shoe season generally begins in April. Stocks of shoes are then quickly absorbed by the market. This did not happen in 1974 and the company found itself holding a stock of 1.8 billion yen at the end of spring. The end of summer saw this figure increase to 3.1 billion yen.

This inventory naturally played havoc with the company finances. The situation was reminiscent of the company's fiasco with diversification ten years earlier. Unless corrective action could be taken immediately the company might well face the same fate again.

At the time, Onitsuka Corporation had a range of over four hundred different designs in shoes for thirty-six different sports. Of these, 35 per cent were produced at their own factories and the rest, 65 per cent, were produced at the subcontract factories. The usual approach would be to cut back production in the contracted factories, but this was not Onitsuka's policy. The members of the Onitsuka Circle had always been co-operative and supportive under all circumstances. They were an indispensable part of Onitsuka Corporation, not to be cast aside to keep the parent company afloat.

It was imperative, however, to cut back somewhere. Before asking for the co-operation of the subcontract factories, it was necessary to set an example at the company's own factories. All that was possible would be done there and only then would the company ask for the co-operation of others. Over the summer months production was reduced by 50 per cent at the company factories, and a 20 per cent reduction was requested of the subcontract factories.

As well as decreasing production, and consequently stock, efforts were made to increase sales. The surplus staff resulting from the cutbacks were transferred to the sales department. As on a previous occasion, all the employees, and sometimes their family members, were involved in the clearance of excess merchandise. They followed the same strategy they had used ten years earlier. The employees took the products directly to government offices and major corporations and sold them for as low as three-quarters of the cost price. As a result of these efforts, the stock decreased from 3.1 billion yen in the summer of 1974 to 2.7 billion yen at the end of the year, and yet further to 2.0 billion yen by the end of 1975.

Nevertheless, the problem was not to be solved that easily. The accounts for the fiscal year 1974 showed that the figure for total sales, 7.3 billion yen, had increased 15 per cent over the previous year. The consumers, however, were paying for the inflation, and the number of sales was lower than in the previous year. Before-tax profits were 360 million yen, 19 per cent below those of the previous year. This was due to inflation: for example, the cost of labour had gone up about 30 per cent that year.

When all this had been assessed, a clearer picture began to emerge. The consequences of the inflation were much more penetrating than Onitsuka and his staff were willing to accept. All hoped that it was only a passing phase, and that soon the thriving economy would return. Many managers prefer to take an optimistic view of a bad economic situation, or rather to suppress their uneasiness by thinking in this way, but Onitsuka asserts that nothing is more dangerous than such an attitude.

The first sales forecast for 1975, prepared in the fall of 1974, reflected the initial optimism. The figure indicated was 9 billion yen. Towards the end of 1974, Onitsuka realized that this would be impossible and suggested a 15 per cent decrease, to 7.7 billion, making the forecast virtually the same as the year before. There was even the chance of a decrease in income. At the same time, costs were rising. There could be no profit with expenditures increasing and income remaining the same. Onitsuka recognized the need for a more intensified 'state of emergency' for the following year.

The 'Diet'

The aim of the company was to achieve a decrease in expenditure to compensate for the lack of increase in sales. It was an attempt to lower the break-even point. Calculations showed that a cutback of 26.9 million yen per month was required to maintain the profit margin of previous years. The only option available was to cut back on wages.

Reductions in the monthly salaries were instigated. In January, pay cheques were reduced by 15 per cent for the president, 10 per cent for the executive managing directors and 5 to 6 per cent for the managing directors. In February, these rates were doubled: 30 per cent for the president, 15 per cent for the executive managing directors, and 10 to 12 per cent for the managing directors.

February was also the month for salary increments at Onitsuka Corporation. That year, all salaries for the posts higher than section and department heads were frozen and all other raises were to be kept at less than 10 per cent. The guarantee that the minimum annual bonus, paid semi-annually, would be equivalent to four months salary was rescinded and the laying aside of 18 million yen each month for bonuses stopped. To reduce labour costs still further, Onitsuka asked for voluntary resignations—on this occasion of his part-time staff. Fifty people responded.

The use of part-time employees as a buffer against changing external economic conditions is a common practice throughout the manufacturing sector in Japan. Many male part-time employees have previously been employed on a full-time basis until they reached mandatory retirement age, somewhere between fity-five and sixty, depending on the organization. A relatively early retirement age for employees below the managing director level is universal in Japan so that opportunites may be provided for younger men. A sizeable lump sum retirement allowance is given to each retiree, but increasing life expectancy coupled with severe deficiencies in the social security system force many retirees to work part-time.

Finding work with another company is not common within Japan's organizationally-centred, inward-looking tradition. As a result, companies commonly re-hire their retired employees on a part-time basis, at a reduced salary. Women working to supplement family income and/or fulfil needs for social interaction and recognition after child rearing responsibilities have lightened make up the major component of the part-time sector. In times of restraint, the part-time employees are the first to be let go.

Very few companies reacted as quickly as Onitsuka Corporation to combat the dangers of inflation. Too many had become comfortable in the warm waters of economic growth. Reductions in wages were unheard of. The media was highly critical of Onitsuka's policy.

Nevertheless, Onitsuka believed then, and continues to believe today, that the management of a company should not be based on reputation and appearances. It is important to do what one thinks best and ignore the criticism. After all, the critics are not responsible for the company, should it fail: the responsibility lies solely with the president.

The banks were the sole exception: they could not be ignored. Onitsuka had always kept the banks informed of developments within the corporation. He considered this essential if the banks were going to trust the company. Says Teruyuki Okumura, president of the Taiyo Kobe Bank, Onitsuka Corporation's main bank, 'Mr Onitsuka was not obligated to explain in detail company plans. But he considered the process necessary to building good relations and creating an atmosphere of trust so that in difficult times we would allow the company to proceed as it thought best'.

Onitsuka went to the banks to explain his plans. The reaction was one of surprise that the company was contemplating strategies for recovery so soon. Most companies, having still to realize the seriousness of the situation, had not yet developed appropriate measures to deal with it. The banks commended Onitsuka for his foresight and advanced planning.

The ability of Onitsuka Corporation to formulate a recovery strategy so quickly reflected the harsh lessons of past experience. The company had learned the danger of procrastination in analogous circumstances. It had become very sensitive to the symptoms and had acquired a sense of premonition about impending difficulties. One further reason for the speed of effective reaction was the co-operation of the employees.

Initially, there was some uneasiness among the employees, but this was quickly dispelled through sectional information meetings to explain the company's plan of action. This initiative, along with a continued 'open door' attitude in management, secured the support of most of the personnel.

The cutbacks had the biggest effect on management. They forfeited their salary increments and suffered reductions in pay. Nevertheless, they all did a splendid job in maintaining the support and the co-operation of all the employees. They would often stay behind after work to deal with problems and complaints, and once again helped to keep the company afloat. It was their efforts that pulled Onitsuka Corporation through the oil crisis. 'Middle managers', stresses Onitsuka, 'are the cornerstone of corporate management. The performance of the corporation is dependent upon how well middle managers understand the president's management philosophy and how well they communicate with the workers.'

The instigation of salary cutbacks may have been possible only because there was no labour union with bargaining rights at Onitsuka Corporation. The critics notwithstanding, this is not to say that Onitsuka was taking advantage of the situation. He had always believed that management must assume the role of the labour union. He had confidence that the employees were aware of, and satisfied with, a system wherein management, workers and shareholders formed an integrated whole.

This perception is borne out by Teruyuki Okumura:

Onitsuka's way of thinking is not peculiar to him alone. It is prevalent throughout the Japanese business world. As the company grows and becomes stronger the rewards for all in the form of salaries, dividends and profits become greater. This is the way the Taiyo Kobe Bank, with its 15,000 employees in 400 branches, is run as well.

Okumura sees an ideal match between Onitsuka's personal beliefs and this dimension of Japanese management.

During this period, Onitsuka saw the need to provide his young middle managers with the opportunity to develop their leadership skills. Large corporations were continually expanding while weaker and often smaller companies frequently lost their competitiveness and declined. 'We had to stay in the mainstream', says Onitsuka. 'Our company was growing and its personnel increasing. We needed to heighten the leadership skills of our middle managers.'

To do this, Onitsuka chose to enrol his middle managers, a few at a time, in the biannual, four-day programme offered by Japan's naval self-defence force at the Naval Academy in Edajima in Hiroshima prefecture. The Onitsuka Corporation employees were among the forty or fifty participants from various companies in the programme. The majority were in their thirties and most were middle managers. Through lectures and physical activities, the programme stressed self-discipline, the importance of tidiness and good organization, time management, the nature of leadership, endurance and co-operation. While Onitsuka was seeking ways to develop the leadership skills of his middle managers he was also seeking a solution to the problem of profit distribution.

Functions of Profit

Onitsuka perceives the functions of profit to be threefold. The primary goal of corporate management in fulfilling its social responsibility in the free world is, in Onitsuka's view:

> to answer the needs of society by providing products and services which are beneficial to people's lives. In return, the corporation will gain profit as a reward. If profit is the ultimate goal of corporate activity, the corporation may be tempted to act unethically. The corporation must be constantly in tune with societal needs. If the products and services provided are desired by the recipients the corporation will, without doubt, make a profit.
>
> Profit is the proof of societal consensus and successful performance. It is the driving force that propels the company forward into the next risk-taking venture. Not making a profit means that the corporation is providing goods and services which are not appropriate. 'Proper' corporate activity is the involvement in a 'virtuous cyclical process' of recognizing society's needs and then marketing,

product innovation, production, distribution, returns and re-investment.

Although profit is one appropriate summation of corporate performance, Onitsuka questions what he perceives to be an exaggerated emphasis on profit in ranking corporate performance. The methods through which profit is acquired and its subsequent distribution are, for him, equally important issues.

The second purpose of corporate activity, Onitsuka feels, is the provision of an appropriate workplace in which one's purpose in living and one's purpose in working can be fulfilled. With this aim uppermost in his mind, Onitsuka asked himself: 'Why is it that intense labour-management disputes often erupt over disagreement regarding profit distribution?' Such disputes had been increasing steadily in Japan and in 1972 some 65 per cent of six thousand labour disputes nation-wide had centred on salaries and bonuses.[1]

Did some method of dividing profits exist upon which both sides could agree? The absence of a labour union at Onitsuka Corporation intensified Onitsuka's desire to find an equitable means of profit distribution which would bring the employees' interests to the fore. As Seiji Mihara recalls:

> Mr Onitsuka came on a book which I believe was written by the former president of Toto, a large bathroom fixture manufacturer, about how to make a profit. We read it looking for ideas on profit distribution. Although it did not go into this explicitly, it provided a starting-point for our thinking and eventually our solution was to focus on the distribution of the value added.

Value added is that portion of the finished product that has been created through the firm's production processes. It is equal to the sum of profits, interest, depreciation and total labour costs. In other words, it is the difference between total sales and the price of purchased raw materials, semi-finished and finished parts, and services that are used to make the product such as transportation, insurance and energy costs.

Onitsuka Corporation began in the 1960s to allot 55 per cent of value added to the employees annually. Of the remaining 45 per cent, 22.5 per cent was paid in taxes. The final 22.5 per cent of value added was divided among executive bonuses, dividends and internal reserves. When a recession occurred, however, as it did in the 1970s with the oil crisis, the employees' portion was increased from 55 per cent in order to ensure that they received a reasonable sum. The executive bonuses were decreased drastically.

Kobe's rubber industry was well-known for its low wages, but with the implementation of this scheme Onitsuka was able to rectify the situation in his company, placing the corporation at the top of the wage scale for similar-sized rubber product manufacturers in the city. 'Compared with bigger industries of this kind, however', says Kazunori Kanzaki, 'Onitsuka Corporation was just on a par and when judged against other types of industries our company still had a way to go to catch up.'

Onitsuka considers that, while it might be exaggerating somewhat, this method of distributing profits to employees, management and share-holders could be called 'adjusted capitalism' or 'new socialism'.

The third purpose of corporate management is to exist harmoniously within the regional community by using profits to provide employment, both at the parent corporation and at the affiliated factories, and to contribute to society through taxes and donations, limiting industrial pollution, and improving morale. Onitsuka believes firmly that a healthy corporation can only exist in a healthy society; a healthy corporation and a sick society cannot coexist.

At the start of 1975, the company had prepared for the worst: no profit, no bonuses. The result was that actual sales exceeded the estimate and totalled 10.3 billion yen instead of the estimated 7.7 billion yen. Thus the total after-tax profit was 300 million yen. The company had realized a record 41 per cent increase in sales and a 36 per cent increase in profits. This was greater than the growth-rate during the high growth economy period.

By May 1975, the consumption of leisure items had picked up again. Almost overnight, corporate policy changed from reducing production to increasing it. The staff continued to work as hard as ever, and this was probably the reason for the year-end figures being so impressive. The banks were full of praise for the company's foresight in planning a year ahead.

All cutbacks and freezes in salaries and bonuses were lifted. The losses in income due to the cutbacks were made up. Everyone was paid what they were due. Furthermore, the biggest bonuses in the history of the corporation were issued, equivalent to 6.6 times the monthly salary. Instead of the normal 55 per cent of the value added, 61 per cent was allotted to the employees. Onitsuka felt that the increase in profits in spite of the recession was due to labour–management co-operation.

The 20 per cent reduction in production requested of the subcontract factories was a great burden to them. Onitsuka felt that he wanted to make up for this loss in some way in accordance with his conception of profit sharing. He decided that, for the Onitsuka Circle factories that had co-operated by reducing production, he would pay the deficit that had resulted. There were twenty-one such factories. The subsidies came to a total of 50 million yen.

Subsequently, Onitsuka was informed that six representatives of the processing sector of the Onitsuka Circle had come to see him. He was apprehensive as he went to meet them, wondering what the Circle members wanted him to do. But the representatives had come, not to ask for more, but to personally express their gratitude for his treatment of them.

With most companies, the subcontractors would have been the first to be dispensed with in difficult times. Onitsuka, however, had made greater reductions in his own company, thereby minimizing the effect of the recession on the Circle members. Furthermore, when these reductions led to deficits, he offered to fully compensate the subcontractors.

Onitsuka had often spoken of the Circle and the company sharing a common destiny, co-operating and working together as a single unit. But the Circle members had remained sceptical. Now, however, they knew that he meant what he said. The six representatives had come to present him with a certificate of their appreciation.

This most unexpected and pleasant surprise overwhelmed Onitsuka. He did not know what to say. In 1974, he had been presented with the National Blue Ribbon Medal for his contribution to the country's economy and with the Japan Academy's Distinguished Service Medal for Industrial Development, but this testimonial meant even more to him.

Says Hiroyoshi Tajima, president of the Hiroyoshi Shoji Company Limited and long-time chairman of the Kobe ASICS Circle, formerly the Onitsuka Circle:

> In the early days I had some doubts as to whether Mr Onitsuka was being completely honest with us. It was a rare occurrence for a manufacturer to take his subcontractors and affiliates into his confidence. But as time passed it became increasingly apparent that what he said and what he did corresponded. We were true partners through good times and bad.

Diversification Rechallenged

The oil crisis ushered in a new era. The market was changing. In order to keep up with the times, adjustments were made in the company's management policies, operations were streamlined, and increased efforts were directed to product development.

Among the new products introduced were the 'Tiger Paw', an all-weather spike shoe for track events; the 'Emperor', a deluxe golf shoe; and the 'Gaelic', a new type of spike shoe for baseball. This latter shoe came in specialized styles for different positions and was immediately adopted by seven of Japan's twelve professional baseball teams. The demand for these shoes was much greater than expected.

In order to pursue appropriate inventory control at this time with product lines increasing, Onitsuka launched the construction of a computer-controlled distribution centre in Kakogawa city in Hyogo prefecture. The 6,600 square metre building was completed in 1974 and replaced the much smaller Suma distribution centre in use since 1965. With the establishment of the Kakogawa distribution centre, the sales component of Onitsuka Corporation became much more tightly controlled.

Within a few years, two more distribution centres had been added—the Hokuriku centre in Fukui, originally a Jelenk distribution centre, and the newly built Kashiwa centre on the outskirts of Tokyo. The former handles distribution in the Japan Sea coastal region, the latter in eastern Japan, while the Kakogawa centre concentrates on distribution throughout western Japan.

Since the oil crisis, Onitsuka Corporation had replaced half of its range of items with improved products. This led to the suggestion that a second attempt at diversification should be made. The 1972 Munich Olympic Games provided the impetus for the idea. Onitsuka noted that Adidas had supplied the uniforms for the Munich Olympic Organizing Committee. Not only that, athletes from many countries appeared in co-ordinated sportswear and shoes. 'Total fashion' was the trend.

Onitsuka was determined that his company would not fall behind. There had been requests for totalization at Onitsuka Corporation as well. Consumers had begun to ask for sportswear to go with their shoes. Many in the sales department felt that sportswear to co-ordinate with the shoes would be a guaranteed success. This opinion was voiced by retailers as well. Onitsuka began to feel that perhaps there was a limit to specializing in shoes alone. He had been giving some thought to the question of expanding the company portfolio. With this in mind he broached the subject to his senior executives. The response was somehow predictable. Remembering the fiasco of the earlier diversification attempt, they pronounced the idea too risky. They also pointed to the fact that the garment industry was far from flourishing. 'Better judgement' held that it would be dangerous to enter that field.

Onitsuka admitted to himself that there was some truth in their views. The oil crisis had adversely affected the Japanese economy. The garment industry, which had been in trouble for a number of years, was now additionally burdened by a mountain of excess finished goods. The sportswear segment was suffering the same fate as the rest of the garment industry. Attempts to reduce stock, lightly disguised as 'special invitation sales', were commonplace.

The memory of the last bitter attempt at diversification still lingered. On that occasion only a return to specialization in shoes saved the company. The reluctance of management to try again was not surprising.

Onitsuka's intuition, however, suggested that this occasion would be different. The diversification of 1964 had been carried out by a company that was still relatively immature. The company had had insufficient capital and personnel for the endeavour. Furthermore, expansion had been attempted in fields unrelated to that of sports, such as mini tape recorders and diamonds. Now they had a brand name that was known, their financial resources bore little resemblance to those of ten years ago, the personnel was much improved, and there was a good sales network. Most importantly, total fashion was in demand in the market.

Onitsuka decided to proceed with diversification only if he could obtain the co-operation of the whole staff. Eventually he was able to gain their support with the caveat that the attempt would be made only after a detailed plan of operation had been prepared. With this, the second attempt at diversification began.

Examples abound of companies going bankrupt because they fail to read the market correctly and to diversify at the right time. One such middle-sized corporation was Nekosu, one of the first steel office chair manufacturers. Founded in 1947 by Koichi Negami, an office efficiency expert, this Tokyo company was engaged in the development of business chairs and used the direct sales method to meet large-scale office demand. The name Nekosu became synonymous with reduction of office fatigue. In 1960 sales totalled 1.4 billion yen, increasing to 1.8 billion yen in 1961 when their market share reached 50 per cent.

Steel office furniture was in high demand in the early 1960s as the trend in business moved away from wooden furniture. With the increasing demand and relative simplicity of production, steel office furniture manufacturers sprang up rapidly. Nekosu expanded its operation using borrowed capital and established three factories outside Tokyo. Eventually, with the intensified competition, rising labour costs, and a large bank loan, Nekosu found itself in financial difficulties. Nekosu's crucial mistake, however, was failure to respond to market demand for 'totalization': the demand for chairs, desks, filing cabinets and lockers as an ensemble. By the time the error in marketing strategy was realized it was too late. The corporation's debts were too great and the competition was too severe. The company went bankrupt in 1964.[2]

Success

The most important lesson Onitsuka learned from the initial failure of diversification was 'gimlet' management, namely, to always maintain a point-of-focus and to proceed cautiously, one step at a time. Diversification was initiated with sportswear for track and field events. This was because Tiger shoes were most widely accepted in this sector. As the other companies had not reached the stage of specialized outfits for the different events in this sport, Onitsuka Corporation decided to make separate uniforms for track events, field events and road races. The production of these items was to be with the full co-operation of Goldwin Incorporated, a sportswear manufacturer that had expressed its support for this scheme.

Founded in 1951 as a knitwear manufacturer, Goldwin became a sportswear producer in 1952. Goldwin's president, Tosaku Nishida, feels that his company's subsequent success in this area is attributable to his recognition of the fundamental differences between the traditional Japanese garment, the kimono, and Western clothing. 'The kimono', says Nishida, 'is a two-dimensional garment designed to lie flat. The back and front are the same size and one kimono fits several different figures. As a result of the long kimono-making tradition, Japanese-made Western style clothing tended to be flat, the same front and back, when I first started business in the 1950s.' Nishida remembers the early Japanese baseball uniforms. 'Every time a player bent over, his shirt would come away from his pants, exposing his lower back.' Japense garments often looked alright on the hanger; their appearance on the body was another matter. With regard to ski wear, Nishida comments, 'Compared with the trim silhouettes created by European ski wear, Japanese skiers looked like they were wearing garbage bags.'

While Western clothing was contoured to the body, Japanese clothing remained flat. The problem, Nishida felt, was that Japanese manufacturers had not mastered the art of creating fullness only where it was required through the use of gussets, gores, and similar techniques. To learn more about Western clothing manufacture, Goldwin entered into technical tie-ups with such European manufacturers as Fusalp of France and Ellesse of Italy.

Onitsuka recognized the superiority of Goldwin products. In 1973 Goldwin Incorporated and Onitsuka Corporation jointly established Goldtiger Company Limited (the name derived from Goldwin and Onitsuka Corporation's Tiger brand), with Onitsuka as president, to accommodate product development.

The formation of Goldtiger was the first step in Onitsuka's larger plan to eventually launch his company into the production of a complete line of sportswear. He had broached the possibility of future amalgamation with Nishida but the latter's involvement in the Knitwear Manufacturers Modernization Scheme of Toyama prefecture made a merger out of the question. However, Nishida agreed to provide the production know-how and technology that Onitsuka required by establishing Goldtiger as a production planning corporation.

A major problem was that of sales routes. Feeling that it was inappropriate for a shoe manufacturer to start producing sportswear at this time, the wholesale dealers had turned Onitsuka Corporation down. Consequently, the company turned to the retail stores. Of the five hundred or so major stores selling Tiger shoes, about three hundred expressed interest in handling the new line of track and field sportswear. Most of these stores had a special interest in the sport: either the owners were former track and field athletes themselves, or their children were involved in the sport.

As soon as the arrangements were made with the retail stores, some of the smaller wholesale dealers decided that they wanted to take part in the scheme after all. It was finally decided that about ten wholesalers would deal with, on average, thirty stores each.

In the first year, 1974, sportswear sales totalled 300 million yen. In the following year, this had doubled to 600 million yen and rose to over 1.2 billion yen in 1976. This last figure accounted for 10 per cent of the total sales for Onitsuka Corporation that year. The scale of success, success that was dependent upon Onitsuka's ability to read and react to market indicators, was astonishing.

Nineteen seventy-six was the year of the Montreal Olympics. In April, the official supplier of uniforms for the Japanese national team was to be appointed. In previous years, this position had been monopolized by the leading brands in sportswear in Japan. It had been suggested, however, that this was unfair and it was decided that this year the companies would compete openly. The manufacturer with the best product was to be appointed official supplier.

This was Onitsuka Corporation's big chance. The company was a newcomer to the sportswear field but the employees involved in the design and production of the uniform had over twenty years of Goldwin's first-rate technical know-how to draw on. They resolved to work extremely hard, knowing that Goldwin products of the past had been as good, if not superior to, those of the larger sportswear manufacturers.

The final Onitsuka product was presented to the judges along with the products from the two other leading companies, Mizuno and Descente. Of the three unlabelled products, that of Onitsuka Corporation was preferred over those of the well-established sportswear manufacturers. This was a suprise to all concerned, even to Onitsuka.

The Japan Amateur Sports Association, taking into consideration Mizuno's long-term financial support of various amateur sports activities in Japan, proposed that Onitsuka Corporation delegate half of the official supplier rights to Mizuno. Personally, Onitsuka was prepared to comply with this recommendation. His employees who had so committed themselves to the development of the product felt otherwise, however. They had worked hard and dedicated themselves to winning the contest for official supplier. Their product had been judged better than the others. They considered the request to surrender part of the corporation's earned rights unjust.

Onitsuka agreed with his employees. Onitsuka Corporation would be the official supplier; he would refuse the proposal. Onitsuka expected that this decision would be met with criticism, but he was undeterred. The contest had proved that his company was capable of supplying the team with good-quality uniforms.

Onitsuka Corporation had defeated companies which, until this time, had been the acknowledged leaders in the sportswear industry. Buoyed up by this success, the employees worked hard and enthusiastically for the Montreal Olympics.

Corporate Olympics

'The Japanese–German "Shoe War"—Going for Gold at Montreal.' This was the headline in the *Osaka Shinbun* (Osaka Newspaper) on 20 June 1976. It referred to the rivalry between Onitsuka Corporation and Adidas which started with Onitsuka's success at the Tokyo Olympics. Since then, the 'score' was 2 to 1 in favour of Adidas. They had been victorious both in Mexico City and in Munich. The headline implied that this contest would continue at Montreal, with Onitsuka Corporation trying to make the score even.

The first group of Onitsuka's staff had arrived in Montreal on 9 June and by 5 July all of the eleven-man team had flow in from Japan. A staff of about twenty, including representatives of the local dealers, comprised Onitsuka Corporation's team for the Montreal Olympics.

The event that arguably settled the company's 'victory' in Montreal occurred midway through the games. On that memorable day, Onitsuka was watching the 10,000 metre race in the main stadium. Running in this race was twenty-seven year old Lasse Viren who, at 5 feet 11 inches and 132 pounds, had been nicknamed the 'Flying Finn'. He had been the gold medallist in the men's 5,000 metre race held only a few days previously, and was favoured to win the gold in this race too.

Viren had earlier worn Adidas shoes, and had won his gold medals for the 5,000 and 10,000 metre races in Munich in 1972 with them. Yet he had switched to Tiger shoes in 1973. In that year, he had been invited to race in Japan and the company had taken this opportunity to present him with a pair of Tiger shoes. Ever since his visit, he had been using Tiger shoes in preference to any other. He would send the company his ideas and suggestions for his shoes, and they would design and make them accordingly, and ship them to Finland—about a dozen pairs every year—for Viren's personal use. Also, in 1974, Viren had become the agent/distributor for Tiger shoes in Finland and so had introduced ASICS' products to the Finnish market. Onitsuka recalls:

> As the Olympics were approaching, Viren asked to have a special pair of shoes made for the Games. He wanted the heel made slightly higher, in order to maintain his body at a forward angle for maximum speed. Although this was less common in the case of long-distance races, we followed his instructions and sent him the shoes.

It was with these shoes that Viren won his gold medal in the 5,000 metre race, and ran the preliminary 10,000 metre race. Now he was running in the final 10,000 metre race for his second gold medal at Montreal. However, the shoes that he was wearing for the race were not exactly as they had been for the earlier races.

The day before the big race Viren had appeared at Onitsuka's service store with his shoes, asking to have the heels made thinner by about five millimetres. This was easier said than done. First, the entire sole needed to be removed, then the midsole scraped down and then finally the shoe glued back together. The latex glue had to be applied to both surfaces, air dried and then heat activated before the surfaces were combined. 'While this process is much faster today', says Toshio Shigi, marketing manager of ASICS Tiger Corporation, 'at that time it usually took a few days for the glue to dry completely and become effective as an adhesive.' Onitsuka was worried about making such an adjustment the day before the race.

This did not seem to bother Viren. He said that he wanted it done regardless. He had his way. The staff at the service shop tried their very best with this unexpected request. The conditions they worked under were far from ideal and there was always the slight possibility that something might go wrong.

Onitsuka did not sleep well that night. Yoshiaki Hase, who was in charge of the adjustment, nearly refused to go to the stadium for the race, saying that he could not face being there for fear of a mishap.

Now, the bell rang for the last lap. Suddenly Viren took off. After dogging Portugal's Carlos Sousa Lopes for most of the race, Viren shot past him. With his final dash, he managed to take the lead by nearly 40 metres. He won the gold medal. In so doing he became the first athlete ever to achieve a 'double-double' by successfully defending his 5,000 and 10,000 metre titles. It was a remarkable accomplishment.

A moment later Viren was crouched down, bent over his knees. Men were running towards him with a stretcher. Onitsuka wondered if the shoes had strained his feet and shuddered at the thought.

As the stretcher came towards him, Viren refused it and stood up. In his hands he had his shoes. He held them high above his head and started running towards where the Finnish section of the crowd were cheering in the stands. Four youths jumped down from the benches onto the field. Waving the Finnish flag, running on either side of Viren, they ran round the track with Viren still waving his shoes victoriously over his head. Onitsuka was overcome with joy and surprise.

This event provided great publicity for Onitsuka Corporation. The media contended that Viren had acted improperly, alleging that he must have received money from Onitsuka Corporation under the table, as an advertisement fee. The *Asahi Shinbun* (Asahi Newspaper) of 3 September 1976 carried a story which read in part;

> Until now, the majority of the Olympic gold medallists have worn either Adidas or Puma shoes, the two largest manufacturers of sports shoes, both from West Germany. However, at the Montreal Olympics, Onitsuka Corporation did remarkably well in the 'medal races'. In addition to Viren, with his two gold medals, they also won the gold in the women's 400 metres with Irena Szewinska (Poland) and the silver in the marathon with Frank Shorter (USA). And thanks to the 'publicity' by Viren, Onitsuka has now got ahead of Puma to be ranked second after Adidas. There must have been a lot of money involved for this to be possible.

This assertion was groundless. Onitsuka Corporation did not have the financial capacity to compete in this way even if it had wanted to. They found it necessary to resort to measures other than money. They had no choice but to seek the support of the athletes through the quality of their product and their service.

Viren's victory had great significance for him and for Finland. Although at one time Finland was well-known for its long-distance runners, in recent years, they had not been living up to expectations. Finnish distance runners had won a total of forty-one medals in the six summer Olympic Games held from 1912 through 1936. In the next six Games, however, they had won only one medal, a bronze in the 1956 marathon.

Subsequently, in Munich, Viren, a village policeman, made his meteoric rise to win the gold medal in both the 5,000 and 10,000 metre races, becoming only the fourth man in the history of the modern Olympics to do so. In Montreal, he had already won the 5,000 metre race. Winning the 10,000 metre race gave him his 'double-double', an Olympic first. Also, he had spent considerable time improving his shoes until they were just right for this race. It was his joy and sense of accomplishment that led him to express his happiness by waving his Tiger shoes in the air after the race. The publicity surrounding this incident decided Onitsuka's 'victory' in the 'shoe war' at Montreal and made Tiger shoes world-famous.

For sports equipment manufacturers, the performance of the competitors using their equipment constitutes a type of 'corporate olympics' and corporations keep close tabs on how well they are doing. For example, corporate records show that out of the seventeen times the Fukuoka International Marathon has been run, the winners have worn Tiger shoes fourteen times. At the 1984 Los Angeles Olympics, sixty gold, silver and bronze medal winners were using ASICS equipment.

These 'corporate olympics' received their major impetus from the feud, the details of which have never been disclosed, between the German Dassler brothers, which resulted in the dissolution of their shoemaking partnership in 1948 and the formation of what were soon to become the world's two top-ranking sports shoe manufacturers, Adidas and Puma, founded by Adi and Rudi Dassler, respectively, in Herzogenaurach, a small Bavarian town in West Germany. The rivalry between these two companies, a major stimulus to sports shoe innovation, peaked regularly at the Olympic Games with each company striving to have its footwear worn by the largest number of athletes. The competition between manufacturers continues today but is intensified by the increased number of competitors.

Corporations have sponsored professional athletes for some time. Onitsuka Corporation, and later ASICS, has sponsored a number of athletes, including tennis pros Margaret Court of Australia, Andrea Jaeger of the United States, Anders Jarryd of Sweden and Kumiko Okamoto of Japan. In such relationships, the corporation pays the athlete a substantial sum. In return, the athlete uses ASICS clothing and/or shoes for a specified length of time and ASICS can use the athlete's picture and/or name for promotional purposes. Some of these athletes are also members of ASICS' advisory staff.

The issue of Viren's shoes drew accusations of bribery because of the supposedly amateur status of Olympic athletes. In reality, the days of the independently wealthy sportsman had passed. Financial support was becoming a necessity if the athletes were to devote themselves to the pursuit of excellence. The shoe companies were among the first to realize this. Today the sponsorship of amateur sport is widespread throughout the world, both within and outside the sporting goods industry. Controversy persists over the relationship between amateur sport and corporate money. Alberto Salazar, a Boston Marathon winner, summed up the feelings of many athletes when he said that he would not participate again unless he was paid.

The International Track and Field Association, at its 1982 conference in Athens, modified its rules to allow amateur track and field athletes to receive monetary rewards for their endeavours through trust funds managed by affiliated national associations. The Association felt that such an intermediary buffer was required to protect athletes from being labelled 'professional'. The Japanese Association of Track and Field reluctantly followed their lead and authorized the receipt of prize money and participation fees by Japanese athletes taking part in events held abroad. This money is pooled in a trust fund. Athletes' expenses are paid out of it and, on retirement, each athlete will receive the remainder of his contribution to the fund. This presents unique problems in Japan where the desire to maintain the 'purity' of amateur sport is strong.

Hanji Aoki, chairman of the Japanese Association of Track and Field, explains that:

> traditionally, students were the main focus of sports popularization and development in Japan. Since World War II, however, this focus has shifted to corporate employees. Corporations and the Association look after athletes' expenses both for training and competition. Co-workers support their athlete colleague by covering his job in the athlete's absence and share in the joy of his accomplishments. This system works because the athletes are amateurs and receive no monetary rewards for their efforts. The introduction of such rewards creates fissures within this co-operative relationship. Private industries often discourage the receipt of monetary remuneration for extra curricular activities and in the public sector the receipt of prize money is prohibited by law.[3]

The distinction between amateur and professional has become blurred. The Olympics are now open to professional athletes in specified sports. Increasingly, the Games have become an arena where commercialism prevails, putting sporting goods manufacturers in an awkward situation.

12 | The Birth of ASICS

Totalization Advances

The Montreal Olympics marked great achievements for Onitsuka Corporation. Not only had athletes using Tiger shoes won the largest number of medals yet, but the company had also been the supplier of the uniforms for the Japanese national team. But, on the other hand, Onitsuka discovered that the 'totalization' of the total range of sporting goods, including shoes, sportswear and equipment, in other countries was much more advanced than he had realized.

By this time, Onitsuka Corporation had penetrated deeply into the world market for volleyball shoes. The Polish men's volleyball team, the winners of the gold medal at Montreal, had been using Tiger shoes until the Montreal Olympics. They were now wearing Adidas shoes. Somewhat surprised at this sudden switch, Onitsuka sought an explanation. He was told that, as Onitsuka Corporation was unable to provide the team with either the balls or the sportswear they required, the Polish Olympic Committee had signed a contract with Adidas. The latter could supply all the team's needs. The team felt that its options were limited unless Onitsuka Corporation could match that type of service. They would, however, continue to use Tiger shoes in training.

Onitsuka had not been aware that totalization had advanced so far in other countries. Onitsuka Corporation had only begun to expand into sportswear. It was obvious that they had fallen behind their competitors abroad. Onitsuka realized that something had to be done quickly, but he was sceptical about the company being able to meet the challenge on its own.

Immediately on his return to Japan, Onitsuka initiated a response. He met with his long-time business associates, Mitsuji Teranishi, then President of GTO, and Kazuma Usui, then President of Jelenk, and told them about the trend abroad. The three men had been working together for some time, carefully preparing the ground for possible amalgamation. Their friendship dated back to the early 1960s.

Shortly after the Rome Olympics, Teranishi and Onitsuka collaborated to form a study group for the sporting goods manufacturers of the Kansai district of western Japan. This group was called the 'Seiwa Society'. The name was derived from the *kanji* (Chinese characters) for the names of the two most recent Japanese historical periods, Taisho (1912–1926) and Showa (1926–   ). All the Society's fifty-eight members had been born in one or other of these two periods.

The group met one evening a month to hear an invited lecturer speak on some aspect of management and/or human nature. Discussion would follow. Topics included management ideology, human resource management, production management, societal values, and so on. Strictly a study group, the Society deliberately avoided political involvement.

Teranishi wanted Onitsuka to become Chairman. The time commitment made Onitsuka reluctant to accept the appointment but when Teranishi promised his full assistance in running the Society, Onitsuka agreed. Recalls Teranishi, 'Even though Mr Onitsuka was extremely busy at this time, he never once missed a Seiwa Society meeting and participated fully in the group's social activities as well.'

Usui moved his head office from Fukui to Osaka and joined the Seiwa Society in 1962. The three men were involved in the Society's main activities and a close friendship developed between them. All three were instrumental in the establishment of the Association of Kansai Sporting Goods Industries, an organization that developed in 1965 in response to the demand for a political voice for sporting goods producers. All are active in this association today.

Mitsuji Teranishi and GTO

Mitsuji Teranishi, then known as Mitsuji Tanimura, was born in the town of Heguri in Nara prefecture in 1919, the sixth of seven sons born to Yoshitaro Tanimura and Iwa Okamura. An economics major, Mitsuji graduated from Wakayama High School (presently Wakayama University) in 1941, the same year as he was hired by Matsushita Electric Industrial Company Limited. Here he was engaged in the task of determining how to apply a cost accounting model which had been introduced from the United States to the Japanese military.

In January 1942, at the age of twenty-two, Mitsuji joined the Seventh Regiment of the Osaka Division of the Japanese Imperial Army. After three months training, he was sent with his regiment to Manchuria where they were united with the Fortieth Regiment from Tottori. They were responsible for overseeing the border between Manchuria and the Soviet Union, but never actually engaged in combat. The Tottori officers thought the Osaka 'city boys' weak and virtually useless and gave them an additional three months training.

Successful completion of this programme in addition to the initial training programme qualified those who were middle school graduates or higher to become military cadets. This paved the way to becoming either officers or non-commissioned officers. Mitsuji was selected for officer training and sent back to Japan to the Maebashi Officers' School in Gunma prefecture at the end of 1942. A year later he was made a second lieutenant and was assigned to the Army's *Senpakutai* branch to develop a suicide mission.

The mission's objective was to destroy enemy ships and submarines close to shore. Primitive boats were constructed from plywood and powered by automobile engines. An anti-submarine depth charge was attached to each boat and the manned craft launched from several directions at once at an enemy vessel. Few of the 'pilots' survived. When Japan surrendered, Mitsuji was in Chiba prefecture, still in charge of the suicide mission.

After the war, he returned to Matsushita Electric but, discouraged by the sizeable gap that had developed between himself and those workers who had not enlisted and subsequently advanced through several promotions, Mitsuji left the company at the end of 1946 to pursue his dream of becoming an independent businessman. He was, however, without a clear idea of how he would make his dream a reality. His father's brother had plans for his nephew though. This brother, Genzo Teranishi, had been adopted as a young man by the Teranishi family to carry on the family net manufacturing business founded in 1895.

Adopting a man and installing him as president of a company is an age-old tradition in Japan. During the feudal period, social status was acquired not on the basis of what a person had done in society, but rather from the household into which one was born. Such a system of inherited social status cannot normally coexist alongside a system based on meritorious performance. During the prolonged period of peace and isolation in the eighteenth and nineteenth centuries, manufacturing and commerce became increasingly important in Japan and merchants—formerly at the bottom of the social hierarchy after warriors, farmers and artisans— acquired economic power exceeding that of the upper-ranking warrior class. With the rise of the merchant class, the *ie*, or household-based social status system often proved conducive to the development of a performance based system. In order to maintain the prosperity of the *ie* in the merchant class, a competent manager was essential.

The founder of the family business may have accumulated wealth but there was no guarantee that his successor would maintain and expand the business. When there was no heir, or if the heir appeared to be lacking in competence, an adopted son might be brought in or selected from among the employees.[1] Among the wealthiest merchants, it became common-place for the son to be by-passed altogether and for the son-in-law, often a company employee who married a daughter of the family, to inherit the business. Such an adoption system made possible the continuation of the prosperity of the merchant household.

Genzo Teranishi's wife had died giving birth to their only child, a daughter, Yukiko. Now that she was of marriageable age, her father wished to adopt his nephew, Mitsuji Tanimura, marry him to Yukiko, and install him as head of the family business.

Mitsuji's own father had died in 1941 and five of his six brothers had been killed during the war. His surviving brother, the one immediately older than he, had become an adopted son before the outbreak of the war. The direct lineage of the Tanimura family was ensured, however, by the existence of a grandson, Mitsuji's eldest brother's child. Although his mother encouraged Mitsuji to accept his uncle's offer, he was hesitant. Finally, however, he gave in to the urging of his mother and his uncle and married his cousin in December 1947.

During the war, Genzo Teranishi, in compliance with the government's policy to strengthen small businesses, had merged with another privately owned establishment. Mitsuji Teranishi dissolved the merger in 1948 when it became evident that the other partner was taking advantage of the situation. That same year the company was incorporated as Genzo Teranishi Stores Limited with production focusing on sports nets.

The Teranishi family had been Japan's first hammock makers, borrowing the idea from the French and introducing it to Japan in 1895. The hammocks were primarily used for babies, to keep them away from the ticks, mites and bedbugs that commonly inhabited Japanese homes. When Mitsuji Teranishi took over the business he felt that the hammocks were unsafe—he thought he would never use one for a child of his own. He decided to leave the hammock business and concentrate on sports nets, although he realized that the market for the latter was limited.

Teranishi improved on existing net-making equipment, developing a machine in 1958 capable of producing fixed, immovable intersections in nets. Thanks to this innovation, Genzo Teranishi Stores was asked to supply the ball sport nets for the 1964 Tokyo Olympics and the 1969 Mexico Olympics.

By the latter part of the 1950s, Teranishi was looking for a possible avenue for diversification. He wanted to expand into sportswear but felt he could not do so without coming into direct competition with some of his good friends in the sporting goods industry. Instead, after consulting with twenty mountaineers, he designed and produced a rucksack for rock climbing. In retrospect, Teranishi says, 'I probably made a mistake not getting into sportswear at that time.'

His strong aversion to intruding on what he perceived to be his colleagues' territory continued but his desire to expand into sportswear persisted. A few years later, Teranishi did find a niche for his company where he would not be in direct competition with anyone else. He diversified into fishing sportswear. Until then there had been no such specialized attire—old clothes were the norm. Predicting an upsurge in this sport coinciding with Japan's rapidly progressing economic recovery, Teranishi felt there would soon be a sizeable market for specialized fishing sportswear. His prediction was accurate and his company's fishing wear, along with its rucksacks and sports nets, came to be recognized as top-quality products.

In 1968, Genzo Teranishi Stores merged with Young Man, an Osaka sportswear manufacturer established after the war by Shinichi Onishi. Through this merger, Teranishi felt he could at last launch his company into the production of sportswear. At the time of the merger, Young Man was heavily dependent on subcontractors, employing only fifteen workers, and their total annual sales were 140 million yen compared with Genzo Teranishi Stores' one billion yen.

With the merger, the company entered into the production of ski wear and later expanded into sportswear for cycling and tennis. Technical and design contracts with domestic and foreign individuals and/or companies facilitated this expansion.

Seeking to lessen the emphasis on the family connection, Teranishi changed the company name to GTO Incorporated in 1974. Acronyms were popular for company names but three letters were more common than two. Teranishi took the GT of Genzo Teranishi and the O of Onishi to arrive at GTO. Teranishi then decided that the letters would also stand for Good Taste and Originality. Says Teranishi, 'I consulted with an English language "authority" and was assured that this would make sense to foreigners.'

By the time GTO amalgamated with Onitsuka Corporation and Jelenk, the Osaka-based company with 354 employees had established a branch office in Tokyo, sales offices in seven cities and factories in four locations. The latter are now ASICS factories. By that time ski wear and fishing gear accounted for 65 per cent and 15 per cent, respectively, of the company's total annual sales of 9.1 billion yen.

Kazuma Usui and Jelenk

Kazuma Usui was also adopted. Born in Takefu city, Fukui prefecture, in 1924, he was the second youngest of four sons and one daughter born to Ishiki Nagami and his wife, Masa Maezawa. From a farming family, Usui, then known as Kazuma Nagami, graduated from Imadate Agricultural School in 1941 and went to work for the prefectural agricultural department as an agricultural engineer. During the war, attendance at veterinary school was waived and qualification as a veterinarian required only that the applicant pass the national exam. Kazuma studied on his own for two years and qualified as a vet in 1943. Conscription followed in the fall of 1944. After initial training, he became an officer candidate but the war ended before he could pursue further training.

Returning to civilian life and his veterinary practice, Kazuma was implored by Kinji Hino, a family friend and Takefu tailor, to consider marriage and adoption into the Usui family. Tamajiro Usui had died suddenly of a cerebral haemorrhage two years before, leaving his wife and three young daughters to look after the family silk business. Now his wife had contracted tuberculosis and was not expected to live more than a year. 'I was very young then', says Usui, 'and had no thought of getting married. Besides, I felt my work as a veterinarian was important to the community.' But Hino begged Kazuma just to meet the mother and finally, out of politeness and respect, he agreed.

The meeting was a moving one. 'I was not a doctor', Usui recalls, 'but from my work with animals it was apparent to me that Mrs Usui couldn't live much longer. Still, I was not prepared to marry the eldest daughter and take on the responsibilities of the family and the business.'

Further discussion with Hino and his own father, however, changed Kazuma's mind. For the first time, his father disclosed that five other families had approached him hoping to adopt his son but he had refused each one because Kazuma was still very young. This time, however, his father encouraged him to accept the offer. In December 1946, at the age of twenty-two Kazuma married eighteen-year-old Toshiko Usui. The following month Tamae Usui died.

On her deathbed, Mrs Usui had told her adopted son that he did not need to worry about multiplying the family's assets; to prevent their demise would be sufficient. She had promised in the next world to secure her husband's permission for Kazuma to change the nature of the business, should the need arise, and his forgiveness if, for some reason, the adopted son should lose everything. She had implored him, however, not to let gambling and loose living bring ruin to the family.

Kazuma Usui was now head of the Usui family, responsible for the welfare of his wife and her two younger sisters and for the prosperity of the family silk wholesaling business. The business entailed procuring raw silk from the silk producers, throwing it—that is, twisting and doubling the raw silk to the required thickness to prepare it for the loom—then selling it to the silk textile factories where it would be woven into the *habutae* silk for which the area was famous and eventually used for kimono linings, scarves and dresses.

Under the controlled economy of postwar Japan, silk production and supply were regulated by the Sericulture Producers Association and quotas were assigned according to prewar volume. Because the business had flourished under Tamajiro Usui, the postwar quotas under which it operated were liberal and spared Kusuma Usui from the stiff competition he would have experienced in a free economy.

In the family business records, Usui found the names of the silk producers in Ayabe, Ueda and Okaya with whom his father-in-law had done business. On visiting these producers, Usui was welcomed with open arms. To help Tamajiro Usui's successor, they sold him the short denier testing threads which were not affected by the quotas. Usui made these into skeins to be used in knitting—a lucrative undertaking.

When the controls were lifted in 1950, the price of silk began to drop. Usui went to Tokyo to consult with government officials about the future of the silk industry. The prognosis was not good. Nylon, he was told, would be the fibre of the future. Usui was advised to get out of the silk business. 'By the time I returned home', says Usui, 'I had made up my mind to follow this advice. My relatives were furious but I was not to be dissuaded.' By 1952, the focus of Usui's business had shifted to the production and sale of baseball stockings, undershirts and training shirts, and the company had been renamed Usui Knitwear Manufacturers to reflect this change. This was Usui's entry into the sportswear field. The next year, he established sales offices in Tokyo and Osaka and a second factory in Takefu city.

Realizing the desirability of a larger and more central location, if he was to achieve his ambition of making his products nationally known, Usui first consulted his wife about the possibility of moving the business headquarters and the family headquarters to Osaka. The latter would entail changing the location of the Usui family grave.

Securing his wife's support, he next consulted with the head priest of the temple which held the Usui family grave. While lamenting the loss of the family as members of his congregation, the priest commended Usui for his intentions. The move to Osaka would test the strength of the company and, through adversity, foster its growth into a much stronger entity. Sure of the appropriateness of his decision, Usui uprooted his family and his business and located them in Osaka in 1962. At the time of the move, he renamed the company Usui Textile Industry Limited.

Both Onitsuka and Teranishi, as representatives from the sporting goods industry, were invited to the ceremony to mark the company's opening. Teranishi was out of the country and could not attend but Onitsuka addressed the gathering. From this time on, Usui considered Onitsuka as an elder brother and trusted business adviser. When Onitsuka Corporation was recovering from its diversification disaster two years later, Usui asked Onitsuka why the company had come so close to financial ruin. Hoping to help Usui avoid a similar fate, Onitsuka explained the circumstances in detail, withholding nothing. Based on the lessons learned from Onitsuka, Usui concentrated on knitwear.

In 1963, working in collaboration with Daiwabo, a large spinning company, Usui succeeded in dyeing polypropylene yarn. The resulting colours were vivid, attractive and eye-catching. The yarn was then made into lightweight training wear which rapidly became popular in the market-place, a welcome contrast to the sombre dark blue and black training wear then available.

Towards the end of the decade, feeling that the company would benefit from a more modern, catchier-sounding name, Usui selected a number of possibilities, then conducted a consumer survey, mainly of students and housewives, to see which had the greatest appeal. 'Jelenk' (derived from *gerenuk*, one of the few species of antelope to have increased in number over the last few decades) was the most popular and the company was renamed accordingly.

In 1971, Jelenk Incorporated absorbed Gelico (an acronym for Gentlemen's Lifewear Collection), a men's sportswear manufacturer with a capital of 10 million yen headquartered in Osaka. This move launched Jelenk into the production of casual wear. Realizing the need to expand into the international market, Jelenk entered into a joint venture with Mitsubishi Rayon, one of Japan's biggest acrylic fibre makers, and, using local capital, established a factory in the Philippines in 1972. The following year Jelenk established a sales company in the United States.

At the time of the tripartite merger, in addition to the overseas operations, Jelenk had branch offices in Tokyo and Nagoya, sales offices in four cities and factories in four locations in western Japan. It employed 339 people and had a capital of 550 million yen with a total annual sales of 10.7 billion yen.

From Co-operation to Amalgamation

In 1971, the year before the Sapporo Winter Olympics, Onitsuka Corporation, GTO and Jelenk first worked in collaboration. It began when Teranishi and Usui learned of Onitsuka Corporation's plan to open a new sales office in Sapporo in time for the Games. Onitsuka Corporation had bought a lot of about 2,000 square metres in the city. They inquired of Onitsuka if it would be possible for the two of them to join him in this scheme.

Onitsuka liked the idea. Three companies working together would be advantageous. They could share the latest news and information about the market and exchange new ideas. The delivery of the products could be made more efficient through co-operation. It would no doubt be more convenient for the customers, too. It was agreed that the three companies, which were engaged in different businesses, would work in collaboration in the same building. They could have created a unified sales company. This, however, would have caused too many problems with the established sales routes and wholesale dealers. Instead, arrangements were made for the formation of the Clover Limited Liabilities Company in Sapporo, financed equally by the three firms.

The new corporation built a two-storeyed building and opened offices there, Onitsuka Corporation, Jelenk and GTO each occupying one-third of the space. This was the Sapporo office. In retrospect, it was the first step towards amalgamation. Thinking back on the formation of the Clover Company, Masaaki Uetsuki, now general manager of ASICS' Sales Promotion Division, says, 'the three companies occupied the same building and undertook joint exhibitions. The relationship among the three was excellent.'

In a similar fashion, two more offices were opened in Sendai and Fukuoka. Onitsuka, Usui and Teranishi would meet once a month to exchange ideas and information. Senior executives of Onitsuka, Jelenk and GTO would meet regularly as well. It was not long, however, before the limitations of this combined management began to emerge. Each company had its own 'trade secrets' and was understandably reluctant to share them. This prevented the companies from maximizing the potential advantages of sharing all their resources and know-how. Towards the end of 1973, it became clear that a major decision had to be made. The three companies could terminate their co-operative arrangement and go their separate ways, establish a unified sales company, or move towards formal amalgamation.

There were many meetings and discussions. Usui, Teranishi and Onitsuka felt that the most satisfactory outcome, financially, would be amalgamation. United through amalgamation, they would be in a position to compete against Mizuno, Japan's largest and oldest comprehensive maker of sporting goods, founded in 1906. Individually, none could hold a candle to this mighty corporation that had done much to popularize sport in Japan.

At this point the decision was made to expand the discussions to include one or two senior executives from each of the three companies. Says Yoshihiro Hashimoto, who was then senior executive managing director with GTO:

Each of us was acquainted with the presidents of the other two companies through various sports equipment manufacturers meetings that we attended but it was through the pre-amalgamation discussions that the personalities and values of each of the three presidents became clear. At this time, Mr Onitsuka, Mr Teranishi, and Mr Usui were still hesitant to commit themselves totally to amalgamation. We were unsure at first too, but eventually came to feel that this would be the best course of action and that if we delayed we would miss the opportunity. We strongly urged the three presidents to act promptly.

Obviously amalgamation would not be a simple matter; many aspects had to be considered and many problems solved. The overriding issue was whether each of the presidents, Onitsuka, Teranishi and Usui, could forfeit his individual sense of ownership in his company. After all, they were all men of pride and achievement who were, in a large measure, personally responsible for the success of their businesses. In the case of Usui and Teranishi, the situation was further complicated by their desire, shared by most presidents of small and medium-sized enterprises in Japan today, to pass on control of their respective companies to their sons.[2]

Teranishi had two sons, Shigekazu and Hikoji, twenty-eight and twenty-five, respectively, at the time of the amalgamation. Both were employed by GTO. Usui's eldest son, Yoshiharu, twenty-six, was gaining business experience as an employee of Teijin Limited, a leading manufacturer of synthetic fibres, while his second, Masaharu, aged twenty-four, was pursuing graduate studies at Nagoya Kogyo University.

Onitsuka, who was not concerned with the question of succession by a son was, perhaps, able to take a more objective view of the issue than the others. He suggested that as the first step in overcoming their strong sense of 'possession' they should nurture a more public attitude to their business. Each president had to realize that an enterprise does not belong to an individual. Accordingly, he proposed that Teranishi and Usui should aim at having their firms listed on the Stock Exchange. His own experience had led him to believe that this was the only way a person could appreciate the social responsibility involved in being president of a company. At that time, Onitsuka Corporation was listed in the first section of the Tokyo, Osaka and Nagoya Stock Exchanges.

Onitsuka's preference in management is to 'deprivatize' business. He has followed this line since the beginning, believing that an enterprise can prosper only when it becomes public. Therefore, he thought that it would be best to postpone the amalgamation until all three men agreed with the idea of deprivatization. There was also the additional consideration of waiting until the other companies grew larger through listing. Amalgamation could only be successful when each merging company was strong enough and big enough for a synergistic effect to result from a merger. Onitsuka's suggestion was accepted without objection. Each company embarked on its own separate preparations.

Shortly after, the oil crisis struck the Japanese economy and each company was forced to fight for survival. All were able to weather the storm and, in November 1975, GTO was listed in the second section of the Osaka Stock Exchange. Jelenk was preparing to be listed in 1977.

Onitsuka's observations at the Montreal Olympics in 1976 convinced him that early amalgamation was imperative. On his return to Japan, he met first with Teranishi and then with Usui, informing them of the need for immediate action. The situation had become critical; every minute counted. Three years earlier they had agreed on carrying out the amalgamation only after GTO and Jelenk had been listed on the Stock Exchange, but the global situation had changed drastically since then. The totalization trend was proceeding rapidly within the sporting goods industry. Onitsuka felt that if the amalgamation could not go ahead immediately the tripartite collaboration would have to be dissolved. Onitsuka Corporation would then proceed with totalization on its own in an effort to avoid falling behind the global evolution.

Although the amalgamation proposition had always been tempting, Teranishi had been hesitant to make the decision lightly. In strict confidence he had sought the opinion of a business consultant he respected. The consultant counselled that a merger between two companies is fraught with difficulties; a successful tripartite merger is extremely rare. He advised against amalgamation. Despite this, Teranishi had grown to trust Onitsuka completely. Now, when Onitsuka confronted him with his findings at the Montreal Olympics, demanding that they act immediately on their tentative plans for amalgamation, Teranishi agreed. Together they approached Usui.

Although Jelenk had not actually been listed, the necessary arrangements had been made. Only the formalities remained to be completed. Onitsuka advised that the company was already sufficiently recognized; the Stock Exchange listing was no reason to delay the amalgamation any longer.

Usui naturally hesitated in accepting this suggestion immediately. Reflecting on how he felt at the time, Usui says:

To be honest, I wanted to wait until our company had been formally listed. I wanted to accomplish this aim that I had set for myself and the company, on our own. However, at the same time, I also knew that I should not be so self-indulgent about the company or so inflexible about my short-term aims. I knew that co-operation with the other two was the best decision for the future and, having convinced myself, I decided not to delay the matter any longer.

Each company differed in origin and had developed along separate lines. When different people come together, the critical question is whether they will be able to work together in harmony. This is particularly true in Japanese corporations where the strong, and often very narrow, identification of employees with one enterprise frequently creates obstacles in fostering co-operative endeavours. Onitsuka Corporation had experienced failure in incorporating new managers into a pre-existing framework thirteen years earlier when the recruitment of management personnel had resulted in severe fissures within the management body. Thus, Onitsuka could fully appreciate the difficulties involved when working together with people from different backgrounds. He knew the attendant risks and dangers, but these did not stop him from pursuing amalgamation plans.

His primary reason for pressing ahead in spite of these difficulties was his great confidence in his own staff. Onitsuka had trained them with his 'own hands'. The managerial core was now sturdy enough to withstand the integration of new staff. In Onitsuka's view, the success of the amalgamation would depend almost entirely on the co-operation of upper management. Before asking Teranishi and Usui to commit themselves finally to amalgamation, he consulted his own senior management staff. He felt he could not justifiably make the amalgamation decision without their absolute agreement. They were the pillars of Onitsuka Corporation. The amalgamation would not succeed if they were against the plan. He called them together and told them he would only proceed with the amalgamation if they were prepared to give him their full support.

Having said this, Onitsuka left the room to allow them to discuss the issue among themselves. This differed from the customary executive decision-making process in the company. Yoshiyuki Takahashi says:

Normally the president would remain for the discussion. We would argue to the hilt, expressing our views freely without fear of censure. After a prolonged, intense discussion, we would ask the president to make the final decision. He would give us his interpretation of the situation and explain why he was deciding in favour of a particular course of action. Once the decision had been made, all the executives agreed to co-operate and to act on it to the best of their ability. This decision-making process also provided an environment in which the executives could grow.

The amalgamation discussion was somehow different. Some of the eleven executive directors present felt that Onitsuka's mind was made up irrevocably. The results of their consultation, they felt, would not have a dramatic impact on the final decision. Nevertheless, some of the executives argued that Onitsuka Corporation was capable of expanding its business on its own—that amalgamation was unnecessary and would only result in a cumbersome organizational structure. Others were concerned that their own positions would be jeopardized.

After some time, a representative of the group came to inform Onitsuka of their decision. The executives had discussed the issue fully. Several were of the opinion that the company ought to continue on its own, but in the end, they all agreed to support Onitsuka's decision. If he decided that amalgamation was the preferred course, the executive directors would do their best to ensure that it was a success.

With this vote of confidence, Onitsuka resolved to finalize his decision. He intended to make this scheme a success and was confident that it would be. On 27 December 1976, Onitsuka, Teranishi and Usui met again in a room in the Osaka Royal Hotel. They were to arrive at their final decision on that day.

Onitsuka had already made up his mind. Now he would listen to what the others had to say. Teranishi spoke first. He felt that a corporation would fulfil its social responsibility through continuous development. At the time GTO was listed, the company had been transformed from a private, family-owned corporation into a public enterprise. He had no assurance that his son could successfully take over the company in the future. The best course of action, he felt, was to strengthen the company's human resources through amalgamation and to cultivate capable successors from among them. In this way he would be working to build a corporation that could survive global competition.

Usui offered his opinion. He wanted to wait until after Jelenk had been listed on the Stock Exchange before making his decision on this final step. He had come to realize that privatization works against corporate development. Short-term profit should not be one's main concern. Citing the proverb 'give up minor differences and unite your similarities', Usui acknowledged that amalgamation would be the best course for corporate development.

This was the response Onitsuka had hoped for and expected. He was filled with excitement. All three men wanted to embark on the amalgamation and realized that the time to make the move was right now. Teranishi and Usui had relinquished the idea of filial succession and had wholeheartedly embraced Onitsuka's philosophy of labour, capital and management being equal partners in the corporate endeavour.

It took less than a quarter of an hour to reach a final decision. Fifteen years after first working together in the Seiwa Society and six years after the opening of the Sapporo office, their first common business venture, the three companies were finally to be united.

'One reason Mr Teranishi and Mr Usui trusted me and felt that the proposed venture would be truly an amalgamation of equal partners, not a takeover, was perhaps because years before I had disbursed such a large percentage of Onitsuka Corporation shares among my employees', says Onitsuka. It could be said that the seeds that brought ASICS to fruition were planted in 1959. Today Onitsuka owns 1.3 per cent of ASICS' shares, about half of those owned by Usui and by Teranishi.

Usui and Teranishi recommended that Onitsuka assume the position of president. It was he who had guided them through the entire procedure. They would be his deputies. As the eldest of the three, Onitsuka felt comfortable accepting the recommendation.[3] Usui and Teranishi would be the vice-presidents. All three would be ASICS' 'representative directors'. 'Representative directorship' is a unique tool of directorship in Japanese corporations. In accordance with the Commercial Code, each corporation has one or more directors with legal power to represent it. As ASICS' representative directors, Onitsuka, Teranishi and Usui are authorized to perform all judicial and extra-judicial acts relating to the business of the company.

The style of leadership had to be clarified. Teranishi had given this a great deal of thought and had prepared a statement which he read to the other two:

> Mr Usui and I will give you our full support, Mr Onitsuka. We will, however, freely express our opinions. If one of us has an idea that has greater viability than your intention, we trust you will recognize this and act accordingly. After all points of view have been exhaustively discussed, if you still feel your position is preferable, then we will support you. The success of the amalgamation depends on absolute mutual trust and the integration of our wills.

Usui and Onitsuka agreed with Teranishi's perception of how corporate leadership would work. The three named the proposed leadership style *shugi dokusai*, or 'democratic autocracy'.

At this time there were twenty executives among the three companies occupying the three senior management levels, that is, *senmu torishimari*, or senior executive managing director, *jomu torishimari*, or executive managing director, and *torishimari*, or managing director. The question was how to fairly assign executive status in the new company when the relative ability of each of the executives had yet to be determined. Yoshihiro Hashimoto of GTO, the only one of the twenty to hold the rank of senior executive managing director, suggested that they all start from the same level and, for the first year, all assume the rank of managing director.

Before the amalgamation could be formally announced there were two concerns that had to be attended to. The first was to secure the approval of the companies' main banks for the merger. The second was to secure the transfer of Rawlings' contract for the manufacture of baseball uniforms from GTO to ASICS. At the beginning of January, Onitsuka, Teranishi and Usui flew to Los Angeles to meet with the president of Rawlings. Negotiations went smoothly and ASICS obtained the contract.

Returning to Japan, Teranishi and Usui notified their families of the impending amalgamation. Their sons understood that this course of action was best for their respective companies. Three of the four have since come to work for ASICS: Shigekazu and Hikoji Teranishi from GTO at the time of the amalgamation and Yoshiharu Usui from Teijin Limited in 1980.

Says Yoshiharu, presently co-ordinator of corporate-wide small group total quality control activities, 'My father developed the family business and made his decisions based on his own beliefs. His beliefs have to be respected. Now I want to participate fully in the maturation of the new corporation.' Of Onitsuka, Yoshiharu says, 'He is a dynamic man. He has a clear mission and a management philosophy that propels him ever forward.' Shigekazu Teranishi is presently managing ASICS' Yao factory in Nara prefecture. Originally GTO's factory, it is engaged in the production of sports nets.

Hikoji Teranishi had been looking forward to participating in the management of GTO in the future. 'At the same time, though', he says, 'my father has been constantly reminding me that a corporation has to be managed by those who have management ability, not just "connections".' After the merger, Hokoji was placed first in the baseball section. Recently, he has been transferred to golf, one of the company's weakest sections. Hikoji fully supports the amalgamation. 'None of the three corporations was exceptionally strong on its own,' he says, 'but since the amalgamation ASICS' name and reputation have become known globally. It was an excellent way for each of the companies to get into totalization.'

On 12 January 1977, a press conference was held to announce the amalgamation. It took six months to finalize the merging requirements. On 21 July of that year the amalgamation was formalized and the three companies, GTO, Jelenk and Onitsuka Corporation were officially united as one entity.

ASICS

The new company was named 'ASICS'. ASICS is the acronym for the Latin phrase, *Anima Sana In Corpore Sano*, meaning 'a sound mind in a sound body'. Juvenal, the Roman satirical poet and great rhetorician, wrote this phrase in the tenth of the sixteen satires he penned between AD 100 and 128. In his satires, Juvenal denounces the laxity and luxuriousness, the brutal tyranny, and the criminal excesses of Roman society. In Satire X he writes:

nil ergo optabunt homines? si consilium uis,
permittes ipsis expendere numinibus quid
conueniat nobis rebusque sit utile nostris;
nam pro iucundis aptissima quaeque dabunt di.
carior est illis homo quam sibi. nos animorum
inpulsu et caeca magnaque cupidine ducti
coniugium petimus partumque uxoris, at illis
notum qui pueri qualisque futura sit uxor.
ut tamen et poscas aliquid uoueasque sacellis
exta et candiduli diuina tomacula porci,
orandum est ut sit *mens sana in corpore sano*.
fortem posce animum mortis terrore carentem,
qui spatium uitae extremum inter munera ponat
naturae, qui ferre queat quoscumque labores,
nesciat irasci, cupiat hihil et potiores
Herculis aerumnas credat saeuosque labores
et uenere et cenis et pluma Sardanapalli.
monstro quod ipse tibi possis dare; semita certe
transquillae per uirtutem patet unica uitae.
nullum numen habes, si sit prudentia: nos te,
nos facimus, Fortuna, deam caeloque locamus.[4]

Although Onitsuka was not well acquainted with Juvenal's writings, the phrase *kenzen naru seishin wa kenzen naru nikutai ni yadoru* (a sound mind in a sound body) was well-known in Japan. The achievement of this goal had been Onitsuka's desire when he first became a sports shoe manufacturer in the gutted city of Kobe after the war. In searching for a name for the new company which would reflect organizational culture, Onitsuka turned to the original Latin phrase *mens sana in corpore sano*. But the acronym was difficult to say, so he substituted *anima* for *mens*; both words connote the idea of spirit.

In the last decade many Japanese companies, regardless of their type and size, have redefined their corporate identity and sought to express it in a simplified name and logo. Name changes are also an outgrowth of what has been termed 'the business world crossover phenomenon', the tendency for businesses to expand or shift their activities from their traditional areas of concentration. This phenomenon has occurred for two reasons. First, the greater integration of various technologies has blurred traditional industrial demarcations. For example, corporations that previously concentrated their efforts in the chemical field have moved into the electronics field and electronic concerns have moved into biotechnology. Secondly, slow economic growth and market saturation have induced corporate expansion into sideline businesses.

Today, a company name may not be simply a visualization of corporate ideology; often, it will have become a 'tool' through which basic business ideology is reinstituted.[5] 'ASICS' is the basic belief upon which Onitsuka founded his company and forms the core of present corporate philosophy. It acts as a centripetal force to bind employees and management together to serve both company and public.

Having decided on the new name, Onitsuka next sought to develop a company logo. One representative from each company—Masaaki Uetsuki from Onitsuka Corporation, Minoru Sugitate from GTO, and Fukuo Iwai from Jelenk—comprised the committee to which logo selection as well as many other amalgamation details were assigned. The committee was chaired by Yoshihiro Hashimoto of GTO. The logo was to portray ASICS as a global entity. After examining the work of many logo designers, both Japanese and foreign, and conferring with a number of advertising agencies, the committee selected the New York designer Herb Lubalin (1918–81) to produce an appropriate company symbol.

With the formation of the new company, in addition to a name and a logo, a succinct statement of corporate managerial ideology was required. Onitsuka, Teranishi and Usui settled on the following three-part statement, repeated today by employees at the outset of corporate-wide monthly meetings:

1. As a diversified sporting goods manufacturer, ASICS strives to contribute to the advancement of the global sports culture.
2. All who participate in ASICS Corporation take responsibility for its future. Their destiny and that of the company are interdependent.
3. ASICS strives to contribute to the prosperity of the local community and to fulfil social responsibilities to society at large.

Because GTO had been established in 1948, one year prior to Onitsuka Corporation and four years before Jelenk, 1948 was taken as the year of establishment for ASICS corporation.

The merging of companies was a popular trend at the time. Many consolidations were a result of the 'fall-out' from the oil crisis; frequently, the only solution to failure was to merge in the interests of economy of scale. The case of ASICS was different because it involved the merging of three healthy companies.

The inaugural ceremonies were held on 21 July 1977. Each ASICS employee then, and from then on, wore an ASICS logo pin on his or her lapel. Onitsuka had commissioned the writing of a corporate song and employees sang it now for the first time:

> Where the sacred torch is lit,
> Builders of the corporation gather.

> With sincere hearts, minds, and actions,
> Let us accomplish our mission.
> Let us cultivate the frontier,
> To the four corners of the world.
> Young in spirit, ASICS.

In addition, they joined in the singing of *Takeda-bushi* (Song of Takeda). This song is believed to have been sung by the sixteenth-century *daimyo*, Harunobu Takeda, commonly known as Shingen Takeda, preparatory to each battle. Onitsuka had first heard *Takeda-bushi* many years before when the former chairman of the Kobe Chamber of Commerce sang it at a business party. He heard it again when it was sung by Daisaku Ikeda, at his inauguration as president of the Soka Gakkai Sect. On these occasions Onitsuka failed to comprehend the song's meaning completely, but as the years passed and his understanding of management deepened, he came to appreciate the song's significance.

Of particular appeal were the lines in the second verse:

> People are a foundation wall,
> People are a castle.
> Compassion is an ally,
> Vengeance is an enemy.

Onitsuka believes that:

This was the essence . . . of Shingen Takeda's territorial management. This was how he kept his followers happy and loyal. Other military leaders built large stone walls and castles for defence but Shingen felt this was unnecessary. He maintained that a ruler could retain his 'country' only through compassion for his subjects. Shingen's compassionate spirit created harmony and united his subjects to fight against his enemies during the period of internal strife and civil war in Japan.

Onitsuka applies Shingen's philosophy to corporate management:

The corporation's existence depends on the employees, the shareholders and the customers. The corporation is people. Management can accomplish little on its own. Success depends on the efforts of everyone working together. Management and management policy must reflect this and must be directed towards fulfilling the needs of all the participants.

For Onitsuka, the amalgamation meant that he was now responsible for 3,939 employees, 1,359 in the parent corporation and the remainder in the corporation's fifteen production and sales subsidiaries. The thought crossed his mind that he was now in charge of more than twice as many people as had been in his Army regiment more than thirty years earlier. But he had no time to reminisce about his Army days or about the old Onitsuka Corporation. It was true, he had come a long way. Yet ahead of him was an even longer road, doubtless filled with more hardships and obstacles. At this time he was a proud but anxious man, preparing himself for whatever might come his way.

Onitsuka often reflects on the lesson about establishment versus maintenance to be learned from Emperor Tai-zong (626–649), son of the founder of China's Tang Dynasty (618–906). A superb military commander, Emperor Tai-zong expanded Chinese influence into central Asia and re-established civil order throughout China following two hundred years during which north China had been overrun by a variety of tribes. Emperor Tai-zong was reported to have put this question to his retainers: 'Which is more difficult—to establish an empire or to maintain it?'

Fang-sxuan-ling, Tai-zong's long-time adviser, answered: 'At the time of establishment the turmoil is great and many are competing for power. To be victorious it is necessary to fight until all enemies have surrendered. From this perspective, establishment is the most difficult part.'

On the other hand, Wei-zhen, who held the position of remonstrator under Tai-zong's rule, felt that a new empire usually emerged out of serious mismanagement and turmoil brought on by the previous ruler. Since the new emperor has destroyed the former ruler, the masses usually accept and follow him willingly. However, once the emperor is established there is a tendency for him to become arrogant and to indulge himself in luxury and extravagance, demanding that his subjects, who expect a peaceful life under the new regime, provide him with a strong labour force. Eventually, the ruler will lose sight of his initial determination. This in return will result in the decline of the empire. From this perspective, maintenance is more difficult than initial creation. Tai-zong replied:

> Fang-sxuan-ling worked very hard with me to establish the empire and it is because of his experience that he thinks establishment is very difficult. On the other hand, Wei-zhen is, as I am, constantly thinking about how to maintain the peace and this is why he feels that maintenance is the more difficult task. Both arguments make sense but now the time of establishment is past and from now on I think together we have to seriously consider how to maintain the empire.[6]

Onitsuka often refers to this story of Emperor Tai-zong, especially in his speeches marking ASICS' successive anniversaries, in order to remind his employees that constant effort is required if the corporation is to maintain and expand its business endeavours.

13 | Growing Pains

Corporate Adjustments

The birth of ASICS as a manufacturer of a total line of sporting goods had not come easily. As in the case of any other successful amalgamation, the three presidents had done considerable homework beforehand to ensure that all three corporations were in good health. The financial stability, market position and management strength of each company had been examined carefully. Even more important was to ensure that there were no mismatches in the management philosophy of the three companies.

Onitsuka cannot stress too strongly the virtue of 'harmony among people' in business, especially in amalgamation situations. When two or more people work co-operatively, they can achieve greater results than the sum of their separate individual achievements: such a synergistic effect is the very purpose of amalgamation.

The key to the success of ASICS was the strength of the bond between the three former presidents. This was what the media and the general public seemed to be most interested in. If the three key men could not hold together, then the entire structure of ASICS would collapse. Fortunately, there were few problems in this regard; Onitsuka, Teranishi and Usui worked well together. Doubtless this was due to the mutual trust that had developed between them over their many years of friendship. This cohesiveness, in turn, almost certainly had a positive influence on the employees. They followed the example of their leaders and integrated well.

'In Japan, successful collaboration among corporations dealing in general merchandise is rare', says Terunaga Kawamata, Director-General of the Association of Japan Sporting Goods Industries (JASPO). This observation is the result of Kawamata's long and rich experience with the Ministry of International Trade and Industry (MITI). In his work with MITI, Kawamata was concerned with the formulation of general guidelines, first for musical instrument producers, then for office supply manufacturers, and finally for sports equipment manufacturers. MITI suggested, as part of a modernization programme, that musical instrument producers enter into collaborative endeavours. Likewise it was suggested that Japan's five major office supply manufacturers should establish a co-operative to improve the order and distribution system.

In both instances, before the discusssion had progressed to a consideration of the financial aspects of the proposal, the talks were broken off and MITI's suggestions were abandoned. Kawamata says:

> Before the ASICS merger the only successful co-operative endeavour I recall in general merchandise was in the match industry. Of course, in other areas, agricultural co-operatives have done well for some time. But, overall, the attempts at co-operative endeavours have not succeeded—to the point where I have come to feel that Japanese lack the skills essential for successful managerial collaboration. ASICS' success, I think, is a reflection of the intense commitment on the part of upper management. The individual management ideologies of the three former presidents have merged into a philosophical symphony.

In the beginning, however, there was much that needed working out. In February 1977, after the amalgamation was announced but before it was finalized, Teranishi visited Munich to attend the spring ISPO (International Sports Equipment Fair) exhibition. Away from routine business, he had time to re-examine the amalgamation along with Yoshihiro Hashimoto who had accompanied him.

GTO, Hashimoto reminded Teranishi, had grown to its present strength because of its short- and long-range planning. As yet, no concrete plans had been drawn up for ASICS. They lacked a blueprint for ASICS' growth in the immediate future.

Returning to Japan, Teranishi discussed the need for management by objectives on the macro-scale with Onitsuka and Usui. Senior executives from the three companies were included in the subsequent planning meetings. It was decided that each company would submit a detailed numerical sales forecast for the following year.

One of the most difficult quests following formalization of the amalgamation was the discovery of an organizational structure whose patterns of authority, division of labour, method of control and lines of communication would unify the personnel from the formerly separate corporations, and at the same time be capable of meeting market demand.

To begin with, the units of the three companies, Onitsuka Corporation, GTO and Jelenk were maintained and formed the three business divisions of ASICS. Each former president was in charge of his respective division. This organizational structure was perceived as being the least disruptive to the established distribution channels—the wholesalers and retailers who had made possible the growth of each of the three corporations. The intention was to maintain this structure for three years. It soon became clear, however, that this organizational structure was inadequate to fulfil the potential of amalgamation. The sales forecasts provided earlier by each company proved to be overly optimistic. Says Teranishi, 'Each company tried to make itself look good by setting unrealistic goals.'

Problems arose because the organization was structured 'mechanically', in the most expedient fashion, rather than 'organically', with consideration given to the type of organizational structure the corporate strategy demanded. The structure was not focused towards performance, nor was it advantageous from the human relations point of view. The separation rather than integration of the workers from the three former organizations resulted in a 'we/they' situation and hindered total commitment to the new organization. In addition, there were the inevitable miscommunications and misunderstandings that led to petty conflicts.

The oil crisis of the early 1970s brought about a drastic change in consumption patterns in the years 1977–78. ASICS' products, like others, were subject to waves of selection and change. Consequently, some of the high-profit products suddenly stopped selling and became a burden to the company.

Within each of ASICS' three divisions there was a nostalgic attachment to the products of each former company and a reluctance to eliminate them, even though they were no longer selling. This led to sectionalism and resulted in a lax attitude with regard to responding to changing consumer demand.

The existing organization was plainly ineffective. Onitsuka and the two vice-presidents realized this and agreed to a restructuring of the corporation. The distinctions between the three former corporations were erased and the new company was divided into three departments, namely production, sales and planning. The objective was to dissolve the segregation of the various sections by integrating the staff.

At the factory level, Onitsuka, Teranishi and Usui visited the plants to explain ASICS' corporate managerial ideology. In addition, joint seminars and training programmes were instigated, bringing managers and production workers together from all of ASICS' domestic shoe and clothing factories. Senior factory management met regularly, rotating among some ten factories. Periodically, a senior production worker from another factory would be invited to address the management group and also the workers at the host factory.

'Although the factory personnel had belonged to different companies originally, they shared common values and strong bonds soon developed among them', recalls Katsuharu Kosake, senior managing director of Fukui ASICS and Takefu ASICS, two of the company's clothing factories.

'All the workers were eager to learn from their counterparts in the other factories', says Noritsugu Taiencho, production manager at Fukui ASICS.

'But at the same time, there was a healthy spirit of competition among the factories.'

The ongoing seminars created a feeling of solidarity among the production plants and gave rise to ASICS' integrated production sector. Formerly, each of the factories within the three factory groups, that is, factories originally belonging to Onitsuka Corporation, Jelenk or GTO, had its own historical and regional ties. The restructuring of ASICS and the subsequent joint seminars, together with ASICS' managerial ideology, created a formal horizontal network among the factories. In addition, informal, personal communication linkages strengthened the bonds between the constituent members and organizational units of ASICS' production sector.

The new organizational structure eliminated the sectionalism of the previous system. Better understanding and greater trust among the staff, both vertically and horizontally, was a rewarding consequence of this reform. ASICS' amalgamation was the amalgamation of three companies, but at the same time it was an amalgamation of the shoe industry culture and the clothing industry culture, the bearers of the cultures being the corporate employees with their own values and everyday characteristic business activities.

Onitsuka Corporation employees had been involved in the shoe industry where practicality and function were primary characteristics and the dominant marketing strategy was from the top down. While quality was important at all three former corporations, GTO and Jelenk employees had been involved in the clothing industry, where aesthetics, trend and fashion were emphasized and marketing strategy was designed to bring the products as quickly as possible to as broad a spectrum of the public as possible.

The second corporate structure allowed people involved in each of the two 'cultures' to be exposed to each other, thus making them aware of more alternatives in product development and marketing strategy. Yet, in less than a year, further problems emerged. ASICS was still not able to respond quickly enough to changes in consumer demands. The new organization did not seem to be well suited to this purpose either.

Further restructuring was required. The key goal was to enhance the company's ability to respond quickly to changes in demand. To achieve this, extensive and direct access to consumers was vital. During periods of high economic growth, it is possible for manufacturers to take the lead in determining what products will sell, but not when the economy is stagnant. In the latter scenario, company policies must be oriented towards consumers, and foresight is required.

Pursuant to the above strategy, the entire operational structure was again reorganized, this time vertically with respect to the various markets.

Accordingly, the first division dealt with the production and sale of all types of sports shoes; the second with sportswear; and the third with baseball, winter sports and golf and leisure sporting goods. Each product/clientele division had functional departments for planning, sales and advertising and subsidiary factories. Besides these three divisions, there were also the overseas operations division, and the departments of administration (including accountancy and personnel); corporate planning, promotion and research and development.

Each of ASICS' subsidiary manufacturing corporations was structurally integrated under the appropriate division to meet the diversified demands of consumers. Within each factory, a special production team was set up to produce items required to meet special market demands.

This new system became operational in February 1980. Its effectiveness had become evident by the latter half of that year. By 1981, the rate of annual increase in sales had grown from the estimated 14 to 15 per cent to 24 to 25 per cent. With this third attempt, ASICS finally found the system that met its needs. This is the organization structure that is in place today, with the addition of two more product/clientele divisions: tennis and golf, and fitness, including aerobics. About 35 per cent of the employees of the parent corporation work within ASICS' five product/clientele divisions and its overseas division. Superimposed on the product/clientele structure is the regional sales network with two major branches in Tokyo and Osaka and thirteen sales offices scattered throughout the country. Employees within the sales network make up 45 per cent of those employed within the parent corporation. The remaining 20 per cent include those employed within the aforementioned departments of administration, corporate planning, promotion, research and development, and a small group of parent corporation employees assigned to distribution related activities.

Direct access to consumer needs had always been the policy of Onitsuka Corporation. Having been turned away by wholesalers in the early days, Onitsuka approached the athletes and local schools directly. The underlying principle of the 'top' and 'base' strategies was precisely this direct contact with the consumers. Amid the confusion that followed the amalgamation, it seemed that Onitsuka had lost sight of this principle. In retrospect, ASICS took a roundabout route in coming back to Onitsuka's original approach, but it was not a complete waste of time and effort. Through the 'failures' of the two previous attempts, all the employees from the top down grew to appreciate the importance of an efficient, all-embracing organizational design and to recognize the new structure as the only one that would work. Consequently, they were quick to understand the requirements of this new system. It was not long before everyone settled into the new routine.

Onitsuka was highly cognizant of the wealth of product information that could be sifted from among the complaints of dissatisfied customers. However, preoccupation with orders, shipping and advertising often resulted in the neglect of consumer complaints. Two years after the amalgamation, a consumer consulting section was opened in the research and technology department of ASICS' head office. This was a 'first' for the sporting goods industry. Each item ASICS manufactured was labelled to show the purchaser where to address his complaints and suggestions. This department has recently been incorporated into ASICS' Research Institute.

Each month about one thousand letters, telephone calls and consumer visits are received by the consumer consulting section. Based on this information, the section regularly circulates reports to the appropriate departments and once every two months a meeting is held with production staff. Shigeru Akiyama, head of the consumer consulting section, describes this system as the fastest and most direct way to get consumer feedback. It is a free monitoring system.

A New Role for Onitsuka

Onitsuka decided that he would not get closely involved with the day-to-day operational details of the company. Teranishi and Usui were both excellent businessmen. Onitsuka felt confident at leaving the company in their charge. His personal involvement could do more harm than good, possibly stifling the other two and causing unnecessary friction.

As is often the case in Japanese companies, close to the top of the corporate hierarchy the delineation of responsibility is blurred. There is no formula for the reservation and transfer of clearly established responsibilities assigned to specific administrative ranks. At ASICS, while Onitsuka is the president, Teranishi, Usui and Onitsuka function as one, covering each others' 'territory'. Thus, more important than the delineation and designation of authority is the maintenance of effective everyday communication channels.

It was now time, Onitsuka felt, to turn his attention to the broader matters of general and overall corporate policy that are the appropriate domain of the company president. But, like the majority of corporate executives, Onitsuka excelled in certain areas. He continued to be involved in product development and marketing, facilities planning and expansion, sports events, and corporate ceremonies. Employees directly assigned to projects in these areas sometimes felt that Onitsuka's involvement was too great, his concern with details excessive. Onitsuka encouraged them to be open with him and heated debates often ensued. This itself was a mutual learning process.

Onitsuka realized that he would have to acquire new skills and knowledge to function in his new role. The acquisition of a strong sense of direction was required for the company. Onitsuka believes that should a leader's desires become self-centred the corporation will be stifled. If, on the other hand, the leader broadens his own perspective the employees will come alive and grow in this receptive environment.

Is there any size beyond which ASICS should not grow? Onitsuka feels that the size of the organization will correspond to the 'receptacle' provided by the management body. The extent of corporate development is a function of collective managerial capability. Acting on this belief, Onitsuka determined to emphasize not only employee and managerial training but also his own development.

In April 1977, Onitsuka began a two-year term as Chairman of the Kobe chapter of the *Keizai Doyukai*, or the Committee for Economic Development, an organization he had joined in 1973. This position provided him with the opportunity to come in contact with industries other than sporting goods. Although ASICS had become one of the largest sporting goods manufacturers, it was relatively small by comparison with some of the corporations in other manufacturing industries. His job afforded him the opportunity to meet many able managers and engage in discussions with them. Views and experiences could be exchanged with some of the leading figures of the business world, resulting in an important enrichment for him.

As chairman of the Committee, Onitsuka was frequently required to address seminars for business organizations. This was another valuable experience. As the ASICS staff were fully occupied with their own work, Onitsuka could not rely on them to draft his speeches. Consequently, he wrote them himself, looking up information and statistics in books. This provided him with the occasion to reflect on his past experiences and collect his thoughts on where the company had come from and where it was going. This is something that one does not do enough, Onitsuka feels.

Onitsuka devotes a great deal of his 'spare time' to writing—at home in the evenings, on airplanes, in hotels, and so on. Each of his many speeches is written out in longhand before being delivered and he has several publications to his credit as well.[1]

Onitsuka's involvement in external activities continues to be demanding and time-consuming. Masaaki Uetsuki, general manager of ASICS Sales Promotion Division says:

Proximity to and observation of Mr Onitsuka over the years has provided my colleagues and me with a wealth of decision-making know-how. His physical presence and behaviour at the worksite has served as a living text. His present external commitments, including service on some three dozen committees, take Mr Onitsuka away from corporate headquarters. We all regret that the opportunity to learn directly from Mr Onitsuka has been decreased.

Usui feels the same way. At the same time, though, he realizes that ASICS has benefited from Onitsuka's external involvements. Also, he interprets Onitsuka's frequent absences as an indication of the extent of Onitsuka's trust in ASICS' management body. 'When a matter requires discussion, though', says Usui, 'Mr Onitsuka immediately makes the time. When I tell him what I need to talk with him about, we are usually able to get together the following morning before work begins.'

The wholesalers and retailers also regret having seen less of Onitsuka since the amalgamation. 'But', says Machiko Takahashi, president of Sports Takahashi Company Limited, 'Whenever I contact the president's office with a problem, Mr Onitsuka responds immediately and finds the time to discuss our differences.'

While much of Onitsuka's time following the amalgamation was devoted to his outside involvements, he did not neglect internal activities. Of particular concern to him was the necessity of forging unity between labour and management.

Labour–Management Unity

Unlike the majority of companies with more than five hundred employees, Onitsuka Corporation did not have a labour union. Its employees were shareholders and company executives were selected from among the workers. GTO and Jelenk, on the other hand, had 'enterprise' unions which were members of *Zensen Domei*, the All-Textile Industries Federation to which 1,489 unions representing 502,602 employees belong. This Federation is closely associated with the Democratic Socialist Party and is moderate in its industrial activities.

During the course of the amalgamation, Onitsuka stressed the importance of a union to his workers and familiarized them with the nature of a labour union. With the finalization of the amalgamation, Onitsuka Corporation workers became part of the newly formed ASICS union along with workers from Jelenk and GTO. The union became a member of *Zensen Domei*.

Under Japan's union shop system, all those employed by ASICS Corporation became members of the union, excluding 'workers at the supervisory post having direct authority to hire, discharge, promote or transfer; workers at the supervisory post having access to confidential information relating to the employer's labour relations plans and policies so that their official duties and obligations directly conflict with their loyalties and obligations as members of the labour union concerned; and other persons who represent the interest of the employer', as designated by law.[2]

In addition to the union at ASICS Corporation, three of ASICS' seventeen domestic subsidiaries also had unions. Individually, these rejoined *Zensen Domei* as ASICS' subsidiaries rather than in their former capacity as GTO or Jelenk subsidiaries.

At the time of the amalgamation, *Zensen Domei* took the opportunity to solicit membership from among ASICS' other subsidiary factories. The reaction at Miyazaki ASICS and Omuta ASICS was typical. *Zensen Domei's* regional representative approached Shigeo Ichimoto, senior managing director of Miyazaki ASICS, Omuta ASICS and Yamaguchi ASICS. Yamaguchi ASICS was already a member of the *Zensen Domei* Federation and the union representative was wondering if workers at the other two factories would like to become unionized as well. Ichimoto consulted with the employees at Miyazaki ASICS, the larger of the two factories. The response was negative. The union representative then asked if he could go in by the 'back door' and speak directly to the workers. Ichimoto gave him his blessing but the results were the same.

With regard to ASICS Corporation's union, Onitsuka felt that it was important for members to fully understand his ideas and beliefs, just as it had been important for the employees at Onitsuka Corporation to do so. He talked with the union representatives directly. He wanted them to understand his philosophy of life, his past experiences and his future plans, not so much as those of the president of their company, but more as a fellow human being. He felt that this was the way to create greater understanding and co-operation between people.

The union's attitude initially was one of 'cautious suspicion'. Union members, especially those formerly with Jelenk and GTO, wondered what kind of a man Onitsuka was. He talked about a co-operative body of people, but they were sceptical, feeling that Onitsuka would be the one to benefit in the long run.

At Jelenk, twenty or so members of the union had approached Usui, asking why the company had to go through with the amalgamation. They felt the organization could manage on its own. Usui assured them that the amalgamation would not be to the detriment of the workers. He tried to make them understand that Onitsuka was not a man who pursued personal gain. Rather, he was a man with great concern for the interests of his employees. That was why Usui had decided on the amalgamation.

The employees' doubts remained; their concerns could not be easily dispelled. Onitsuka persisted, holding labour–management meetings every few months for intensive discussions with all involved. Eventually, the reluctance began to dissolve. Discussions became more open, and there was a growing willlingness at least to listen to what Onitsuka had to say.

Two years after the amalgamation, Onitsuka felt the time was right to introduce regular union–management conferences. Initially, a conference consisted of a committee of five union members and some ten executive managing directors meeting to discuss general working conditions and the distribution of profits. Onitsuka was striving to gain the confidence and understanding of the union. Details of company management were made available through regularly published reports in the hope of increasing union members' awareness of ongoing company activities.

On the day each conference was to begin, confidential material from the company administration would be made available to the union representatives. In his efforts to bring about harmony, Onitsuka would advise management to pay attention to the concerns of the workers and to attempt to appreciate their point of view. Despite his efforts, there were few real signs of movement towards understanding. The discussions became platforms for each side to state its position, bargaining for demands without expressing underlying feelings.

Onitsuka was saddened by the lack of progress on this matter of deep personal concern. He regarded improved labour–management understanding as being crucial to the future well-being of the company. Why would two groups of people working together under one roof, sharing a common destiny, find so much on which to disagree? The standard reply for the outsider was that labour–management relations were universally like this. To Onitsuka, this response was unacceptable: it was essential that both sides reach a basis for agreement if the company was to succeed.

Onitsuka sincerely wanted to improve the terms and conditions of employment for the workers. This could not be achieved instantly, however; improvements could only come about gradually as the general situation of the corporation also improved, postulated Onitsuka. On the other hand, the labour union argued that corporate improvement was dependent first upon the assurance of the workers' standard of living.

Correcting one's own faults should be a prerequisite to condemning the faults of others. Onitsuka suggested this approach to management, advising them to continue to try to reach an understanding with the union. The talks could not succeed if the management made little effort to listen genuinely to the desires, demands and problems of the employees: greater concern had to be demonstrated. With renewed efforts, each party began slowly to appreciate the other's viewpoint. In the spring of 1980, three years after amalgamation, agreements on several issues, including salary increments were concluded.

After Tetsuya Abe took over as third union head in 1983, he recommended greater representation at the union–management conferences. This recommendation was accepted. Now each side is represented by about a dozen individuals, but problems still exist. Abe says:

> Management perceives labour–management interaction to be going well because the two groups exchange their opinions regularly. But the management representatives cannot finalize agreements. Matters must always be put before the Board for approval. In essence, our meetings are simply preparatory negotiations, causing some dissatisfaction on our part. Mr Onitsuka is a very unusual man. He puts a great deal of effort into thinking about his employees' welfare. In the past, Mr Onitsuka was able to make decisions based solely on his own discretion but this is no longer the case. As the corporation grows, there are more and more areas in which Mr Onitsuka can no longer act on his own.

An issue of increasing union and management concern is the treatment of female employees. Among the top industrialized nations, Japan is perhaps the worst in its treatment of its female labour force. Although some improvements have been made through changes in societal attitudes, legislation and administrative efforts, discrimination still exists in all aspects of employment, particularly in opportunity and in reward and recognition.

Thirty-eight per cent of ASICS' full-time employees are women. The starting salary at ASICS for female and male university graduates is, in theory at least, the same. In practice, though, because women 'choose' positions that are categorized as 'non-transfer positions', i.e. positions in which they will not be required to move from one geographic location to another, their salaries are lower than their male counterparts who generally opt for 'transfer' positions. Wage disparity exists in about 70 per cent of Japanese corporations, the average difference being around 10 per cent.[3]

The opportunity for promotion for women in Japanese corporations is generally limited. Abe says:

> At ASICS, however, the opportunity is given to both males and females to sit the examination for advancement to the managerial level. If one passes, one receives increased remuneration, and if there is an opening, appointment to managerial position or, in some cases specialist designation. Mitsuko Bungo was ASICS' first female employee to attempt the examination. She did so in 1986. Passing the test, she was classified as a specialist at the deputy section manager level in the winter wear division rather than given managerial responsibility. The focus of her activities is product design.

The issue of equality for women in the workplace is complex. Problems with equality stem from the deep-rooted collective view of Japanese women as subordinate beings, and the corresponding sharp division of roles by sex, nurtured over time. Present-day corporate discrimination against women derives from this view of women held not only by men but by women themselves. Awareness of this issue has been heightened, avenues for change have been identified, and efforts towards change begun in this direction, but barriers remain formidable. Marked improvement in the situation, above all, rests on changes in societal consciousness and is expected to take time.[4]

ASICS' Innovation

Union members anticipated a substantial increase in corporate performance following the amalgamation, the benefits of which would be passed on to the employees. This expected heightened vibrance did not materialize, however. Anxious to reap the rewards of increased performance, ASICS labour union, under its first chairman, Okasis Hashimoto, proposed collaboration with management on a new project based on small group activities.

Prior to the amalgamation, small group activities had been going on in each of the three corporations, mainly in their production sectors. Onitsuka had initiated ZD (Zero Defects) activities at Onitsuka Corporation as early as 1966. ZD had been introduced from the United States in 1965 when the high-tech enterprise, NEC, adopted it in order to bring about product quality standardization. Impressed with the results at NEC, the electric machinery maker, Toshiba Corporation, and France Bed, a leading bed manufacturer, followed suit. Onitsuka Corporation was not far behind and fifty-two ZD project groups were organized throughout the company. The company temporarily shelved their attempts at ZD three years later. At the time of the amalgamation, QC (Quality Control) circles and suggestion systems were operating in Jelenk's factories. Immediately after the amalgamation, presentations of the results of these small group activities were held at each factory but at that time these activities had not 'taken off'.

Quality Control concepts and activities, introduced to Japan from the United States, were initially implemented in the production sector of Japanese companies and gradually diffused throughout the entire organization, including research and development, marketing, finance and accounting, and personnel, and even disseminated, in some cases, to the organization's affiliates.

While ASICS' management were aware of the necessity of activating Total Quality Control (TQC), they had taken few explicit steps in this direction. 'The traditional pattern', says Kazunori Kanzaki, 'has been for management to solicit the involvement of employees in such activities. In our case, however, it was the union perhaps more than management who suggested strengthening and expanding small group activities.'

A project committee made up of representatives from the union and management was formed to discuss ways in which existing small group activities could be given new life. 'ASICS Innovation (AI) was the name that union representatives proposed and was adopted for the productivity improvement movement. AI logo suggestions were invited from the employees at large.

AI was instigated in 1979. The idea did not ignite, however, until 1982 when Yoshiharu Usui took on AI promotion on a full-time basis. At this time, an AI promotion committee was established, chaired by vice-president Teranishi and an AI office set up, headed by Kazunori Kanzaki under whom Yoshiharu carried out his AI work. Four major AI promotion offices were established company-wide as well as AI councils within each of ASICS' divisions, departments, sales offices and subsidiaries.

In 1984, 216 groups, each comprising three or four employees, tackled chosen projects related to cost reduction, improved efficiency, production process improvement, and so on. Of these, 144 completed the projects with varying degrees of success. Most of the work on these projects was carried out in the evening, after working hours. The results were first presented to fellow division workers. The best presentations were repeated at corporate headquarters with Onitsuka and the two vice-presidents in attendance. Says Yoshiyuki Takahashi:

> QC activities, from which AI derived, are a symbol of the Japanese business spirit. If this spirit does not exist, things like QC activities do not stand a chance. The people involved gather after work to work on their projects. Some, I am sure, come reluctantly, but, nevertheless, they participate in activities which bring no over-time pay. QC originated in the United States but it took root in Japan because it complemented Japanese work ethics.

Today, there are close to three hundred small groups company-wide that participate in AI. Enthusiasm for AI runs high, especially in the factories. The economic benefits for the corporation and subsequently for employees are important but of even greater significance is the fact that AI promotes co-operation among employees and heightens their motivation.

In 1985, preparation began for the introduction of AI into the Nichidai factory in Taiwan. Because the workers there had no experience of quality control circle activities, Akio Bessha, back in Taiwan for his second term as Nichidai's head, estimated that it would be three years before AI was fully implemented. Yoshiharu Usui says:

While AI is functioning well at the production level in Japan, there are inherent difficulties in implementing it in many of the company's support activities. We are trying out different approaches and techniques in tackling problems in other areas. For example, in routine office work, the attempt is being made to integrate work analysis and office automation to increase work efficiency. At this level, it seems it is still difficult to show employees quantitatively how they are tangibly benefiting from their efforts in areas like workload release and job satisfaction.

Recently ASICS has begun to look beyond TQC to NPS (New Production System). NPS is a further development of Taichi Ono, the former vice-president of Toyota Corporation, who developed Toyota's *Kanban Hoshiki* system of production and inventory control. NPS is still in the experimental stage with one corporation from each industry—over thirty nation-wide—using it on a trial basis since 1981. So far the results have been very good and at least three hundred more corporations are waiting to receive instruction in NPS from the NPS Research Institute. Teranishi is spearheading the movement at ASICS to pursue this new direction.

In a nutshell, NPS searches for production technology utilizing the minimum facilities and machines, the minimum number of people, the minimum number of items in production, producing the minimum number of defects, and requiring the minimum lead time between receipt of work order and delivery of product. Any factors that prevent meeting product quality requirements, price and delivery date are undesirable and to be eliminated through holistic corporate effort including sales, research and development, production, distribution and management control. While this is common sense and does not sound fresh and different, NPS attempts to actualize it through alteration of the mind set of everyone from top management down.[5]

Maruei Kagaku, a Kobe subcontract factory of ASICS with 160 employees and a daily production capacity of a thousand pairs of shoes, has been experimenting with NPS with the help of Hitoshi Yamada of PEC Industrial Education Centre. The results are excellent, production is up 25 per cent, production lead time has been greatly reduced, and formerly fluctuating quality has stabilized to a defect rate of less than 1 per cent. Yoshihiko Tomizawa, president of Maruei says:

> while the system may be good, ultimately, in production, the quality of the product is dependent on the workers' heartfelt commitment to their jobs, especially for high technology, labour intensive products like shoes. More than twenty-five people are involved in assembling one pair of shoes. After twenty years in this business, I have come to

feel that the quality of the product depends upon the care taken by the people who use the machines.

Becoming Number 1 in Profitability

Another internal ongoing concern for Onitsuka has been the improvement of the company's financial balance. At the time of amalgamation, ASICS was forced to increase its borrowing because of excess stock even though the new company was considered to be one of the Big Three Japanese sporting goods manufacturers, together with Mizuno and Descente. This in turn affected earnings and a great gap in profitability appeared between ASICS and its two closest competitors. Trade journals were quick to point out that ASICS had come into existence relying on borrowed money and they predicted that the company would soon lose its position as one of the Big Three.

The company had an equity ratio of about 29 per cent at amalgamation, not a strong financial footing for a new venture. Nevertheless, ASICS focused its attention on maximizing profitability. By the beginning of 1982 the equity ratio had risen to 47 per cent and, with a current profit of 6.57 billion yen, ASICS overtook Mizuno with 6.36 billion and Descente with 1.29 billion yen to take the lead in profitability. ASICS took the lead in terms of retained earnings, sales margin, and net profit to total sales. In terms of total sales, however, the company lagged behind with 86.5 billion yen, compared to Mizuno's 119.6 billion and Descente's 105.4 billion yen.

Onitsuka attributes the rapid increase in profitability to the diversified product line and the realization of scale merit resulting from the amalgamation. Of prime importance was the concentration on profit maximization rather than simply on sales increase. The performance of a sales department, Onitsuka feels, should not be evaluated solely according to the growth of sales. At ASICS, several criteria are used, including earnings per share, credit recovery rate, year-end stockpile, and rate of merchandise return. Soon after the amalgamation, ASICS' sales departments set as their target a profit ratio of roughly 30 per cent. With a great deal of effort, the profit ratio for the fiscal year 1979 was 26.3 per cent and four years later it had risen to 30.4 per cent.

The attempt to improve sales performance centred not only in ASICS' four sales departments but also in the company's sales offices throughout the country. In the latter, under the ASICS Innovation Programme, small group activity and a performance award system were initiated. Performance measurement criteria, including total sales, gross profit (total sales minus sales costs), stock backlog, payment recovery rate, and rate of merchandise return were established. Each quarter, sales office performance is rated and all the employees in each of the top three offices are given financial rewards over and above salary increments and bonuses—10,000 yen per person in the top-ranking office, 7,000 yen in the second-rank office, and 5,000 yen in the third-rank office—regardless of the employee's position. In addition, the best annual sales office performance is rewarded—10,000 yen per employee. Thus, an employee whose sales office is placed first annually and in every quarter as well could receive yearly awards totalling 50,000 yen.

Of much greater significance than the monetary reward, however, is the satisfaction and feeling of achievement derived from the group effort and the reward of company-wide recognition. From management's point of view, of primary importance is the fact that this scheme provides a potent method of communicating to employees what is meant by effective sales activities and the degree to which one's own unit contributes to the corporation's total sales performance.

The introduction of the quarterly sales performance evaluation and award system was made possible with the installation of a computerized sales inventory control system. At the time of the amalgamation, each of the three corporations had computerized to varying, limited degrees. Incompatibility among the existing systems resulted in the decision to introduce one integrated system. ASICS selected a Fujitsu M160S computer system which was fully operational within a year of the amalgamation. This system made tight inventory control of ASICS' some 120,000 items of merchandise possible and permitted accurate tabulation of team performance in each sales office.

In order to improve its financial situation, ASICS sought the introduction of low-cost foreign capital. The company floated loans first from London and later from Frankfurt, Geneva, Vienna and Singapore, altogether totalling 23 billion yen. Because of changes in currency value over time, there were adjustments in the value of the loans. Onitsuka had denominated his loans in local currencies while the company sold its products in yen. In this way Onitsuka received money in yen from sales but paid back his loans in the weakening local currency. This generated a 15 billion yen premium. To this the company added a 7 billion yen internal reserve and used this 22 billion yen to decrease its high-interest Japanese bank loan.

This strategy not only improved the company's financial balance, it also publicized ASICS' name throughout Europe and Asia via the security and financial markets, thereby complementing and enhancing ASICS' international marketing strategy. Onitsuka feels that, among Japanese sporting goods manufacturers, ASICS' name is now the best-known outside Japan.

This has come about through the careful financial planning necessitated by ASICS' 'poverty'.

With the internationalization of Japanese business and the liberalization of capital markets, more accurate evaluation of financial corporate groups became necessary for both corporations and investors. Under the Securities and Exchange Act, the use of consolidated financial statements was introduced as of 1 April 1977. Until that time, financial statements of affiliated corporations had been kept separate from those of the parent corporation, making accurate assessment of the corporate group difficult. Often the parent corporation would be showing a profit while its affiliates were in debt, or vice versa.

Under the new system, the financial statements of subsidiaries 50 per cent or more owned by a parent corporation were to be consolidated with that of the parent corporation. In 1983, this was changed to include subsidiaries 20 per cent or more owned by a parent corporation.

With the amalgamation and the expectation of greater international involvement, ASICS introduced a consolidated financial system in 1977. As of March 1985, 53 per cent of the 837 corporations using a March fiscal year-end listed on the Tokyo Exchange were using consolidated financial statements.[6]

Winter Olympics

One of Onitsuka's ambitions was to see ASICS enter the global winter sports market. Preparatory to ASICS expanding its own ski wear and equipment production, in 1978 it established a technical tie-up with Amber Incorporated of Austria. In January 1980, the company entered into an agreement to sell Dachstein ski boots and in the spring of the same year introduced Peter Steinebronn brand ski wear.

The thirteenth Winter Olympics, held at Lake Placid, New York, in February 1980, provided an appropriate opportunity to introduce ASICS' new range of winter sportwear. The first winter Olympics had been held in Chamonix, France, in 1924, with successive meets occurring every four years after that in various locations. This, however, was the first time that ASICS had participated.

ASICS' target was to become the official supplier for the total outfits, including outer wear and boots, of the staff for the Lake Placid Olympics. Accordingly, it approached the Organizing Committee at a very early stage. Fortunately, the American manufacturers were not particularly interested in supplying the needs of the staff and Adidas and Mizuno were too late in making their proposals. ASICS therefore secured the rights with much effort and a little luck. When the other manufacturers discovered that ASICS had been chosen as the official supplier, they quickly became concerned and active, but to no avail: the contract was firm.

Lake Placid is a small town, with a population of about three thousand. During the games, the population increased to approximately fifty thousand, of whom about six thousand comprised the Olympics' staff. With its Lake Placid debut, ASICS spearheaded the visible involvement of Japanese corporations in sports events in the amateur arena.[7] One in eight persons in the town wore an ASICS product displaying the ASICS trademark.

Today, ASICS' winter sports division is flourishing. The returns for the fiscal year 1985 for this division accounted for nearly 20 per cent of total net sales. Its best-selling products include skis, ski boots, *après-ski* boots, winter weather running shoes, and the Killy line of ski wear.

Lake Placid assumed significance for another reason, relating to China's declaration of its intention to take part in the Games. China had been a regular participant in the Summer Olympic Games until political disagreements over the recognition and representation of Taiwan in international sports competitions provoked Chinese withdrawal from several international sports governing bodies, including the International Olympic Committee in 1958. China did not compete again internationally until 1970, when her athletes participated in basketball and table tennis competitions. Four years later, China participated in the Seventh Asian Games held in Teheran. Since then, China's participation in international sport has increased substantially.[8] The Lake Placid Games of 1980 were China's first Olympic appearance since the Helsinki Games in 1952.

At the time, the Chinese had little experience of international competition for the winter events. They were behind, not only in technical aspects, but also in their knowledge of equipment and outfits. If world class excellence is to be achieved and maintained in amateur sports, participants must gain experience by competing against top players and learning about their training methods and strategy. The Chinese decided to send their athletes abroad before the Olympics so that they could receive instruction about techniques and equipment.

Initially, they had considered sending the speed skaters to Norway, the alpine skiers to France, and the biathlon participants to Sweden, but subsequently the decision was made to send all the athletes to Japan. ASICS was chosen as the supplier of their equipment. Onitsuka had met with the Chinese when their business missions had visited Onitsuka Corporation on several previous occasions. It is conceivable that these business missions had left a favourable impression on the Chinese visitors.

When the Society for Japan–China Cultural Exchange delivered this request, Onitsuka decided to offer the Chinese a helping hand. There had been many historical occasions when Japan had quite unjustly inflicted misfortune on China. Onitsuka considered this as he made his decision. Although the past could not be erased, the least Japan could do was to try to make up for her sins by doing some good to her neighbour. As a Japanese, Onitsuka wanted to make his contribution, however small.

ASICS not only provided the Chinese national team with all the equipment for the Olympics, it also financed the team's trip to Japan and their thirty-seven day stay in the country. The entire cost, although estimated at 10 million yen, was nearer 40 million yen. Onitsuka has no regrets about the expenditure. It was worth every yen.

The Chinese team totalled forty-three, including skiers, skaters, biathlon participants, coaches and staff. The team arrived on 23 December 1979. Immediately, the athletes split up into their respective groups and started training with their full-time Japanese coaches. The skaters went to Karuizawa and the skiers to Nagano. After more than a month of training and practice matches, they gathered in Tokyo on 28 January. From there, they flew directly to the United States and the Olympics.

The assistant leader of this party was Li Mu-hua, the Chinese Deputy-Minister of Education. In 1981, he was appointed head of the Physical Culture and Sports Commission (*Tiyu Yundong Weiyuanhui*). Established in 1952, this is the central government ministry responsible for policy setting, financial planning, personnel training and public relations. It acts as a liaison with other government ministries such as Education, Public Health and National Defence.[9]

In 1981, Li Mu-hua invited Onitsuka, Usui and Hitoshi Yoshida, ASICS' director of general affairs in Tokyo, to China. By then, ASICS had a down wear subcontractor in Changsa and a sports shoe subcontractor in Shanghai. Hirotsugu Kaku was in charge of these operations. Usui was unable to make the trip to China at the time so Kaku went in his place. The three men spent nine days in China and visited ASICS' two subcontract factories.

Recognition

Onitsuka's achievements in several areas have been recognized publicly both at home and abroad. On 21 February 1983, Onitsuka was awarded the Grosses Silbernes Ehrenzeichen für Verdienste um die Republik Oesterreich (the Grand Silver Order of Honour for Service to the Republic of Austria). This award is presented in recognition of outstanding contributions in the areas of politics, culture and economics.[10] Onitsuka was selected as a recipient in honour of his contribution to the development of the Austrian economy through the improvement of the balance of trade resulting from ASICS' introduction of Amber and Hoover ski wear, Dachstein ski boots, and Atomic skis to the Japanese market. At that time, nearly 50 per cent of the skis imported to Japan came from Austria.[11]

ASICS' Austrian connection dates back to 1968 when GTO established a technical tie-up with Hoover corporation. In addition, Onitsuka Corporation had imported shoe materials from Hoover for some years. Today, in addition to its links with Dachstein, Atomic and Hoover, ASICS imports cross-country ski boots from Hartjes, ski sweaters from Steffner Company, and sailboards from Peter Brochause. In addition to his economic contribution, Onitsuka was instrumental in laying the foundation for the Japan–Austria Cultural Exchange Association established in November 1985. Onitsuka is presently serving as the Association's vice-president.

On the domestic front, in the fall of 1983, Onitsuka was chosen by the *Mainichi* newspaper as one of the two 'Men of the Year in Economics'. This award is bestowed on individuals or groups who breathe new life into the industrial world and activate a particular sector of the economy while at the same time advancing international co-operation and contributing to the betterment of Japanese life.

Dr Chikara Hayashi, founder and president of ULVAC Corporation, a leading company in the development and application of advanced vacuum technologies, was the other recipient of the *Mainichi* award that year.[12] Like Onitsuka, Hayashi's initial motivation and dedication to hard work partially derived from his war experience. A graduate of Tokyo University in physics, Naval Technology Lieutenant Hayashi was engaged in research into improved periscope design at Toyokawa Naval Factory in Aichi prefecture when an air raid on 7 August 1945 killed some two thousand of his fellow workers. Hayashi felt that he, too, had died and resolved to work extra hard to compensate for the loss of his colleagues. If the defeat of Japan contributed anything to the economic recovery and subsequent transformation of the nation into a dominant economic power, it instilled in people's minds a determination to ensure that their fellow countrymen had not died in vain.[13]

National and International Association Involvement

In 1974, Onitsuka assumed the vice-presidency of the newly formed Association of Japan Sporting Goods Industries (JASPO). JASPO's roots can be traced back to 1921 through various regional and use-related sporting goods organizations. Today it serves as an umbrella organization for two regional and eighteen use-related associations encompassing some two hundred corporate members.

Through improvements in the quality and safety standards of sporting goods, JASPO aims at effective consumer use of sports equipment and improved production and trade. These in turn, it is hoped, will bring about increased levels of national fitness and growth and development in the sporting goods industry.

In 1982, when Takeo Ishimoto of Descente stepped down from the presidency of JASPO, Onitsuka succeeded him. As president, Onitsuka also became Japan's representative to the World Federation of the Sporting Goods Industry (SGI). Headquartered in Zurich, this body, founded in 1978, is made up of representatives from national sporting goods industry associations in twenty-five countries and 150 corporate affiliates world-wide. SGI's first president, from Britain, represented European and African countries, while its second, from the United States, represented North and South American countries. When the office was vacated in 1983, it was decided that a representative from an Asian country should head the organization for the next three-year term and Onitsuka was appointed president. Serving with Onitsuka as vice-president was Armin A. Dassler, president of Puma of Germany, and second vice-president, Peter K. Martin of Canada's Fred Martin Agency Company Limited. Each of these men was also the president of his country's national sporting goods industry association.

Business associates in Kobe teased Onitsuka about his lack of fluency in English. Says Shoichi Yamada, managing director of the Kobe Chamber of Commerce and Industry, 'Mr Onitsuka was often asked how he managed to fulfil his responsibilities as president of SGI when he lacked a working knowledge of English. But he never seemed to feel this was a problem. "I just conduct business in Japanese and use a translator", he would say.'

There was no one within ASICS with the necessary language fluency and sufficient free time to take on the nearly full-time job of translator. Onitsuka turned to Yamaichi Securities, ASICS' long-time underwriter, for assistance. Yamaichi Securities selected Hajime Onoda, an executive working at the time at the company's New York office, to assist Onitsuka in fulfilling his duties as president of SGI. Since his appointment as head of the Office of the President of ASICS, Onoda, with his forecasting skills honed in the securities business, has been involved in corporate strategic planning in addition to his work as translator.

'Mr Onitsuka may not be able to speak English fluently', says Onoda, 'but he has an acute sense of the content of any discussion as soon as a small portion is translated.' Sometimes when the debate is heated, Onoda has time to translate only the essence of what is being said, omitting many details. 'Mr Onitsuka', says Onoda, 'absorbs information swiftly. He's often working out solutions in his head and mumbling under his breath the outcome he anticipates, long before the discussion has concluded, and he seldom misses the mark.'

The SGI is involved with such issues as membership credentials and fees, import taxes and imitative products, co-ordination of fairs and exhibitions, statistics and market data, international standardization of sports equipment and rules, and co-operation with international sports organizations. In this last capacity, SGI's Board of Directors, acting on Onitsuka's initiative, met with Juan Antonio Samaranch of Spain, president of the International Olympic Committee (IOC) to arrange for the equitable distribution of fifty-thousand sporting goods items to national sports associations in developing countries. These associations will in turn distribute the equipment to athletes preparing for the 1988 Seoul Olympics.

14 | Meeting the Escalating Competition

Modernizing Garment Production

While Onitsuka Corporation's tripartite amalgamation with Jelenk and GTO brought many advantages, it also gave rise to several concerns, one of which was the establishment of a total on-line production system integrating product development, production and sales. The system would require minimum stock and would be capable of supplying required products in the required quantity at the appropriate time. Onitsuka launched this system in the garment sector of ASICS.

The garment industry in Japan was losing its international competitiveness as lower labour costs gave the advantage in this labour-intensive industry to companies in other South East Asian countries. The Japanese corporations that were able to compete were those that took the initiative in introducing new production systems, improving equipment operating rates, educating and training their human resources, and reducing production management costs. Traditionally the garment industry had been characterized by mass production and limited selection. In order for companies to adjust to today's diversified market demand, however, the capability for multi-product, small-batch production is essential.

The sporting goods industry, especially, is characterized by a variety of wear and equipment that extends over many types of sports and categories of users. This has inhibited the growth of companies controlling a major share of the market and has resulted in severe competition among both domestic and foreign suppliers. In order for firms to gain market strength, accurate demand forecasting and inventory controls, product innnovation and material development, and good merchandising, backed by a flexible production system are required.

After the 1973 oil crises, recognition of technological innovation as the means to break through the economic stagnation heightened and the trend within the industrialized world was to move towards the establishment of a more advanced technological society. Like all other industries in Japan, the character of the garment industry was changing from labour-intensive to knowledge-intensive. ASICS Corporation was in step with this trend.

The first robots, Unimate (universal automation) and Versatran (versatile transfer), appearing in the United States in 1962, were introduced to Japan in the latter part of the decade. Versatran was imported from the United States in 1967 and the following year Kawasaki Heavy Industries, currently Japan's leading robot manufacturer, produced the country's first robots under licence from Unimation, now part of Westinghouse. In the early 1970s robot production was relatively slow but escalated late in the decade. After a period of trial and error, the production and use of robots gradually increased until, in 1980, a tremendous upsurge occurred. This diffusion take-off year, 1980, has been labelled in Japan as 'Robot Year Number One'.

In 1978, when Onitsuka was first considering automating sportswear production, some four thousand robots were already operating in Japanese companies. The vast majority of these, however, were at work within the automobile, electrical and electronic equipment, and the plastics industries. More than two hundred types of robots had been developed and were available for practical application but none were well suited to the needs of the garment industry. Nor did the appropriate Japanese computer controlled equipment required for automated production at ASICS exist.

Instead of a fully-automated production system, ASICS settled for an advanced integrated manufacturing system known as SAW (System of ASICS Wear) manufacturing supported by foreign-made computer controlled equipment and its own production workers. SAW's fundamental concept had been developed by Jelenk prior to the amalgamation and its further development and implementation were guided by ASICS' research department.

Pattern making is the initial step in garment manufacturing. The basic pattern has to be modified in order to accommodate a variety of sizes and customer categories. In the 1970s and 1980s, more and more people have become involved in sport as leisure time has increased. The age range of participants is widening rapidly and as the involvement of the generations at both ends of the age spectrum increases, so do the size variations required in sportswear. Widespread improvements in postwar nutrition in Japan have resulted in a generation of teenagers and young adults noticeably taller and heavier than their parents and grandparents. To systematize pattern making and grading, ASICS introduced the Marker-Matic Computer Aided Design (CAD) System from Camsco Corporation (presently Gerber-Camsco) of the United States. This was introduced into ASICS' research headquarters. Here computer programmes were developed and sent to the garment factories on magnetic tape.

Prior to automation, there were many chronic problems associated with pattern cutting. Fabric waste, cutting time loss, lack of precision, and a shortage of skilled labour were among the most predominant. In order to reduce these problems and to fully utilize the CAD system, ASICS introduced computer controlled automatic cutters made by Gerber Garment Technology of the United States. As a result, the cutting time was reduced dramatically, the precision improved, repeated production facilitated, costs reduced, and the use of unskilled labourers made possible.

Given the improvements that the new technology had brought about in pattern making and fabric cutting, the decision was made to implement the next stage of the plan—to automate the most labour-intensive area of all, the sewing component. Within the sewing segment of traditional garment production the time during which the sewing machines operate represents only 20 to 30 per cent of production time. The remainder of the time is spent in handling the material, moving the garments from one work station to the next. Efficiency improvement in this area was critical for ASICS if the company was to gain a competitive edge in garment production.

After considerable study, it was thought that the Eton 2000 System from Sweden would best meet ASICS' needs. Researchers and factory managers who were involved in system development and implementation went to Sweden to see the hanger conveyor system in operation. On their return, a twenty-five station experimental system was set up and run in ASICS' research department to allow system designers, and later operators, to become familiar with the equipment. Ninety-five per cent of the operators introduced to the system at this stage liked it.

The Eton 2000 System was introduced to Kita-Kyushu ASICS in 1982 and later to Fukui ASICS and Miyazaki ASICS. Its use in all three factories has subsequently expanded. Each installation is tailored to the specific factory layout and incorporates the specified number of stations required for production. Routine maintenance is carried out by ASICS employees. Equipment repair is done by engineers with C. Itoh Texmac Company Limited, Japan's major importer of textile machinery and the agent for Eton.

The Eton System is integrated with an ASICS developed production control system. Work stations are linked by optical fibres and are connected to computer terminals located throughout the production process as well as to the central host computer. Yoshio Nishikawa, president of Kita-Kyushu ASICS says:

Prior to the installation of this system, we relied on human observation of the production process for information regarding bottle necks, slack areas, and so on. With the new system, real-time production control became possible. It is easy now for production managers to regulate production flow and operators can readily see their team's performance on the computer screen. With this objective data in mind, the individual and the team can respond to meet production goals.

In this way, the new production system has decreased production lead time and, with the increasing use of computers in product design, order reception and merchandise distribution control, managerial lead time, that is, the time between product conception and the receipt of payment, is also being reduced.

The success of ASICS' production system is dependent upon the availability of materials, the maintenance of the hardware in top running order, production planning, and dependable, committed, co-operative employees. The Eton System itself is not unduly complex; however, precise production planning is required to maximize its capabilities. Noritsugu Taiencho, production manager at Fukui ASICS says:

> The key to its success lies in the appropriate process control, balancing the manufacturing process to meet the requirements of specified products. To achieve this, it is necessary to have a competent production planner, skilled in analyzing the production requirements of different garments and recognizing the varied skill levels of employees, and integrating these with inherent machine capabilities.

Prior to the introduction of the new system, ASICS consulted with the subcontractors affiliated with its garment factories. Fukui ASICS, for example, had thirteen subcontractors employing, 1,500 workers, while Kita-Kyushu ASICS had five employing 300 workers. In the course of these discussions, the corporation's intentions were outlined and the ways in which the subcontractors could assist in realizing these intentions explained. While ASICS did not provide capital or managerial staff for these subcontractors, the corporation was involved in information provision, employee training and equipment loans. There was a strong symbiotic relationship between ASICS and the garment subcontractors and Onitsuka tried to accommodate them as much as possible.

The production processes of ASICS' garment sector gradually evolved into a highly automated, computer integrated, flexible production system. Following the dominant pattern of successful adopters of microelectronic production systems, ASICS experimented with one machine, confirmed its usefulness and then adopted other machines to gradually build up a dependable system able to balance the seemingly opposite requirements of high productivity and high flexibility.

This system reduced by about one month the time required from the inception of a new product to its production. Also, it facilitated faster production, improved accurate product delivery date prediction, improved product quality, and facilitated accurate inventory control. Costs were reduced, the accuracy of cost management improved, and technological know-how accumulated. The streamlined production line resulting from the introduction of the system not only made the maintenance of production line balance and operational management control easier, it also improved the morale of factory workers. Now each worker could determine the way in which his input related to total factory production.

The Eton System is not without problems, however. 'Controlling variation in material colour is a concern', says Tatsuaki Kondo, head of ASICS' Strategic Planning Office. 'Even within the same dyelot there are colour variations.' ASICS considers each of the different textile roles in a dyelot to be a different colour and tries to avoid mixing fabric from different rolls in any one garment. Within the same roll, there is colour variation as well and, strictly speaking, ASICS attempts to make each garment from fabric from the same section of the roll. Controlling this within the Eton System is certainly possible but it reduces productivity considerably. Kondo says:

In the United States I have observed that garments with slight colour variation between sections are often sold. In Japan, such products are considered defective. It seems that the Japanese consumer is much more disturbed by such minute imperfections than is his American counterpart. The productivity level of the garment assembly industry in Japan is only about one half of that of the United States or West Germany. This low productivity level is, in part, the necessary outcome of overly fussy customers who are willing to pay for high quality goods.

'Automated apparel production is not yet the norm in Japan', says Katsuharu Kosake, senior managing director of Fukui ASICS. 'Ninety per cent of manufacturers are still moving the materials by hand.' ASICS' special project teams—work groups that fill special orders such as team uniforms—work without the assistance of automation. ASICS' Takefu factory, for example, is not automated as workers there are primarily engaged in special product production. Kosake points out that the six thousand pieces required for the team uniforms that ASICS produced for the 1981 Los Angeles Olympics were made in the Takefu factory.

In 1985, ASICS installed an on-line computer order system where customers can select the style, fabric, colour and size from a computer display set up in select retail outlets. Replacing the catalogue, the hand-written order form and the telephone, the on-line order system has reduced the margin of error in custom-made sportswear. Baseball teams are a prime user of the system. Ninety per cent of the baseball uniforms ASICS makes are custom made and the computerized order system gives the company an edge over its competitors. The use of this system by soccer and volleyball teams is also increasing. All these orders are handled by the special project teams and are generally filled within two weeks.

The efficiency level achieved through the automated, flexible production system would seem to make ASICS' garment factories suited to *Kanban Hoshiki*. Under this system, all necessary parts are delivered, in just the right amounts, just before they are to be used in planned production. Unlike the automobile industry in Japan, however, where just-in-time production was first introduced and where there is a vertical relationship between the parent companies and the parts suppliers, the component parts of the garment industry—spinners, textile makers, knitters and dyers—are horizontally organized. Thus, according to Yasuo Watanabe, a production technology manager at ASICS Sports Research Institute, it is not possible to instigate total just-in-time production. However, the fundamental idea can still be incorporated into production within each factory.

ASICS' situation in the forefront of technological advancement in the garment industry has led to involvement, along with twenty-eight other enterprises, in an automated sewing system project. The project, begun in 1982 and terminating in 1989, was initiated by the Ministry of International Trade and Industry's (MITI) Agency of Industrial Science and Technology. It is one of the Agency's many large-scale, national projects and has a budget of 13 billion yen.

Intended to ensure the growth of a garment industry appropriate for an industrially advanced nation, the project is aimed at the development of a flexible, efficient, automated sewing system capable of supplying highly diversified individualistic apparel in response to rapidly changing consumer preferences.

The specific goal of the project is to reduce by more than half the per-piece manufacturing time for small quantities of a variety of goods in small and medium-sized sewing enterprises. Research is being undertaken in sewing preparation, sewing assembly, fabric handling, system management and control, and total system technology to establish an integrated manufacturing system.[1] ASICS' involvement in this project centres on sewing preparation technology and system management and control technology. In the former area, research focuses on fabric spreading and cutting techniques. In the latter, it is on the provision and recognition of control information that will allow automated sewing equipment to process fabric.

Changes in Merchandise Distribution

ASICS' traditional pattern of merchandise distribution has been through wholesalers to retailers. Both wholesalers and retailers have made a comfortable profit from this arrangement and, of course, ASICS' growth has been dependent upon their sales. Thus, ASICS' executives feel the corporation is indebted to the retailers and wholesalers.

Recent increased concern with health has changed the character of the market, expanding it much beyond the traditionally confined sports equipment market. The vast increase in interest in sporting goods and sportswear in recent years has attracted the attention of 'big capital' large chain store retailers. Stores such as Daiei, Ito-Yokado and Nichii have added sporting goods to their traditional merchandise: food, clothing and light electrical appliances.

For some time, ASICS resisted pressure to sell to the chain store retailers, fearing that their tendency to undercut prices would be detrimental to the image of the merchandise and also harmful to ASICS' loyal small retailers. Recognizing the first objection, shared by many manufacturers, as a valid one and wishing to secure a stable supply line from the manufacturers, chain store retailers standardized prices, matching those of the small retailers. Now ASICS could no longer justifiably refuse to supply the chain store retailers. These retailers were handling many foreign products; if ASICS was to compete, its products had to be on their shelves.

The bulk purchasing capacity of these mass market retailers has resulted in the establishment of distribution channels which, for some commodities, bypass the wholesalers. Competition among the wholesalers has escalated in recent years and the resulting intermittent price wars have, in some instances, threatened their survival. 'Co-operation among the wholesalers', says Katsuto Izuno, president of Hiroun, 'is lacking, and we cannot collectively agree on measures to improve the situation.'

This has raised the ire of some of the small retailers. They feel they cannot compete with the variety and convenience offered by the chain stores. In 1984, 120 small sporting goods retailers went bankrupt. Small retailers condemn the emergence of their giant competitors and they condemn manufacturers who are responding to these competitors. In order to offset their lack of variety and convenience, small retailers are cutting prices to attract customers at considerable expense to their profit margins.

Onitsuka has suggested that, as is often done in Europe, the small retailers, with or without the co-operation of the wholesalers, should band together and jointly establish a large-scale purchasing co-operative.

This co-operative would produce a retail catalogue, negotiate with the manufacturers, and serve as a distribution centre. Through such equalization of the distribution structure, small retailers could adjust to changing rules of competition. The retailers' response thus far, however, is that such a course of action is unrealistic. Onitsuka and ASICS' management group continue to seek workable solutions to the problems associated with the emergence of new distribution channels.

Concern over apparently high distribution costs led ASICS, in 1982, to investigate commodity flow and associated expenses. The study showed that 4.65 per cent of total sales was spent on merchandise distribution. To reduce this cost, it was decided to establish a new corporation, ASICS Distribution, in a joint venture with Senko Corporation, a comprehensive land, marine and air distributor. The new Hanshin distribution headquarters was built in Nishinomiya, half-way between Kobe and Osaka, in 1983, at a cost of 2.8 billion yen. Presently, 202 people are employed there.

Fully computer-controlled, the centre is capable of storing and processing 6 billion yen worth of merchandise. Shipping activities previously carried out at ASICS' thirteen regional sales offices and at its Osaka and Tokyo offices are now controlled from Hanshin and take place either there or at one of ASICS' three regional distribution centres in Tokyo, Fukui and Kakogawa. These centres are now integrated with the Hanshin distribution headquarters.

Marketing Lessons from Descente

In 1985, ASICS Corporation's net sales topped the 100 billion yen mark for the first time. This was the realization of yet another dream that Onitsuka had held for sometime. Such an achievement, however, does not guarantee continued market success. It is possible for the performance of a corporation in this position to crumble suddenly. The recent and sudden decline in Onitsuka's long-term competitor, Descente, Japan's largest sportswear maker, is an example.

Descente's present chairman of the Board, Takeo Ishimoto, established the company in 1935 as a retail store selling men's outfits. Listed on the Stock Exchange in 1977, Descente established its present operation primarily through ties with major foreign corporations—Munsing of the United States and Adidas of West Germany. It also introduced such foreign brands as Fila of Italy, NCAA of the United States, V de V of France, and HCC of Switzerland.

Descente overtook Mizuno, Japan's top manufacturer of sporting and leisure-time goods, and became the country's number-1 sporting goods manufacturer by sales in 1982. At this time, nearly 40 per cent of Descente's total sales were in Munsing golf wear—in retrospect, much too high a concentration in one line. Descente became number-4 in the world in terms of total sales, after Adidas, Nike and AMF, and was followed by Mizuno, Wilson and ASICS.[2] Among these top seven companies, Descente was the only corporation exclusively manufacturing apparel.

In November 1981, Kiyoshi Oda, president of Descente, died suddenly and Takeo Ishimoto, the founder and chairman of the Board, resumed active control of the company. Descente announced that total sales would be raised from 112.8 billion yen with a profit of 4.1 billion yen in 1982 to 150 billion yen in 1985. Yet two years later the company recorded a deficit amounting to 14 billion yen. Projected sales could not be realized. Why? Descente's decline was the result of loose stock control and misreading the market environment.

Descente's inventory control could not adequately accommodate the large quantity of returned stock which, as is customary in the apparel industry, came back from the retailers, particularly the large department stores. The inventory system largely made the time of delivery of the goods to the retailer, rather than the purchase of the goods by the consumer, the preferred point of sale. This was the same mistake that led to the bankruptcy of both Van Corporation and Hanasaki Incorporated. The former produced the Van jacket which popularized the Ivy League look for men throughout Japan while the latter was a well established dress manufacturer.

In retrospect, it was possible to survive and even prosper despite the hidden problems inherent in the type of loose stock control practised by Descente during the 1970s when the success of the company was riding on the sports boom in the Japanese economy. Between 1970 and 1979 Descente's total sales increased more than ten times. Based on this success, Descente developed a production plan focusing on their best-selling items.

Their marketing strategy was similar to ASICS', that is, it was a 'top strategy' focusing first on the top athletes, and then eventually capturing a broader spectrum of the potential market. At about this time, streetwear manufacturers throughout Japan began to produce sportswear. This coincided with the popularization of sportswear for everyday casual wear. In particular, Descente's main line, Munsing, ceased to be worn exclusively by golfers, gaining popularity among the general public as casual wear. The demarcation of the use of sportswear for specific occasions became blurred.

Descente named the new market the 'sports apparel' market and accelerated the production and sales of Munsing wear, inadvertently flooding the market. Munsing wear became commonplace, soon losing its appeal, and this resulted in a tremendous amount of dead stock. The fatal blow was struck when Descente, in order to move the excess merchandise, offered it at bargain basement prices. Forty per cent off discount sales were very popular at that time. While such a strategy may have been unavoidable, it unfortunately resulted in a sudden decline in the prestige attached to Munsing wear.

In order to rebuild Descente, the Board has brought in senior executives from three major corporations closely associated with the company. Two of these corporations are major shareholders, C. Itoh and Company, one of Japan's 'Big Three' commercial houses which traditionally excels in textile transactions, and Sumitomo Bank, Descente's major bank, well-known for its efficient management. The third corporation from which executives were recruited was Toyobo Company Limited, a leading spinner which has grown into an integrated manufacturer of natural and synthetic textiles.

The restructuring strategy designed by the executives from the four corporations has resulted in the establishment of a fully computer integrated point-of-sales management information system, tighter stock control, improved and seasonally adjusted production strategy, and better-trained sales representatives. Munsing items are now mainly order produced while the focus is on creating good selling lines out of sub-brand items. It is now recognized that Descente failed to investigate other possible pillars in addition to Munsing wear around which to concentrate its energy at a time when sales were up and resources could be directed to the exploration of new avenues.

At first glance ASICS and Descente appear to follow similar marketing strategies, in that they both focus on the 'top strategy'. ASICS' advantage, however, was in its ability to integrate specification and diversification. In addition to diversification induced by the market, as exemplified in ASICS' response to the athletes' demand for 'total fashion', ASICS also succeeded in diversification of another kind, namely technology-based diversification.

ASICS succeeded in the production and sale of shoes for basketball, volleyball, baseball, wrestling and running, to name but a few categories, and it now markets more than five hundred different styles of sports shoes. Onitsuka developed this type of diversification by linking his fundamental corporate strategy—based on his strong ethical convictions—with the basic technology of shoe making, the skill he struggled so hard to master and is constanty trying to improve.

R & D in Sports Shoes

From the beginning, when Onitsuka the travelling shoe salesman was talking directly to the athletes to learn how his shoes might be improved, research has played an integral role in product development. Unable at first to acquire his own production facilities, his shoes were manufactured at a subcontract factory and it was here that he learned everything he possibly could about shoemaking. Pattern making, stitching, last making, the chemical composition of cement—nothing escaped his attention. This accumulated know-how provided the impetus for future improvements and new product development.

Onitsuka believes that, no matter how a company excels in management strategy, if its product is not the very best, then its market competitiveness will be almost nil. A quality product is essential to industrial survival. Production technology is the foundation upon which quality products are developed. Unfortunately, such technology cannot be acquired overnight. When he founded the company in 1949, Onitsuka was a novice. He had to devote an extraordinary amount of time and effort to technology and development. In return, Onitsuka gained a great deal of respect for the opinions of others, particularly technical experts.

ASICS' product development is distinctly different from that of the majority of shoe companies because ASICS is attempting not only to improve existing design ideas but also to bring revolutionary changes to the shoe industry world-wide. This involves novel designs, materials and production methods. ASICS' products are the result of the efforts of its research and development teams scattered throughout the corporation. ASICS' products influence and are influenced by material improvements, product innovation and technology transfer around the world.

A major portion of the scientific and technological research carried out in Japan is conducted by private enterprises, with universities and special research institutions playing a lesser, but none the less significant, role. In 1980, for example, 59 per cent of the total funds spent on scientific and technological research were accounted for by private industries and this share continues to grow annually. Fifty-five per cent of academic research funds are allocated to basic research, 38 per cent to research in application technology and the remaining 7 per cent to development-related research. Private industry, on the other hand, devotes three-quarters of its research funds to product development, one-fifth to application technology and the remaining amount to basic research. Research and development expenses for private industries average about 1.5 per cent of total sales.[3] ASICS, according to Seiji Mihara, the company's head administrator, spends 3 to 4 per cent of its total sales on research and development.

It is uncommon for shoe companies to have their own research facilities beyond a machine or two to determine whether or not the materials arriving from suppliers are of uniform quality. Peter Cavanagh, a professor in biomechanics at The Pennsylvania State University, grades shoe research A for advanced, B for better than average, C for caution and D for dangerous.[4] In the first category are companies that sponsor research projects at private or university laboratories designed to determine the effects of a specific feature of the shoe on the wearer. Cavanagh rates the company as A-plus if it has its own laboratory. Such a facility is indicative of the company's commitment to product improvement through careful research which demands a considerable expenditure of both time and money.

In the second category, B for better than average, Cavanagh places those companies that utilize the expertise of a technical adviser or a group of experts to serve as an advisory panel. Podiatrists, orthopaedists, biomechanists, coaches and athletes often serve in such a capacity, acting as sounding boards and as sources for new ideas. The shoe that results incorporates ideas that are not substantiated by experimentation.

Given C for caution—the caution the runner needs in assessing these companies' shoes—are those companies that select for inclusion into their product those ideas that will differentiate it from other shoes on the market. The primary goal is to be different, to stand out. The benefit of the new feature to the runner is of much less importance. As Cavanagh says, 'The "design team" in this case might be an individual with an MBA who has never run a step. It might also be someone who is an avid runner and a good thinker. So caution is the word.'[5]

The D for dangerous category is reserved for companies whose sole regard is for profit. The most distinctive features of other shoes are copied with minor modifications to satisfy patent requirements and incorporated into their products. There is no research and often little understanding of how the features function. The results could be very dangerous for the runner. The lack of regulation within the sports shoe industry makes it possible for manufacturers to incorporate any idea they see as profitable into their shoes even though the idea may prove harmful to the runner.

At ASICS Corporation, before a new product is introduced on to the market it is tested and retested, checked and rechecked. As ASICS' consultant Ian Whatley, a British bio-engineer and industrial designer working in North Carolina, explains:

The time taken to introduce a new shoe concept depends on the complexity of the final product. A slight revision of an existing model may be brought to market in a matter of months. Major changes that require extensive testing or new production techniques can take three years to finally reach the market. Recognizing that most new models are requested only six to twelve months before they need to be finalized, the American product development group now have several shoe ideas which are not slated for specific shoes but are expected to be market ready in two or more years. An example might be the use of a new last or a very unusual outsole pattern.

This thoroughness results in a very high-quality, durable product. 'ASICS' return rate due to defects is the lowest in the industry', says Dr Joe Ellis, ASICS Tiger Corporation's marketing consultant. 'Many of the other sports shoe manufacturers look to ASICS for their technology.' As well as product innovation, ASICS is engaged in research into product testing equipment and in biomechanical studies.

In recent years, biomechanical studies, that is, studies of the way in which the bones, muscles and joints of the body react to movement in sport, have yielded innovative designs that help prevent injury and reduce muscle and cardiovascular-system fatigue, thereby improving performance. They have also resulted in the development of new materials that enhance product performance.[6] ASICS' team of Japanese researchers is supplemented by the expertise of Dr Barry Bates, a kinesiologist at the University of Oregon, Eugene, and the aforementioned Ian Whatley and Dr Joe Ellis, a California podiatrist.

Joe Ellis, the company's first American consultant, joined ASICS Tiger Corporation (ATC) in 1981 as a product research and development consultant. His title has since been changed to marketing consultant. He still maintains his private practice as a podiatrist and writes monthly columns for two sports magazines. A runner himself, Ellis invented a machine to measure force and motion some years ago. With the aid of this machine, he provided shoe ratings based on shock and motion for *Runner's World* for a year and for *Running Times* for three years.

When sports magazines began publishing shoe ratings in the mid-1970s they were based virtually on one person's opinion. By 1977, when Ellis became involved with *Runner's World*, testing was carried out by a ten-member panel (three runners, three retailers, two podiatrists, an orthopaedic specialist, and the magazine publisher) as well as in the laboratory. Ellis did 'scientific' testing with his machine and helped establish *Runner's World's* criteria for panel judging. Today the judging is done by a three-member panel, all of whom are podiatrists, and a reader survey. Several companies, including Nike and Adidas, approached Ellis about consultancy work. When ASICS asked him to join their staff in 1981 he accepted a position as an exclusive consultant, suspending his work on shoe ratings.

Asked why he went to ASICS rather than to any of the other companies, Dr Ellis says:

I chose the ASICS Tiger Corporation (and 'Japanese Philosophy') because of their team work approach and making the 'I' less important than 'We'. Also, the loyalty of Japanese companies to their employees is well known. Finally, the pride that the Japanese companies and employees place in their product was also an important factor. All of these are what I call 'Japanese Philosophy'.

Ian Whatley, in response to the same question said:

After a long period of work in the athletic shoe industry, I had a wide choice of companies I could work for. I was honoured to join ASICS. Most companies have one person responsible for each shoe; the team approach yields a better final product. The British concept of loyalty to the company and inter-personal relations are more similar to the Japanese approach than the U.S. ASICS has a genuine desire to produce innovations. This is a philosophy for the twenty-first century.

Whatley joined ASICS in 1984. His role in research and development is to come up with new design concepts and to work with the rest of the product development team to polish each others' inspirations into feasible ideas that will evolve into high-performance shoes.

Today, researchers continue to expand their knowledge of biomechanics. Applied to sports shoes, biomechanical research focuses on such features as weight, fit, shock absorption, heel stability, traction, durability, flexibility and ventilation. Each sport demands shoes with particular characteristics. For example, running shoes must accommodate one-directional, forward movement as freely and as smoothly as possible, whereas tennis shoes require lateral movement and sliding attributes but need to sustain relatively little vertical impact. Thus, running shoe design emphasizes light weight, vertical shock absorbancy and flexibility while tennis shoes are firmer than running shoes and offer greater traction but less bottom cushioning.

Since most athletes, whatever their sport, train by running, and since running has also gained widespread popularity as a form of exercise among the population at large, sports shoe manufacturers focus much of their research on running shoes.[7] Research into shoe design aims at developing products to meet unique podiatric and biomechanical requirements and to minimize such injuries as knee strain, tendonitis, shin splints, bone bruises, hip problems, heel spurs, metatarsal bruises and stress fractures. To reduce the possibility of injury, sports shoe research, in which ASICS is in the forefront, has led to a number of innovations, particularly in shoe midsoles and outsoles.

Since it provides both cushioning and stability, the midsole, a layer of foam padding between the upper and the outsole, is the most important part of the shoe. Today, running shoe midsoles are usually made of EVA, a plastic foam that is a combination of ethylene, vinyl and acetate. Ethylene allows for mouldability, vinyl provides resilience, and acetate adds structure and stiffness. The softness, weight and resiliency of an EVA midsole can be adjusted by varying the chemical composition as the foam is manufactured.

ASICS and many other sports shoe manufacturers now use a dual density midsole patented by Dr Barry Bates. The basic concept of the dual density midsole is to use a softer EVA on the lateral (outside) portion of the shoe where the heel first strikes the ground. This provides maximum shock absorption. On the medial (inside) part of the shoe the EVA used is firmer, allowing for better stability and support. There have been considerable advances in shoe outsoles since the day when Onitsuka was inspired by octopus suction cups and, later when he sent Tokio Sakaguchi to the automobile show to study tyres. About that time, in the late 1950s, Russian athletes began to come to the fore, excelling in many different sports. This was a result, in part, of the Soviet national sports policy. Onitsuka heard, too, that the Russians trained on the tundra and that the springy consistency of the earth's surface was ideal for developing the leg muslces. How to duplicate tundra conditions in Japan? Onitsuka concluded that the closest surface would be grass. In Japan, however, where land is limited, the only areas large enough were golf courses. To use a golf course as a training ground was impossible. Consequently, Onitsuka decided to 'grow grass' on the sole of the shoe and thereby create the effect of running on grass.

Eiji Nagai, president of Shinei Kako, a company specializing in the manufacture of shoe soles, remembers Onitsuka telling him to make the very best soles possible, regardless of the cost. At that time sponge rubber served many purposes in everyday life but was too soft for Onitsuka's needs. After some experimentation, Onitsuka succeeded in combining hard, artificial rubber and softer natural rubber to create a sponge with the appropriate elasticity. A sole made from one layer of this sponge material, however, was still not ideal. The weight of the body is not uniformly distributed over the shoe sole, but rests on certain pressure points. To remain balanced on a spongy sole requires the use of leg muscles, resulting in fatigue. Onitsuka solved this problem by sandwiching the soft spongy layer between two layers of hard sponge on the top and bottom.

Today, most running shoe outsoles are made of styrene butadiene rubber. ASICS has developed the 'runaway tread' which follows the entire movement of the runner's foot, increasing traction from heel to toe on all surfaces. At the same time it helps to control excessive pronation while maintaining flexibility.

Flexibility is also enhanced by the air channels that run through the midsole under the ball of the foot. Perhaps the greatest contribution to increased flexibility, without decreasing the stability of the shoe, has been the development of combination lasting. Combination lasting is a recent attempt to combine the benefits of the two traditional standard lasting methods, board lasting and slip lasting. In board lasting a piece of fibreboard is attached to the last and the uppers are fitted over the last, then glued on the underside. Board lasted shoes provide excellent stability but limited flexibility.

In slip lasting, the board is omitted. The upper is stitched together before lasting and then slipped onto the last like a sock. The result is a light, close-fitting shoe with a very flexible forefoot but less stable than the board lasted shoe.

In combination lasting, the rear part of the shoe is board lasted for maximum stability while the forefoot area is sliplasted for maximum flexibility. As flexibility is only required in the metatarsal area where the foot has a major joint, combination lasting is effective because it makes the shoe rigid up to the ball of the floot and flexible from there forward.

Rearfoot stability has always been the Achilles' heel of running shoes. To keep the foot and ankle in the correct position during pronation, ASICS uses a heel counter and, in models specifically designed to reduce the rate and range of pronation when it is excessive, a stabilizing pillar. It 'centres' the foot and keeps the shoe stable. The hard rubber stabilizing pillar at the instep side of the heel in some models was developed with the assistance of Joe Ellis. Yet, as Ellis says, 'Probably the easiest thing is coming up with the idea, the concept. Putting it to work is a whole other story.'

An example of the collaboration between American consultants, 'coordinators', and the Japanese research team in the area of running shoes is the best-selling X-Caliber GT. The latter was the first running shoe on the market to attempt to control pronation. The X-Caliber GT was also ASICS' initial attempt at controlling excessive motion while still allowing rearfoot shock absorption through the incorporation of an early version of the dual density midsole. Like many of ASICS' other innovations, competitors subsequently copied these ideas, with slight modifications. 'In the sports shoe industry patents are easily circumvented' notes Joe Elllis. 'It is not unheard of for other companies to market ASICS' ideas before ASICS does.'

Information leaks most often occur in the Asian subcontract factories where it is the norm for production lines supplying three or four well-known sports shoe companies to operate side-by-side. In these factories, those responsible for production planning for the various shoe companies often share an office and information exchange is unavoidable. Also, new product specifications with diagrams are generally posted on the factory walls for the workers to refer to. Without subjecting a new product to rigorous tests, it is possible for one company to have another's shoe on the market before the company has developed it.

The problem of blisters on the soles of the feet, which so concerned Onitsuka in the late 1950s, has virtually been eliminated through improved construction techniques and shoe materials. A heel collar made of water-resistant interwoven fabrics covered with soft pile provides blister resistance at the back of the heel. As early as 1967 Onitsuka Corporation introduced an all-nylon upper on their Olympiad XIX track spike and on a new version of their Marathon shoe. This innovation made the shoes 'machine washable' and also enhanced breathability. Nylon uppers caught on and in a little more than ten years they had been incorporated into almost all running shoes.

As new materials are developed, manufacturers are quick to incorporate them into their products. Gore-tex, developed by Wilbert L. Gore, formerly a chemist with DuPont, is one such material. Promoted for its ability to release perspiration while at the same time being waterproof, ASICS marketed a shoe with Gore-tex uppers in 1983. This turned out to be a disaster. Although Gore-tex releases perspiration, it proved unable to handle adequately the excess moisture produced by the feet during strenuous exercise.

Today ASICS running shoe uppers are constructed from tri-layered nylon at the rear and breathable mesh at the forefoot. This combination maximizes stability and control during pronation while allowing ventilation. Greater foot breathability is provided by additional holes in the Tiger stripes.

Nowadays almost all sports shoes are distinguishable by their lines, patterns or alphabetical symbols. For example, New Balance's 'N', Nike's 'Swoosh', and Adidas' three vertical, slanted stripes make their products readily identifiable on the athletes' feet as well as on the retailers' shelves.

Onitsuka developed ASICS Tiger stripes in the early 1960s to identify his shoes and to improve their fit around the instep. Tiger stripes made their debut at the 1964 Tokyo Olympics. Over the next four years, Onitsuka worked to perfect their design and they appeared in their present form in the 1968 Mexico Olympics. The stripes, ASICS' registered trademark, appear at first glance to be exclusively decorative. Closer inspection, however, reveals their function. The two vertical lines that wrap around the arch support the instep and help prevent fatigue. The two horizontal lines extending from the heel to the instep support the heel and at the same time inhibit stretching in the uppers. Onitsuka considers the Tiger stripes to be one of his masterpieces.

As running has gained in popularity, the provision of a wide variety of shoes to meet individual needs and preferences has become economically justified. Runners differ in age, anatomy, physical condition and running habits. Ian Whatley notes:

Sports shoe development is starting to hinge more and more around the idea of market segmentation. This involves the identification of and meeting the specialized needs of participants within different sports. For example, runners can need shoes for pronation control, road racing, track racing or for forefoot striking in training. Each design has to be different to meet their needs.

No longer is it possible to select one shoe as 'the best' running shoe on the market.

Consumer recognition of the success of ASICS' efforts can be measured by the popularity of such shoes as the Alliance, the Tiger Extender, the Tiger Tigress LT, and the X-Caliber GT. ASICS' achievements in bio-mechanical shoe design have been recognized by *Runner's World*, the popular American running magazine and by the German running magazine *Spiridon*. Several Tiger shoes have received top ratings in both magazines.[8] Over the years distance runners from many nations have used ASICS shoes, including Karel Lismont of Belgium, Carey May Edge of Canada, Joyce Smith and Ian Thompson of Great Britain, Jack Foster and Allison Roe of New Zealand, Rosa Mota of Portugal, Juma Ikangaa of Tanzania and Frank Shorter of the United States.

When asked if he feels that improvement in the human running record is a function of human effort more than of the improvement in shoes, Dr Ellis agrees that it is. He points to Zola Bud, the South African-born British runner whose level of running has improved substantially over the last five years, yet she wears no shoes at all. The primary contribution of improved shoe design and construction, Ellis feels, is a reduction in the severity and number of injuries runners experience.

Data collected from the University of California shows that, the lighter the shoe is, the less energy the runner must expend and, theoretically, the better his time will be. In 1985, ASICS developed a marathon shoe which, at 100 grams, was the lightest in the world. Tokio Sakaguchi, head of product development, suggests that an extremely light shoe gives the runner a psychological advantage in that the knowledge that his shoes are helping him conserve energy will propel him even faster.

The running shoe market, at least in the United States, is accepted now as having reached a plateau and may be falling slightly. The market for aerobic shoes, on the other hand, has grown very rapidly in the last two years. As Ian Whatley observes:

The very fast changes in the shoe demands require the ability to refocus development in a matter of months. ASICS has occasionally been slow in noticing trends but the increased size and diversity of backgrounds of the shoe marketing and development teams has dealt with this shortcoming. ASICS has always been a performance rather than a fashion oriented company. This has pushed R & D to a very functional approach to design but cosmetics have not been ignored. Another outcome of being a non-fashion company is that ASICS is less vulnerable to rapid changes in taste. While this tends to give lower annual sales, the market is more stable and it is more responsive to ASICS' strength in product than to clever marketing methods.

Changes in taste, and particularly differences in taste between markets, do not go unnoticed, however. 'The recent trend in North American taste', says Mikio Kuwata, president of ASICS Tiger GmbH, ASICS' wholly owned subsidiary in Germany, 'is towards softer soles and more vivid colours in running shoes. In Germany, though, there is a preference for firmer soles and more reserved colours.' Information of this nature is forwarded to ASICS' Overseas Operations Division in Kobe. Together with information acquired through ASICS' network of professional (sports pros) advisers, retailers, wholesalers, salesmen, consumers and external research advisers, this information is integrated into product development.

'Products developed for defined targets', Onitsuka points out, 'should be patented as soon as possible. Patent acquisition for inventions and design is one method of recording the company's progress.' At ASICS, monetary awards are presented annually to employees to whom the original ideas for innovation can be attributed. In 1984, ninety-four individuals received such awards.

15 | Ongoing International Expansion

Taiwanese and Korean Licensees

Onitsuka's first attempt at foreign expansion occurred as early as 1961 and was aimed at penetration into the American market. As the corporation had not then developed in-house expertise in foreign trade, he chose to use a trading company to facilitate initial market entry. The large Japanese trading companies such as Mitsui, Mitsubishi, Sumitomo and C. Itoh, which handle a major share of the Japanese import/export business, are excellent distributors of goods and services and facilitators of trade. They also provide extensive market coverage, credit reliability and stable financial service capabilities. Yet, they had little interest in small-bulk items such as Onitsuka's shoes. There were, however, literally thousands of smaller trading companies and Onitsuka decided to use Chatani Sangyo.

The disadvantages of this option soon became apparent. Onitsuka had little control over the market and received virtually no direct feedback concerning market information. The blame for all product imperfections, even those that were clearly the result of improper storage and handling on the part of the trading company, was placed at Onitsuka Corporation's doorstep. Onitsuka realized that his product was relatively unknown and that the profit margin for the trading company was not large. He felt that his product's reputation would be severely damaged were he to continue with the trading company. He terminated the relationship and in 1965 signed an agreement with Blue Ribbon Sports making this company the exclusive distributor of Tiger shoes in the United States. This contract was renewed periodically until the aforementioned legal dispute between Onitsuka Corporation and Blue Ribbon Sports in 1972.

In 1966, Onitsuka Corporation's exports totalled only 50 million yen. In the decade following, however, exports soared and by 1976 exports to foreign countries had risen to 1.8 billion yen, accounting for 18 per cent of total sales. By this time, Onitsuka Corporation's contract agents around the world numbered close to thirty and the company was exporting to sixty-two different countries. Two-thirds of their export business centred in the United States.

The first foreign factory, intended to serve the American market, was the Nichidai factory, established in Taiwan in 1969. The advantage of this course of action became apparent when the value of the yen started to rise in 1971, making made-in-Japan goods less competitive in the foreign market. Later, trade friction arising from Japan's large trade surplus further underlined the expedience of manufacturing in Taiwan. Since the establishment of the Nichidai factory in Kaohsiung's Export Processing Zone, however, the advantages of locating within this zone have decreased significantly to the point where it is almost a disadvantage to be located there.

Through the establishment of a bonded storage system, factories outside the zone can now enjoy tax advantages on the manufacture of products for export similar to those afforded firms within the zone. Taiwanese banks capable of handling foreign transactions have increased in number and efficiency. Within the Export Processing Zone, labour laws are more strictly imposed and the entry and departure of materials and goods tightly monitored, making use of subcontractors outside the zone economically unjustifiable as such activities are badly hampered by red tape. This severely outweighs the theft control advantage of strict monitoring.

Impressed with Taiwanese workmanship at both the Nichidai factory and at Johnson Rubber, and in order to meet the increased American demand for ASICS shoes, ASICS contracted with two more factories in Taiwan, but these arrangements lasted only a short time. In 1978, ASICS approached R. S. Tseng, director of the Chung Chyun Industry Company Limited. 'At that time', recalls Tseng, 'many Taiwanese factories were reluctant to do business with Japanese corporations, especially with ASICS, because of their high quality standards. It was rumoured that 50 per cent of any product batch would be considered to be defective by ASICS.'

Tseng thought he could meet ASICS' standards if production proceeded slowly and carefully. He was determined to try. The defective rate of 10 per cent on the test batch of 10,000 pairs of soccer shoes was still high by Japanese standards but much less than if it had been at other Taiwanese factories, and a 10,000 and then 50,000 pair order were forthcoming. ASICS is now the primary customer of the Chung Chyun Company and its recently established sister company, Chung Shyong Industry, of which Tseng is also the director.

'Today', says Tseng, 'our policy is to fill ASICS' orders first and then take orders from other corporations to utilize fully our production capacity. We have no written contract with ASICS. There is mutual trust between our companies.' Together Chung Chyun and Chung Shyong produce between eight and nine times the number of shoes produced by Nichidai.

There is an ongoing exchange of information between the Nichidai factory and the Chung Chyun/Chung Shyong companies. Personnel visit back and forth and technical information is shared. ASICS' inspectors and technical assistants spend prolonged periods of time in Taiwan checking materials, appearance and shoe construction.

Osamu Sasada joined Onitsuka Corporation in 1971 and is now an inspector and technical consultant for Taiwan. He spends between six and eight months annually in Taiwan. Says Sasada, 'Product quality at the Chung Chyun and Chung Shyong factories is excellent. The employees are well disciplined, hard working and highly skilled; the machines are made in Taiwan and are of good quality; if problems do occur they most often relate to the materials, usually Taiwanese, used in production.'

Product quality is also satisfactory at the Chung Hsing Company and the Hsyu Tai Company. The former has been a subcontract producer since 1983, making ASICS' junior sports shoes, and the latter has been producing snowboots for ASICS since 1984.

In addition to its present licensing agreement with five Taiwanese shoe manufacturing corporations (these agreements are not necessarily supported by detailed written contracts), ASICS has licensing agreements with five other corporations which make ASICS' sportswear, sports bags and tennis racquets. Similar licensing agreements exist with Korean manufacturers.

R. S. Tseng is grateful that ASICS has subcontract factories in Korea as well as Taiwan. 'The Korean factories keep us on our toes', says Tseng. 'If we don't do our job well, we will lose out to the competition. The Koreans seem to be able to make shoes a little more cheaply than we can but we can make them faster and I feel our quality has an edge over theirs.'

In addition to the difficulties imposed by the rising value of the yen, limitations are often imposed on Japanese exported products by high customs tariffs, quotas and controls on the issue of import licences. To overcome some of these obstacles, ASICS has entered into licensing agreements with a number of Korean companies.

While ASICS has no production facilities of its own in Korea, it has licensing agreements with several Korean shoemaking factories, including Sewon, Chin Woo, Honan Rubber, Yae-yang and Jin-yang, all of which produce shoes for other manufacturers as well as ASICS. ASICS shoes produced in Korea are for both the local market and for export.

While the licensing agreements between ASICS and the Korean subcontractors provide the contractual basis for their relationship, their interaction encompasses mutual understanding and shared values. B. C. Kim, president of the Sewon Company established in 1976 and now ASICS' major Korean shoe producer, approached Onitsuka Corporation in the mid-1970s hoping to learn about its technology and manufacture its shoes. At that time, the company's overseas manufacturing focus was on Taiwan. It was not until 1983 that Kim received an affirmative response from ASICS.

Through his career as a naval officer, a coast guard education administrator and a businessman, and through the university executive management courses in which he subsequently enrolled, Kim came to realize the importance of managerial values in economic pursuits.

Says Kim, 'The more I learn about Mr Onitsuka's philosophy, the more I find I am in accord with him. When we entered the licensing agreement with ASICS, I told Mr Onitsuka that I wanted to learn not only about technology but also about his philosophy.'

'In the area of shoemaking technology', says Jang Kil Kim, Sewon's vice-president, 'ASICS does not simply admonish us not to produce a poor product. Rather, the company's resident shoe technology specialists are constantly suggesting how we might improve and how we might reach even higher levels of excellence. This is the real basis of the bond between us.'

Dong Chil Kwon, Sewon's deputy export manager, points out that other companies for whom Sewon produces shoes have inspectors who visit occasionally while ASICS has technical specialists on the site most of the time. 'In addition to teaching us about shoe construction', says Kwon, 'the ASICS men keep us ever in mind of sound ethical values.'

Recently, the importance of appropriate managerial values has been strongly felt in Korea. There is a growing demand for shorter hours and higher wages, which would narrow the gap between white-collar and blue-collar incomes. Sewon's president, B. C. Kim, says:

> To improve the situation, company owners must let go of the idea that corporations exist solely for their benefit. Profits must be used to improve the company and shared with the employees. The way in which a husband and wife can improve each other applies in the corporate context as well. Instead of saying to his wife 'you are not good for me, I wish you would change', if the husband improves himself and becomes a better husband, then his wife will no doubt become a better wife. By the same token, if an employer thinks about the well-being of his employees and thereby becomes a better employer, his employees will contribute more. My ideas have their roots in my Buddhist beliefs and have been enriched by my relationship with Mr Onitsuka.

Kim admits that not all his employees are completely happy with Sewon Company. Working hours are long—more than fifty hours a week is the national norm—and employees work 302 days a year. 'But', he says, 'I believe that there is a fundamental trust between management and employees. We are not suffering from the serious problems that stem from an underlying distrust of management on the part of the workers.'

Today, Sewon, with 2,800 employees and three factories containing eleven lasting production lines and forty stitching lines, has a monthly production capacity of 550,000 pairs of shoes. Of these, 30 per cent are for ASICS and the rest are for American and European corporations, including Kangaroos, Buster Brown, KAEPA, New Balance, Elgreco, Adidas, Lecoq Sportif, and PBI (Marks & Spencer).

Ki Deuk Park, president of the Chin Woo Company, another of ASICS' Korean licensees, predicts that the increasing cost of shoe production in Japan will eventually force the Japanese to abandon shoe production altogether. As he sees it, ASICS would then concentrate on research and development, contract production abroad, import, export and sales.

In the area of sportswear, Wonchang Moolsan Company, which also produces garments for J. C. Penny Company and Japan's Ito-Yokado, is ASICS' largest Korean manufacturer. Their relationship dates back to a 1974 licensing agreement between Jelenk and Wonchang. Having worked for two Japanese corporations in Korea—Mitsubishi Steel before the war and Kanebo after—the chairman of the Board of Wonchang, Seung Ryoum Kim, feels a close affinity with the Japanese. A Christian, he has built both a church and a school for his employees. Employees attend the school in the evenings to improve their general educational level. He also stresses the importance of employers looking out for the well-being of their employees and is in accord with Onitsuka's management philosophy.

Wonchang Moolsan is run by Kim's youngest brother, Woon Ryoum Kim, who studied labour economy at graduate school at the University of Wisconsin. He feels that Korea's economic progress is dependent upon the ability of its workers to produce goods superior in quality to those of any other country. 'Korean workers', says Woon Ryoum Kim, 'work harder than their counterparts in Taiwan, Mainland China and Japan.'

Increased demand in Korea for ASICS products, coupled with the desire to take advantage of the opportunity provided by the Asian Games and the Summer Olympics to be held in Seoul in 1986 and 1988 respectively, led, in 1983, to the establishment of ASICS Sports Corporation. This is a joint sales venture participated in by ASICS, Sewon Company, Wonchang Moolsan Company and Soon-sik Yong. Yong is the main investor and also serves as president of the corporation.

Born during World War II, Yong grew up at a time when anti-Japanese feeling was running high in Korea. After graduating from Kyunghi University in Seoul in 1966, Yong worked for the government, had his own electronics business, spent ten years in the Army, and participated in food industry management. During the course of his varied career, he had no contact with Japanese until, in the early 1980s, he met Masaaki

Uetsuki, who was responsible for ASICS' entry into the Korean market, and Takemi Tanaka, head of ASICS' overseas operations. Says Yong, 'I had heard nothing but bad reports about the Japanese and I tended to believe them until I met Mr Uetsuki, Mr Tanaka and, eventually Mr Onitsuka.' Unlike many of ASICS' older-generation Korean business associates, Yong is not fluent in Japanese. Jae-bok Byun, formerly the editor of a Korean newspaper and a basketball magazine and in this capacity acquainted with ASICS personnel, acted as go-between and interpreter. 'Through discussion of management philosophy with Mr Onitsuka', says Yong, 'I came to realize that not all Japanese were as I had been led to believe. I agreed with Mr Onitsuka's idea of co-prosperity and I trusted him as a human being.'

ASICS Sports Corporation now has a workforce of more than eighty and 1985 sales were up 30 per cent over the previous year. Determined to improve the company and at the same time make the company's success of direct benefit to the employees, Yong reinvests 60 per cent of the annual profits in the company and distributes the remaining 40 per cent among the employees.

German and Brazilian Subsidiaries

In addition to ASICS Tiger Corporation, ASICS' wholly owned subsidiary in the United States, there are ASICS Tiger GmbH and ASICS Tiger do Brasil Industria e Comercio Ltda., ASICS wholly owned subsidiaries in the Federal Republic of Germany and in Brazil, respectively.

No attempt was made to penetrate the vast European market until 1975 when Onitsuka Corporation established a sales company in Neuss, just outside Düsseldorf. The first president was Masayasu Miyata. Düsseldorf was selected because it was a financial centre and a geographic and economic focus of the European Community. In addition, many Japanese corporations were already established there and it appeared to be a good place for gathering information that would support the work of the company's European liaison office. Further, there was the hope of delivering a damaging blow to Adidas and Puma.

In 1978, ASICS Tiger GmbH absorbed the floundering Möbus Co., KG., a shoe manufacturer located in Crailsheim. Möbus' sixty employees were to produce soccer and training shoes but, in 1981, after Akio Bessha assumed the presidency of ASICS Tiger GmbH, Möbus failed. Shinji Fuwa, an ASICS employee fluent in German, has managed the European liaison office since its inception. He cites several reasons for Möbus' bankruptcy, including high production costs, and the lack of a developed sales distribution system.

Bessha's successor, Masaru Yato, focused on ASICS' lack of recognition in Europe. 'Adidas and Puma were all-pervasive', says Yato, now acting head of ASICS' Overseas Operations Division. 'In comparison to these giants, ASICS was invisible.' Yato applied Onitsuka's point-of-focus strategy geographically, concentrating on expanding business from the immediate neighbourhood to targeted retailers and various regions in Europe. In 1985, ASICS entered into a contract manufacturing agreement with an Italian shoe manufacturer. This has resulted in a small annual production of eighty thousand pairs of tennis shoes.

Today, ASICS Tiger GmbH functions as an importer and wholesaler to German retailers and supplies wholesale distribution agents in other European countries. ASICS Tiger GmbH provides marketing know-how and financial assistance to ASICS' agents who hold exclusive distribution rights in each country. Mikio Kuwata assumed the presidency in 1985 and oversees seven Japanese and twenty German employees. While ASICS' reputation is growing among professional European athletes, widespread mass-market penetration has yet to be achieved. Says Kuwata, 'In the ten major European running events for 1985, 24 per cent of the participants used ASICS' shoes, making our shoe the most popular. Mr Onitsuka's "top strategy" is succeeding here but we still have a long way to go, especially with the general public.'

While ASICS Tiger GmbH was making inroads into the European market, ASICS Tiger Corporation handled the American and Mexican markets and Canada was looked after by ASICS' trading department in Japan. South America, with its population of approximately 400 million, remained a virtually untapped market until 1984. In that year, ASICS established its wholly owned subsidiary, ASICS Tiger do Brasil Industria e Comercio Ltda. in Sao Paolo. It is one of some 630 Japanese companies operating in Brazil.

The groundwork for this was laid by Akira Kato. A graduate of Keio University, Kato worked for Yahata Steel Corporation (presently Nippon Steel Corporation) from the mid-1950s until 1969. For the decade following, he acted as manager and/or coach for a number of national volleyball teams, including Brazil, Chile and Peru. He joined ASICS in 1979 and from then until his sudden death in 1982 was involved in data collection and business negotiations regarding the South American market.

ASICS Tiger do Brasil was incorporated to work in co-operation with Cambuci, a local shoe manufacturer. Since the licensing agreement became effective, production engineers from Cambuci have visited ASICS' Japanese factories to observe the production process. As a result, improvements have been made in Cambuci's production system. ASICS Tiger do Brasil oversees various aspects of the licensing agreement, including technology transfer, manufacturing processes, and marketing arrangements. The company is presently a two-man operation, headed by Fumio Hirao, who stays in close touch with ASICS' head office through monthly reports and regular telex communication. A similar company was established in Australia in 1986 to cover the Oceania market. As of the end of 1986, ASICS had licensing agreements (sometimes as the licensor, sometimes as the licensee) with foreign establishments in some twenty countries world-wide.

Through trial and error, ASICS is writing the international marketing chapter for the management textbook of the future. The company's plans for further penetration into the international arena are expansive and include permeation of ASICS' products into communist bloc countries beyond their top athletes. The company's immediate goal is to gain access to the mass market in China where, as previously mentioned, ASICS already has subcontract factories producing shoes and sportswear, primarily for export. Towards this end, ASICS staged a six-month exhibition of its products in a leading Beijing Department store in 1986.

Onitsuka sees sport as contributing to the promotion of healthy nations and to the growth of understanding among nations. However small his contribution, Onitsuka feels his responsibilities to his war comrades, to his employees, to his shareholders and to the public at large are being fulfilled.

In recent years, Onitsuka has been invited to share his management know-how by speaking at business and academic gatherings. In 1983, he accepted an invitation to deliver the keynote address to a Japanese Management conference in Lethbridge, Canada. The following year, he was invited to address a gathering of Austrian businessmen and politicians in Vienna. Although the ideas he put forward at both presentations have been expressed in different parts of this book, his Canadian speech is contained in the appendix as it is indicative of those points he feels are of interest and importance to a foreign audience. Also in the appendix are comments by Konosuke Matsushita on Onitsuka's philosophy of management.

A New Corporate Office

Since the amalgamation, ASICS had been making do with existing office space owned by the former Onitsuka Corporation, GTO and Jelenk. There was a pressing need for a new facility designed to accommodate ASICS' present and future needs. Teranishi first looked for a site near the former GTO headquarters in Osaka. At that time, in 1982, land in the area was selling for 3 million yen per *tsubu* (3.3 square metres), but within a short period it had increased by 30 per cent. The decision was made to purchase a lot on Kobe's Port Island instead, at a cost of 0.9 billion yen. The same size lot in Osaka would have cost five times that amount.

Port Island is a man-made island constructed near the city of Kobe. Begun in 1966, construction of the 436 hectare area took fifteen years to complete, at a cost of 530 billion yen. Systematically laid out, the island's container terminal serves as the core of the whole Port of Kobe. International, residential and business sections are contained in the heart of the island. In the International Square are convention/meeting facilities, including the International Exchange Hall, and a luxury hotel. Serving the needs of the island's twenty thousand inhabitants, the Community Square includes apartment compounds, schools, shopping centre and a hospital.

At the very centre of Port Island is 'Kobe Fashion Town'. Nearly forty corporations have offices here. Among these are representatives from the garment, pearl, footwear, audio equipment, computer softwear, furniture and food industries. Onitsuka has been the chairman of the Kobe Fashion Town Planning Council since its inception in 1983.

The various areas of Port Island are linked to each other and to downtown Kobe by Portliner, a computerized, driverless, elevated train. When the new Osaka airport and the offshore highway leading to it are completed, the airport will be only half an hour's drive from ASICS. The company's new location created commuting difficulties for some employees, however, and 107 left in 1985, many of them because of the inconvenience. In an average year there are about eighty resignations, 90 per cent of them female employees leaving to marry or have a baby. ASICS hired 112 new employees in 1985, 75 per cent of whom were female.

ASICS' new head office, opened in July 1985, has eight stories, and a total floor space of 19,000 square metres, providing twice the office area of the previous headquarters. It was constructed at a cost of 6 billion yen, none of which had to be borrowed. A forerunner of the new 'information age', the building's state-of-the-art electronic technology, including high-speed digital service communication circuits and optical fibre cable LAN (Local Area Network), facilitates instantaneous information transfer between both internal departments and with external offices. Television conferences between the head office and Tokyo, Osaka and California are also possible.

The building's multi-purpose, four-storeyed central atrium accommodates large-scale meetings, parties, fashion shows, exhibitions and indoor sports events. Located on the eighth floor are the adjoining offices of the president and two vice-presidents. Onitsuka is most often found in the Port Island headquarters, Teranishi divides his time between Port Island and the Osaka office, while Usui spends much of his time at the company's Tokyo headquarters.

Addressing the employees when the building was opened on 15 July 1985, Onitsuka spoke of the distance the company had come in thirty-seven years. He told his employees:

> Our target now is to challenge our own limits. The degree to which the company can take advantage of its new surroundings depends on the harmony and co-operation that exist among us who work in it. Sun Tzu's three conditions for success—opportune timing, geographical advantage, and harmony among participants—are required for ASICS' success. The time is ripe for us to challenge the future.

Research Institute of Sports Science

In Onitsuka's view, research is fundamental to the survival of sporting goods manufacturers as they advance towards the twenty-first century. Consequently, in 1982 Onitsuka proposed the establishment of ASICS Research Institute of Sports Science (RISS), and the following year a committee chaired by Yoshihiro Hashimoto was formed to determine the basic functions and research policies of the proposed Institute.

With the opening of ASICS' new head office building in Kobe's Port Island, the core research and product development departments that had formerly operated in the Kobe and Osaka offices were amalgamated into the Research Institute of Sports Science. Onitsuka continues to be directly involved in research and, as with the former research departments, the new Research Institute is linked directly to the Office of the President. Opened in November 1985, the Institute has seventy-five employees under the directorship of Hirotsugu Kaku.

A month earlier, the Tokyo R & D Centre opened on the outskirts of Tokyo, adjacent to ASICS' Kashiwa Distribution Centre. The Tokyo R & D Centre functions as a service depot for skis, ski boots and golf equipment from all over Japan. Custom-made golf clubs are also produced here. The centre is close to a number of championship golf courses and serves as a liaison office between ASICS and professional golfers. Presently, the Tokyo R & D Centre employs ten people under the directorship of Mamoru Murakami. The information gleaned through service and through customized production is passed on to the Research Institute.

The Research Institute is also closely linked with some fifty researchers working on product development in ASICS' five product/clientele divisions. Says Kaku, 'The Sports Institute is engaged in basic research activities while the research teams in the product/clientele divisions are engaged in research directly connected with the products marketed by their respective divisions, especially those for the coming season.'

The functions of the Research Institute are threefold. First, it accommodates holistic and systematic studies in biomechanics through research into kinematic physiology, anatomy and dynamics. Second, it investigates the application of new organic and inorganic materials in the production of sporting goods. Finally, it facilitates research into high-technology based, multi-product, small-batch, just-in-time production systems, particularly for the garment sector, to respond to diversified and changing user needs in a timely fashion.

The Research Institute comprises four departments. Three of them—the departments of basic biomechanical research, materials research and production technology—correspond to the Institute's three basic functions. The fourth is the department of administration and planning. In addition to the administrative and planning work directly linked to the Institute, this department is responsible for patenting procedures, consumer consultation and quality control as it applies to finished product testing.

The Research Institute operates according to a policy of close internal and external co-operation. It co-operates with industry, government and academics; however, its basic policy is to conduct its own research studies. Kaku sees himself walking a tightrope between the researchers who are always asking for more funding and ASICS' head corporate administrator, Seiji Mihara, who calls him 'a money eater'.

'Excellent research facilities and adequate funding make it easy for ASICS to attract top researchers', says Masanobu Fukuoka, assistant manager of the fundamental research section. 'No other sporting goods corporation in Japan has a research department like ours. Generally, we are satisfied with the funding. Most importantly though, results are not assessed on a short-term basis.'

There have been some complaints, though, about the salary system. Fukuoka points out:

> ASICS still adheres to the traditional Japanese salary system whereby everyone is paid virtually the same starting salary regardless of qualifications. Thus, those with masters degrees in science are paid on the same scale as those with bachelor's degrees. Even so, there has been no shortage of highly qualified applicants.

The salary system is presently under review by the corporation.

Onitsuka continues to utilize his direct involvement with athletes and coaches at the many meetings and sports functions he attends to ascertain which aspect of sports equipment need improvement. Says Fukuoka, 'Mr Onitsuka often comes into the Institute to scold us for not having solved a particular problem that he has heard about directly from an athlete. In this way, he keeps us constantly aware of the direction our research should be taking.'

One area in which Kaku feels the Research Institute would do well to increase its strength is product design. 'While there are many well-designed Japanese products', says Kaku, 'it appears that design is not well-established academically nor is it well rewarded financially. The integration of aesthetics and function in product design is an important research area of our Institute but we lack the appropriate personnel.'

Sound Minds in Sound Bodies

Onitsuka's territory has undergone global expansion since the early days when he travelled by train throughout Japan selling his shoes to retailers. But Onitsuka still travels extensively. In this day of advanced communication networks, he continues to feel that personal contact with his business associates is of primary importance. Not only does he stay in close touch with ASICS' domestic operations, Onitsuka travels widely outside Japan, visiting ASICS' foreign operations, meeting with government officials, clients, sportsmen and technical experts and fulfilling his responsibilities to the various associations which he represents.

Through long experience 'on the road', Onitsuka has learned how to make the best use of this time. Travelling domestically, usually by train or chauffeur-driven car, he reads reports, journals and newspapers and remains in touch with each ASICS division and with external business associates by telephone. On international flights he reads, writes manuscripts for his speeches, public lectures and publications, and with the aid of his tape recorder, learns *enka*, popular Japanese ballads, which, following Japanese custom, he will perform at business parties around the world.

Says Tosaku Nishida of Goldwin Corporation, 'Over the years I have travelled a great deal with Mr Onitsuka. I usually have a drink and relax but Mr Onitsuka always works when he travels, processing corporate documents, writing speeches, and keeping up with his reading. I sometimes wonder when he sleeps.' But travelling, both internationally and domestically, does provide time to rest. Onitsuka is well-known for his ability to nap anywhere and to awaken feeling invigorated and ready to go.

Onitsuka attributes his good health to regular habits maintained wherever he is. He says:

I eat well, have regular bowel movements, and sleep well. This is the essence of how I stay healthy. Furthermore, no matter what happens I refuse to worry. However serious a situation may be, it is not life-threatening. Therefore, there is never a time that I am too worried to eat. When you get used to a busy life it becomes a natural rhythm.

To accomplish all that he wishes to, Onitsuka is constantly on the go. 'The concept of time off does not exist for Mr Onitsuka', says Koichi Shiba, executive secretary. Abroad or at home, Onitsuka's approach to stress is simply to get things done rather than worry about things that have to be done. He falls asleep each night thinking of the things he has accomplished during the day. His outdoor relaxation is golf, for which he occasionally makes time on Sundays.

Each of ASICS' executives seems to have his own approach to stress management. Yoshiyuki Takahashi finds that golfing on the weekends sets him up for Monday morning. 'By Thursday, I find that late nights at the office and all the concerns of the workplace are beginning to take their toll,' says Takahashi. 'I struggle through Friday and most Saturdays but a day on the golf course on Sunday takes my mind off the company and leaves me refreshed and eager to face the coming week.'

Seiji Mihara developed health problems in his late thirties. To combat these, he took up table tennis, a sport in which he had excelled while at university. He continued to play table tennis until the age of fifty when he felt he was too often defeated by younger competitors. 'For two or three years I didn't engage in any sport', says Mihara. 'I found the pressure of work very hard to handle so, at the suggestion of my doctor, I joined a health club and now I run regularly. On average, I participate in six marathons a year.'

Toshihiko Niki, who now heads ASICS' fitness division, has a more holistic and philosophical approach to fitness. He defines fitness as harmony between body and spirit and nature and society. He watches his diet, swims and reads a great deal. In a variety of ways, ASICS' executives are living ASICS' philosophy: a sound mind in a sound body.

The High Cost of Corporate Success

In order to make ASICS what it is today, Onitsuka has, from the very beginning, devoted every ounce of his energy to corporate development. His hard work has borne fruit and he is admired and respected within the business world. Looking back, though, Onitsuka realizes how dearly his family has paid for his corporate success. Onitsuka says:

I was never able to spend time playing with my children or even having quiet family evenings together. When I look at young fathers now devoting so much time and energy to their children, I realize how much my family missed. But in those days, after the war, providing food for the table meant the difference between life and death. For someone like me, who knew nothing and had to start from the very bottom at a time when materials of all types were so scarce, providing a livelihood for my family and my employees took all my time. But those were the conditions then; very few had an easy life. Later on though when the situation improved, I still focused my attention on my work. I'm sure my daughters saw other fathers spending more time with their children and wished I would do the same.

As a little girl, Emiko, Onitsuka's eldest daughter, thought that an absent father was quite normal. 'Later, though', she recalls, 'my friends would tell me about going to the zoo and on other outings with their fathers and I longed to spend more time with mine.' Takako, however, does not remember missing her father's presence as much.

Both women say that their father never pushed them as far as education was concerned. In fact, he was so busy neither can recall ever showing him a report card. Emiko does remember one evening in her last year of high school when she was studying late at night for a test the next day. Concerned about her health rather than her grades (Emiko was never a robust child), her father came in, unplugged the light, and sent her to bed despite her protests that she had to finish memorizing the material for her examination. Neither Onitsuka nor his wife were what is known as 'an education papa' or an 'education mama'—a parent who relentlessly drives their children to excel at school. Both Emiko and Takako were free to choose their own schools and set their own pace. And both children did very well, graduating from university in the latter part of the 1970s.

Learning from their father the importance of broadening horizons through travel, Emiko and Takako asked that they be allowed to travel while they were at university, not with a group but by themselves. Onitsuka and his wife complied with this request and each year during the summer vacation encouraged their daughters to go abroad and mix with people in other countries.

Onitsuka's daughter, Emiko, born when the company was in its infancy, married in April 1980. Before the wedding, Onitsuka held a family conference and explained to Emiko that her marriage would not automatically provide her husband with an executive position, nor would it necessarily ensure their financial stability. Motoi Oyama, Emiko's fiancé, was then employed by the trading company, Nissho Iwai, but was hoping to get into sports related work. He subsequently joined ASICS and is now based in California.

The wedding took place at the Kobe Portopia Hotel. Onitsuka recalls his feelings:

It seemed only yesterday that I got off the train at the Sannomiya station and saw the city of Kobe as a charred wasteland. The same city today, as seen from the hotel on Portopia Island, is flourishing and vital. It is the port of welcome for this great economic nation. The memories flashed through my mind: the city of Kobe, my daughter in her wedding dress, ASICS—a dream come true. I could feel the tears welling up in my eyes.

'Do I have any regrets about not spending more time with my family? No, not really', says Onitsuka. 'If I had been more of a family man, given conditions in postwar Japan, I fear my business would not have survived; ASICS would never have come to be.'

Epilogue

ASICS' retirement age is sixty for regular employees, sixty-three for managing directors, and sixty-five for executive managing directors and executive senior managing directors. Presently, there is no set retirement age for the vice-presidents and president, but as Onitsuka approaches seventy, the question of the succession is increasingly at the fore. As is the case with many of the founders of successful corporations, Onitsuka is a charismatic leader. Will the organization crumble with the departure of such a leader? Says Onitsuka:

> This depends on how well the leader has nurtured the organizations' human resources. The issue is the continuation of the organization's ideological foundation. If the founder has succeeded in developing personnel who understand and act on corporate values then the corporation will continue to develop based on the shared, accumulated corporate culture.

Onitsuka believes that ASICS has a competent managerial body that will propel the company successfully into the twenty-first century. The presidency of the company should, he feels, be transferred soon, while he has the energy to oversee the transition and guide the corporation into this new phase.

Onitsuka's strong value system has had a profound impact on the nature of the corporation. Teranishi and Usui held values similar to Onitsuka's. Over the years these have been absorbed into what is now commonly referred to as 'Onitsukaism'. Onitsuka is the spiritual pillar of ASICS as an economic entity with a strong ethical flavour. In general, ASICS' corporate behaviour is characteristic of small and medium-sized corporations where people are very visible. The corporation operates according to traditional Japanese values where emotions, mutual trust and verbal promises still dominate.

'Onitsukaism', to a certain extent, has been maintained and transmitted through managerial policy over the last ten years. Once a month, 160 executives from the deputy departmental manager level upwards, meet to present and hear evaluations of performance in those areas for which they are responsible and make proposals for the future. The evaluations and plans are in turn discussed in the light of corporate philosophy. Through this exercise, middle managers are actively exposed to 'Onitsukaism' as it functions in the daily life of the corporation.

ASICS' executives who are responsible for the corporation's future recognize the emergence of a new generation whose 'modern' values are very different. At ASICS, automation, both in the factory and in the office, has been the recent trend. To a greater and greater extent the corporation is being run by the 'system'. ASICS' executives are concerned about the best way to pass on 'Onitsukaism' and are searching for a new framework of corporate values for future corporate endeavours.

To plan for future business developments, a committee has been formed to work out an appropriate strategy. In 1985, a total of 1.3 trillion yen was spent in Japan on sports equipment, wear and shoes.[1]

Estimating a 5 per cent increase in labour costs, a 2 per cent increase in number of employees, and taking into consideration the redistribution of value added, the committee concluded that ASICS needs to be generating 320 billion yen worth of sales by the year 2000. Tatsuaki Kondo feels that about half of this amount can be realized through improvements in existing products and expansion, particularly within the youth, female and elderly markets.[2]

For the remainder, new products and ventures into new domains are required. Mitsuji Teranishi conceptualizes sports-related industries as the sporting goods industry, the sports facility industry and the sports information industry. These three, together with the health-related industry and the education-related industry, Teranishi feels, ought to become ASICS' new frontier, and the company is working on formulating future blueprints.

Looking back over the path he has traversed from the founding of Onitsuka Corporation in 1949 to the present, Onitsuka is reminded of the maxim of Ieyasu Tokugawa (1542–1616), the first Tokugawa Shogun, a skilful warrior and shrewd politician. Ieyasu said, 'Man's life is like going on a long journey under a heavy burden: one must not hurry.'[3] 'The heavy burden I carry', says Onitsuka, 'is the burden of social responsibility. The purpose of my journey is to strive for the well-being of as many people as possible.' Onitsuka's effort in actualizing his corporate mission continues.

Appendix

Onitsuka's Speech

Theories and Practices of Japanese Management

I am honoured to be speaking to you this evening on the topic of Japanese management.

Before I go into detail on my own methods used in ASICS, I would like to touch briefly on the background that has caused the Japanese style of management to become such a popular subject these days.

As you know, Japan had a very late start in its drive towards modernization, yet within a fairly short period of time it has emerged as one of the advanced industrial nations.

After defeat in World War II, Japan was able to arise from incomparable ruins to achieve a miraculous recovery. Through technological co-operation with the United States and Europe, together with a large, young labour force, Japanese industry sustained a period of high growth from 1950 to 1973.

Then, in 1973, the beginning of the oil crisis affected numerous countries, and Japan alone was able to regain her balance quickly enough to sustain favourable economic conditions.

This ability to adapt quickly to changing circumstances has led a number of people to wonder if it might be the style of management that is the cause and, if this is the case, these people feel that Japanese managerial methods should be examined more closely.

I believe that it is necessary to understand the fundamental differences between the structure of Japanese companies and that of American and European companies. These differences, I believe, lie in the history, philosophy and customs that make up the society in which companies mature.

Japanese companies in general are run on the theory that all the employees share a common bond, in a clan fashion. A term that describes this situation is *gemeinschaft*, or 'community'. The employees of a Japanese company are expected to share the company's goals and share its profits and losses. The ties that bind an employee to the company are much deeper than simply a paycheck. Without signing a contract, a new employee is guaranteed employment until retirement, seniority-based wages and promotions, social welfare and other fringe benefits.

The company also instils in its employees the understanding that their new company is a worthwhile, humanistic place. Except in rare circumstances, an employee will not be fired, and so the new employees are better able to accept lower starting wages and strive to create an atmosphere conducive to productive work. Towards this end, white-collar and blue-collar workers work together in enterprise unions to promote 'coexistence and co-prosperity' within this familiar structure.

In contrast, American and European companies are run on the basis of turning a profit. The term for this is *gesellschaft*, or 'corporation'. The importance of individualistic values necessitates the use of specific contracts to tie the employee to the company.

Under this *gesellschaft* system, workers are seen as commodities in the form of manpower rather than as human beings. Companies try to procure labour as cheaply as possible. On the other hand, the workers divide themselves up into lateral unions, depending on their specific craft or industry, and attempt to sell their skills for as much as possible. Here the emphasis is not on what company people work for, but rather what type of work they do.

This is just a simple explanation of some of the ways that Japanese companies differ from American and European ones. Both types have strengths and weaknesses, so it is not possible to judge which is superior.

Since entering the prolonged slow-growth period, the gaps between the various Japanese companies have become more pronounced. Many small and medium-sized enterprises are now facing bankruptcy because of the intensification of competition in the market-place. The Japanese companies that have been given high ratings, in general, have adopted the Japanese style of management as their basic framework and have added to it parts of American theories of expertise. By creating an innovative form of management, these companies have been able to retain the strengths of the purely Japanese style of management, supplemented by the American system's strengths. These companies have been able to adapt to and cope with the changing circumstances.

My company has been very fortunate in its successful development. At this point, I would like to take the opportunity to present my managerial methods to you.

I established Onitsuka Corporation, ASICS' forerunner, in 1949, and struggled bitterly for ten years before I was finally able to exhibit clearly the style of management that enabled our company to grow and prosper.

The purpose of our top management is to identify and explain to our employees our company goals, establish and maintain common bonds among all our employees, and make our company the central point for the attainment of our goals.

The goals that have been set for our management are as follows:

1. Rather than simply promoting sport, we want to become the type of manufacturer that can offer good-quality, low-priced, safe sporting goods that will be beneficial in raising outstanding citizens for our community.
2. We want to ensure that our company has the proper atmosphere conducive to our staff's well-being and productivity. For this end there must be continual and close co-operation between our top management and staff—in other words a *gemeinschaft* approach—so that we can cope readily with the changes in

society, continue to serve our community and in this way make an honest profit.

I would like to explain this point in more detail.

(a) There are three factors, or strengths, that work together in a company: top management, employees and shareholders.

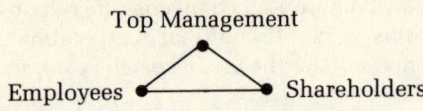

These strengths form the vertices of an equal-sided triangle, and cannot function in competition with each other. Workers and top management must have a deep sense of confidence in each other. The future of the workers is tied directly to the success of the company, and therefore it is imperative that the individual reflects the company goals and guidelines.

After ten years doing business, I voluntarily reduced my private holdings of company shares from 100 per cent to 30 per cent. Of that 70 per cent, 50 per cent was distributed to my employees at no cost, and the other 20 per cent was sold at a fair market value to my employees. This was done to ensure better co-operation with top management, because these stock-holding employees would now be working both as labourers and as 'capitalists'.

(b) In order to promote greater motivation among the workers, we initiated a system that emphasizes human esteem by promoting motivation and technical capabilities. To give credence to this idea, we did away with preferential treatment for blood relatives and university graduates, and instead instituted an open in-house education system of examinations that allows motivated staff to advance through the ranks at an accelerated speed, depending on their initiative and ability.

(c) In order to establish a fair system of profit distribution we introduced a bonus allotment programme.

(d) Top management and workers must work together to ensure that the lines of communication are kept open. To achieve this goal we have established a friendship club, which organizes social activities to bring workers and management together.

(e) Through these various systems the workers are united with the top management in a community of common desires and concerns—reflecting the *gemeinschaft* system—and this, in turn, has led to more prosperous expansion.

(f) Furthermore, we opened our company shares to our affiliated companies and kept them fully informed about corporate operations. While doing so, we also made clear the associated responsibilities and obligations attached to such a relationship. In this way we were able to protect our mutual dependence and form a co-operative system for 'coexistence and co-prosperity'.

Now, having explained the second goal of our management, namely ensuring close contact between staff and top management, I would like to turn to the third goal. This is to provide a good environment for the surrounding community by fighting pollution, raising morale, paying taxes, contributing to the development of the community, and being able to coexist in a socially responsible manner.

I also set three rules for myself to obey so that my management theories could actually be put into practice.

The first rule is that there must be absolutely no misrepresentation by the top management. We have set up a 'glass pane' approach where it is clearly seen that decisions are impartial, where achievements are announced within the company, and where we do not lie about the company's situation. Our staff must be aware of the true situation so that they will respond to our needs.

The second rule is that the top managerial staff must constantly practise direct, personal contact with their subordinates. By using a bottom-to-top approach to decision making, all managerial staff will feel they are making a valuable contribution to the company, and will be able to understand the full weight of their responsibilities and the level of their authority. In other words, the top management must have strong networking skills.

The third rule is that there must not be any conflict between or any overlapping of business and personal matters. Since owners have absolute authority, they have a tendency to use company finances to pursue their own private interests. Also, they might hire an incompetent relative over someone who is much more capable.

If you follow the 'glass pane' approach to management it will be much simpler for managers to avoid abusing their power and pursuing their private interests. The employees will be more motivated because they can see readily that they will be rewarded for good work, and that bonuses and promotions are open to all on the basis of merit. In this way, we at ASICS have been able to correct some of the negative aspects of a seniority based wage and promotion system.

I would now like to summarize my ideas. We have established a *gemeinschaft* system where labour, shareholders and management form a perfect triangle. The introduction of employee shares gave our company a broader perspective so that we came to think of ourselves as a public institution for the community's benefit, rather than simply as a family-type operation. Responsibility and authority have been passed down to lower management in order to encourage greater involvement, and our in-house education system rewards individuals who exhibit initiative and ability. Through this system of modified capitalism, we have been successful in increasing motivation and institutionalizing this innovative form of management.

I must also add that it is necessary for top management to undergo continual personal development to expand their horizons. The company's development depends on the quality of the time that the top personnel devote to the company.

Finally, I would like to raise five points that I have found to be relevant from the point of view of top-level management.

1. You must have a code of ethics. You must have good interpersonal skills, but beyond that you must be able to execute decisions promptly and decisively. This means that you must understand your obligations to society and not be tempted to confuse business and personal interests.
2. You must have foresight and highly creative powers. You must be able to look

at the present situation and see beyond to what kind of developments will occur. A top-level manager should neither imitate nor fall behind others, nor should he expect others to do his dirty work.

3. You must have a sense of frontier spirit and determination. Winning means gaining the upper hand. In order to produce for the company you must have the type of personality that is hungry, willing to take risks and continually trying to open up new territory.

4. You must have the ability to handle leadership. This means being able to soothe hurt feelings, to convince your customers, staff and management that your decision is the correct one, and then to implement your decision. Constant communication allows your staff to feel confident in you, and in turn, trusted by you.

5. Think of others before yourself, and in this way you will accumulate virtue. Think first of your duty towards your community and fellow workers, and then think of yourself lastly. If you work to help others you will find that you are helping yourself at the same time. You should strive to become the type of person in whom others can put their faith.

As the president of ASICS, I deal daily with people who practise the foregoing philosophy. I hope that each member of our company has a full understanding of his role in its success, and that ASICS will become a very exciting place where we can use this sense of solidarity to work towards our own happiness as we serve our community.

I sincerely hope that some of what I have presented will be of some use to you. Thank you for your kind attention.[1]

Matsushita's Comments on Onitsuka's Management Philosophy

In 1979, Konosuke Matsushita founded the Matsushita School of Government and Management to prepare top university graduates to become the business and government personnel who will lead Japan into the twenty-first century. The major components of the five-year programme are: fundamental philosophical inquiry, moral education, development of an international perspective, and practical training. The programme includes field case studies at Japanese corporations whose prosperity is rooted in a solid corporate philosophy. ASICS is one such corporation. Kenji Yoshida, a graduate of Osaka University who enrolled as a Matsushita student in the first year the school opened, spent some time at ASICS in 1983. Later, he and Konosuke Matsushita discussed Onitsuka's management style.

Matsushita observed that the main reason why ASICS has grown to its present status is that, from the outset, Onitsuka has never considered that his company belongs exclusively to himself. He has always managed the company as a public institution. Matsushita, too, has always considered his business to be a public, not a private, matter:

Because I started my business with just my wife and my wife's brother, I understand how easy it is for the manager/owner of a small company to think that the company is his to do with as he pleases. There is a tendency to think only about one's own income. Employees, customers, business associates all become secondary. This is one of the pitfalls of managing a small or middle-sized business.

In order to demonstrate to his employees that the company did not belong solely to its owner, after his company numbered ten employees, Matsushita set up an accounting system showing how much money was to be used by himself, and how much was to remain with the company. Sales, company expenditures and profits were clearly delineated and the books opened to the employees. The employees were sceptical. At that time, shortly before the outbreak of World War II, most small business owners did not have a clear idea of company earnings and they would customarily take whatever they needed for their own use from company funds. Clear records were seldom kept and employees remained in the dark about company finances.

With Matsushita's system, company earnings and expenditure were reported monthly. This made employees aware of the way in which their work related to corporate income and fostered a growing eagerness on their part to do their best for the company.

Matsushita believes that:

distinguishing between private and public is the foundation of any business. Whether you employ only yourself or tens of thousands of people, so long as you are making use of societal resources in the form of people, material and money, then you are engaged in a public, not a private, task. As long as a corporation exists in harmony with society it will grow and develop. If it doesn't it will recede. This is true regardless of the size of the corporation.

Matsushita finds many similarities between Onitsuka's management style and his own. In each corporation, management, employees and affiliated firms are *unmei kyodotai*, that is, they are interdependent entities with a common fate. Matsushita emphasizes that this term does not refer to attributes such as friendliness and harmony. Rather, it refers to 'the integration of the mission of the corporation as a public tool, and the mission of the employees to carry out their assigned tasks. In other words, the synthesis of each employee's commitment to fulfilling his mission leads to the fulfilment of the corporate mission.'

Matsushita stresses that, in order to achieve *unmei kyodotai*, the manager must not be preoccupied with his own immediate benefit. Instead, he must identify and clarify the corporate mission. Likewise, employees must understand, comply with, and respect the corporate mission and work together with management to actualize it. If there is to be trust and confidence between employees and management, it must be reflected in actions. This is how Onitsuka has always run his corporation.[2]

Notes

Preface

1. A succinct discussion of various hypotheses that attempt to explain the apparent effectiveness of Japanese management practices is provided by J. Bernard Keys & Thomas R. Miller, 'The Japanese Management Theory Jungle', *Academy of Management Review*, **9**, No. 2 (1984), pp. 342–53.
2. The importance of history to managers and to the study of management is reviewed in Alan M. Kantrow, ed., 'Why History Matters to Managers: A Roundtable Discussion on the Value of Having Managers Study History and a Graduate School of Business Administration Teach It', participants: Alfred D. Chandler, Jr, Thomas K. McCraw, Alonzo L. McDonald, Richard S. Tedlow & Richard H. K. Vietor, *Harvard Business Review*, **64**, No. 1 (1986), pp. 81–8.
3. Japan Ministry of International Trade and Industry, Small and Medium-Sized Enterprises Agency, *1985 Chusho Kigyo Hakusho* (1985 White Paper on Small and Medium-sized Firms), Tokyo: Ministry of Finance, 1985, Statistical Appendix pp. 2–3.

Chapter 1

1. Born in Niigata prefecture, Okura moved to Edo (present-day Tokyo) at the age of eighteen and sought employment in a dried-seafood store. Three years later, he opened his own dry goods store. In 1865, he opened a gun store and supplied weapons to both the Imperial Army who supported the opening of Japan to the outside world and the corresponding end of domestic feudalism, and to the *bakufu* forces who opposed these objectives. After amassing a small fortune from this venture, Okura travelled to the United States and Europe in 1872 and on his return to Japan opened a general trading company, Okura-Gumi Shokai. In 1874, the company became the first Japanese firm to establish a branch in London. In 1887, in partnership with Denzaburo Fujita, Okura became established as a government purveyor and supplied military provisions, particularly during the Sino–Japanese war (1894–5) and the Russo–Japanese war (1904–5). With the wealth accumulated from these undertakings Okura invested in a wide range of businesses. Domestically, he financed a number of corporations, including Tokyo Dento (now Tokyo Electric Power Co., Inc.) and Imperial Hotel. Internationally, he established a variety of businesses in China and Korea. The Okura-Gumi Shokai expanded together with the Okura Public Works Company (now Taisei Corporation) and

the Okura Mining Company, and the three firms formed the foundation for the Okura *zaibatsu*, a family-controlled financial combine. Okura also established the Okura Commercial School (now Tokyo University of Economics) and the Okura Shukokan Museum.

2. For a comparison of military management in various countries and its application to contemporary corporate management, see Keitaro Hasegawa, *Guntaishiki Management Hikaku: Kigyo Keiei ni Do Ikaseruka* (A Comparison of Military Management in Japan, Germany, U.S., U.S.S.R., and China: Applications to Corporate Management), Tokyo: President-sha, 1983).

3. For further discussion of the Matsushiro Imperial Headquarters, see *Matsushiro no Shiseki to Bunkazai* (Historical Sites and Cultural Properties in Matsushiro), Nagano: Matsushiro Kankojigyo Shinkokai, 1984, pp. 89–102.

4. According to Taizo Akiyama, Director of the Matsushiro Seismological Observatory, Matsushiro's underground tunnels, totalling some 3 kilometres in length, with diameters varying from 2.5 to 6 metres, proved ideal for seismological observation. The tunnels are in a remote location, 60 kilometres from the nearest sea coast, thus the site is free from surf disturbance and railroad and traffic vibrations are relatively low.

5. These figures came from the Peace Museum in Hiroshima. For further discussion of the impact of the bombings, see 'The Committee for the Compilation of Materials on Damage Caused by the Atomic Bombs in Hiroshima and Nagasaki', *Hiroshima and Nagasaki: The Physical, Medical and Social Effects of the Atomic Bombings*, Tokyo: Iwanami Shoten, 1979.

6. 'Back Mirror', *Nikka Times*, 4 October 1985.

7. Kôbe Chamber of Commerce, *Kôbe Shoko Kaigisho Hyakunen-shi* (100 Years of the History of the Kôbe Chamber of Commerce), Kôbe Chamber of Commerce, 1982, p. 357.

Chapter 2

1. John Durant, *Highlights of the Olympics From Ancient Times to the Present*, New York: Hastings House, 1969, p. 18.

2. David B. Kanin, *A Political History of the Olympic Games*, Boulder: Westview Press, 1981, p. 83.

3. Ichiro Oshikawa, Ichiro Nakayama, Hiromi Arisawa & Kiichi Isobe, eds, *Chusho Kogyo no Hattatsu* (The Development of Small and Medium-sized Industries) (Tokyo: Toyokeizai Shimpo-sha, 1962, pp. 195–6.

4. M. Y. Yoshino, *Japan's Managerial System: Tradition and Innovation*, Cambridge: MIT Press, 1968, pp. 96–7.

Chapter 3

1. Diana Rowland, *Japanese Business Etiquette*, New York: Warner, 1985, pp. 7–8.

2. The stages in the development of Japanese marketing are discussed by William Lazer, Shoji Murata & Hiroshi Kosaka in 'Japanese Marketing:

Towards a Better Understanding', *Journal of Marketing*, **49** (Spring 1985), pp. 69–81.

3. Today, the Hyogo prefecture Credit Guarantee Association guarantees loans to a maximum of 70 million yen within the manufacturing sector. To qualify, the corporation must not have more than three hundred employees and 100 million yen in capital. For a brief discussion of small business financing in Japan, see The Bank of Japan Economic Research Department, *Money and Banking in Japan*, New York: St Martin's, 1973, pp. 241–4, 268–79.

4. Edward G. Seidensticker, 'Satsumaimo' in *A Hundred Things Japanese*, Tokyo: Japan Culture Institute, 1975, pp. 56–7.

5. The custom of *miai kekkon*, or arranged marriage, spread from the *samurai* class to the commoners when marriages between people living in distant parts of the country became common. At the request of the family of either of the prospective marriage partners, the *nakodo*, or go-between, seeks out a suitable mate. If the proposal is acceptable to both families involved an *o-miai*, or marriage meeting, is arranged for the man and woman, usually accompanied by their parents. If all parties are satisfied, wedding plans proceed accordingly. Nowadays *renai kekkon*, or love marriages, are the norm in Japan, but *miai kekkon* is still practised. Even in *renai kekkon* the *nakodo* still plays an important though symbolic role, particularly in the wedding ceremony itself (*Mock Joya's Things Japanese*, Tokyo: Tokyo News Service, 1960, pp. 374–5).

Chapter 4

1. Shigeo Okinaka, *Naikagaku* (Internal Medicine), Vol. 3, Tokyo: Nanzando, 1954, pp. 496–7.

2. Manfred F. R. Kets de Vries, 'Stress and the Entrepreneur', in *Current Concerns in Occupational Stress*, C. L. Cooper & R. Payne, eds, New York: Wiley, 1980, p. 57.

Chapter 6

1. Onitsuka Corporation's Board of Directors consisted entirely of full-time operating executives. This is a common occurrence in Japan, though largely a postwar phenomenon. As Yoshino explains, immediate postwar economic reforms, especially those aimed at the deconcentration of corporate power and the purge of key executives, resulted in a large number of vacancies on Boards of Directors of major firms. These were soon filled by full-time operating executives. Once established, this practice was further facilitated by the wide diffusion of postwar stock ownership. M. Y. Yoshino, *Japan's Managerial System: Tradition and Innovation*, Cambridge, MIT Press, 1968, p. 211.

2. Kaoru Kobayashi, *Japan: The Most Misunderstood Country*, Tokyo: The Japan Times, 1984, p. 67.

3. Japan Ministry of Culture, *Shukyo Nenkan: 1984* (Annals of Religion: 1984), Tokyo: Gyosei, 1985, pp. 118–19.

4. Kenneth K. S. Chén. *Buddhism in China*, Princeton: Princeton University Press, 1964, pp. 378–9.

5. Keigo Okonogi, 'Nichiren and Shinran: Two Faces of Buddhism', *Japan Echo*, **10**, No. 4 (1983), p. 70.

6. Nichiren Shoshu International Center, *Lectures on the Sutra*, Tokyo: Nichiren Shoshu International Center, 1978, p. 76.

7. Yasuji Kirimura, *The Fundamentals of Buddhism*, exerpted in *New Century*, **4**, No. 12 (1985), p. 13.

8. Yasuji Kirimura, *The Fundamentals of Buddhism*, excerpted in *New Century*, ibid., p. 13.

9. The bonus system is universal in Japan. The bonus is part of a worker's regular pay, normally representing a large portion of his annual salary, which he receives in a lump sum twice yearly, usually in June and December. This appears as a genuine 'bonus' to the worker, whereas it is really part of his basic salary, unlike in North America where bonuses are typically over and above the regular wage.

10. The evolution of Tadao Yoshida's managerial ideology and its expression in corporate behaviour is described in Sohachi Yamaoka, *Zen no Junkan* (The Cycle of Goodness), Tokyo: Chihiro Kikaku Rinjin Chuppanbu, 1964 and *Zoku Zen no Junkan* (The Cycle of Goodness, continued), Tokyo: Kagamiura Shobo, 1974. For information about Konosuke Matsushita, see Rowland Gould, *The Matsushita Phenomenon*, Tokyo: Diamond-sha, 1970.

11. For a brief discussion of the necessity of erecting a proper grave, see Mock Joya, *Mock Joya's Things Japanese*, op. cit., pp. 336–7.

Chapter 7

1. Sun Tzu, *The Art of War*, trans. by Samuel B. Griffith, London: Oxford University Press, 1963, p. xi.

2. Sun Tzu, *The Art of War*, ibid., p. 79 and p. 84.

3. Peter R. Cavanagh, *The Running Shoe Book*, Mountain View: Anderson World, 1980, p. 9.

4. R. Turner Wilcox, *The Mode in Footwear*, London: Charles Scribner's Sons, 1948, p. 29 and pp. 34–5.

5. Peter R. Cavanagh, *The Running Shoe Book*, op. cit., p. 16.

6. Ibid., p. 17.

7. Ibid., p. 18.

8. Ibid., p. 23.

9. A large collection of footwear, particularly Japanese, is on display at Nihon Hakimono Hakubutsukan (Japan Footwear Museum) in Fukuyama city, Hiroshima prefecture. A discussion of Japanese traditional footwear is contained in Tetsuo Ushioda, *Hakimono* (Footwear), Tokyo: Hosei University Press, 1985.

10. Peter R. Cavanagh, *The Running Shoe Book*, op. cit., p. 24.

11. Ibid., p. 30.

12. Ibid., p. 138.

13. For a summary of the importance of small enterprises, particularly sub-contractors in the Japanese economy, see Japan Ministry of Foreign Affairs, *Small Businesses in Japan: Underpinnings of Economic Vitality*, 1982.

Chapter 8

1. M. Y. Yoshino, *Japan's Managerial System: Tradition and Innovation*, Cambridge: MIT Press, 1968, pp. 32–3.
2. Takehiko Kobayashi, *Gendai no Tosan* (Contemporary Bankruptcies), Tokyo: Nihon Keizai Shibunsha, 1971, pp. 137–8.

Chapter 9

1. Toshio Saeki, ed., *Gendai Sports no Shakaigaku* (Sociology of Contemporary Sports), Tokyo: Fumaido, 1984, p. 265.
2. Ibid., p. 265.
3. Peter F. Drucker, *Management: Tasks, Responsibilities, Practices*, New York: Harper & Row, 1973, p. 104.
4. For a recent, new interpretation of this battle arguing that Nobunaga's victory was not the result of a deliberate surprise attack, but rather of a misreading of the situation combined with good fortune, see Masayuki Fujimoto, 'Okehazama no Tatakai: Naze Nobunaga wa Imagawa-gun ni Katetaka' (Okehazama Battle: Why Nobunaga was Able to Win Against the Imagawa Army), *Rekishi Dokuhon*, 1984, pp. 64–71.
5. Associated Press and Grolier, *The Olympic Story: Pursuit of Excellence*, New York: Franklin Watts, 1979, p. 254.
6. Lord Killanin & John Rodda, *The Olympic Games 1984*, London: Willow Books, 1983, p. 166.
7. In freestyle wrestling, Y. Yoshida took the flyweight title, Y. Uetake the bantamweight title, and O. Watanabe the featherweight title. In Graeco–Roman style wrestling, the flyweight and bantamweight titles went to T. Hanahara and M. Ichiguchi respectively.
8. The men won their gold medal as a group, and Yukio Endo won the overall individual gold as well as the gold on the parallel bars. H. Yamashita won the gold in the long horse vault and T. Hayata took the title on the rings.

Chapter 10

1. In its seventeen years of operation, the Nichidai Sports Shoe Company has experienced no strikes or demonstrations.
2. Anne Elizabeth Murase, 'Keiyaku', *A Hundred Things Japanese*, Tokyo: Japan Culture Institute, 1975, p. 109.
3. For further comments on socio-cultural aspects related to Japanese attitudes to law, see H. Tanaka, 'The Role of Law in Japanese Society: Comparison with the West', *UBC Law Review*, **19**, No. 2 (1985), pp. 375–88.

4. High-context low-context cultures are explored in Edward T. Hall's *Beyond Culture*, Garden City, N.Y.: Anchor Press/Doubleday, 1976.
5. The disagreement between Onitsuka Corporation and Blue Ribbon Sports was complex. A sketchy outline of it from the Japanese perspective is presented here to illustrate the difficulty of conducting business between two parties from different cultures. For further comment on the disagreement see Peter R. Cavanagh, *The Running Shoe Book*, op. cit., pp. 39–41, 329–30, 366.
6. Chie Nakane, *Japanese Society*, Harmondsworth: Penguin Books, 1973, p. 15.
7. Yasutaka Matsudaira, Naohiro Ikeda & Masaru Saito, *Winning Volleyball*, Vanier, Canada: Canadian Volleyball Association, 1977, p. 5.

Chapter 11

1. *Labour-Management Relations in Japan*, JETRO Business Information Series 4, Tokyo: JETRO, pp. 15–16.
2. Takehiko Kobayashi, *Gendai no Tosan* (Contemporary Bankruptcies), op. cit., pp. 151–3.
3. Hanji Aoki, *Athletes yo Eien nare* (Athletes Forever), Tokyo: Waseda University Press, 1986, pp. 29–30.

Chapter 12

1. Another alternative was to designate a competent employee as *banto* or head clerk. The *banto* had a great deal of authority and actually ran the business, often in the absence of the owner. The wisdom of the owner was said to lie in his ability to recognize the capability of the *banto* and in his magnanimity in giving the *banto* free reign to run the business. Although he was still an employee, the *banto* had the power to veto the owner's capricious intentions, the understanding being that the long-term maintenance and prosperity of the *ie* was more important than the immediate gratification of the current head of the household's whims.
2. According to the 1983 White Paper on Small and Middle-sized Industries, the presidents of 89 per cent of small and middle-sized industries in Japan expect that their sons will succeed them.
3. Age of individuals is a significant factor in business and personal relationships in Japan. An individual's age is usually known to his associates and increasing years command increasing respect.
4. In *Juvenal's Sixteen Satires*, Harmondsworth: Penguin, 1970, Peter Green translates this as follows:
   Is there nothing worth praying for, then? If you want my advice,
   Let the Gods themselves determine what's most appropriate
   for mankind, and what best suits our various circumstances.
   They'll give us the things we need, not those we want: a man
   Is dearer to them than he is to himself. Led helpless
   By irrational impulse and powerful blind desires
   We ask for marriage and children. But the Gods alone know

What they'll be like, our future wives and offspring!
Still, if you must have something to pray for, if you
Insist on offering up the entrails and consecrated
Sausages from a white pigling in every shrine, then ask
for a sound mind in a sound body, a valiant heart
Without fear of death, that reckons longevity
The least among Nature's gifts, that's strong to endure
All kinds of toil, that's untainted by lust and anger,
That prefers the sorrows and labours of Hercules to all
Sardanapalus' downy cushions and women and junketings.
What I've shown you, you can find by yourself: there's one
Path, and one only, to a life of peace—through virtue.
Fortune has no divinity, could we but see it: it's we,
We ourselves, who make her a goddess, and set her in the heavens.

5. For a brief discussion of Japanese corporate name changes, see 'C.I. Stratagem for the Multifaceted Management Age', *Focus Japan*, **12**, No. 11 (1985), p. 3.
6. This story is recounted in *Zhenguan Zhengyao*, political statements of the Jinkwan Period of the Tang Dynasty.

Chapter 13

1. Two of Kihachiro Onitsuka's representative publications are: *Onitsuka Yakushin Keiei no Himitsu* (The Secret of Onitsuka Management), Tokyo: Asuka Shuppansha, 1977, and 'Hichiten Hakki no Uta', *Keieisha Kaiho*, March 1981 through March 1982.
2. Japan, *Labor Union Law*, Chap. 1, Art. 2.
3. The Japan Institute of Labour, *Problems of Working Women*, Tokyo: The Japan Institute of Labour, 1981, pp. 12–13.
4. For a discussion of the situation of Japanese women in the labour force, see Hiroshi Tanaka, 'Working Women in Japan', *Equal Opportunities International*, **5**, No. 1 (1986), pp. 1–7.
5. For further background on NPS and examples of its implementation, see Isao Shinohara, *NPS no Kiseki* (The miracle of NPS), Tokyo: Toyo Keizai Shinposha, 1986.
6. Instead of the Japanese systems of consolidated financial statements currently operating, it is acceptable to use the American Financial Accounting Standards Board critiera overseen by the Securities Exchange Commission. Thirty-three companies on the Tokyo Stock Exchange, including Sony Corporation, Mitsui & Company Limited, and Hitachi Limited were using the latter system as of March 1985.
7. Later, in 1980, NEC Corporation, the world's second largest semiconductor producer and a major maker of computers and communication equipment, sponsored the Federation Cup Inter Soccer Four and the following year bought out the eighty-year old Davis Cup tennis tournament at a cost of 420 million yen. Toyota introduced the Toyota cup to determine the world's number-1 soccer team. TDK, the world's largest ferrite core and magnetic tape

producer, sponsored the First World Track and Field Event held in Helsinki. Sanyo, Brother, Fuji Film and Canon were the main Japanese sponsors for the 1984 Los Angeles Olympics, collectively assuming nearly 20 per cent of the costs. Toshio Saeki, ed., *Gendai Sports no Shakaigaku* (Sociology of Contemporary Sports), p. 250.

8. James Riordan, ed., *Sport Under Communism: The U.S.S.R., Czechoslovakia, The G.D.R., China, Cuba*, Montreal: McGill-Queen's University Press, 1978, p. 129.

9. Ibid., p. 115.

10. Onitsuka was only the second Japanese to receive this award and the fourth to be recognized for his service to Austria. Motohiko Ban, chairman of the All Japan Ski Association, had received the Grand SIlver Order of Honour for Service to the Republic of Austria while Yoshizo Ikeda, adviser to Mitsui & Company Limited (Mitsui Bussan), one of Japan's top commercial houses, and Takayuki Fukuoka, the late chairman of the Japan–Austria Ski Association, had received the Grand Gold Order of Honour and the Grand Bronze Order of Honour, respectively.

11. Hiroshi Takeuchi, *Ski Keizaigaku* (Ski Economics), Tokyo: Jitsugyo no Nihonsha, 1986, p. 115.

12. Hayashi established his company in 1952 with ten employees. ULVAC's products include equipment for producing semiconductors and other microelectronic devices; thin-film and metallurgical equipment for the automotive, aerospace and machine tool industries; systems for the production of pharmaceuticals and freeze-dried foods; mass spectrometers and helium-leak detectors; and vacuum pumps and gauges. These items are marketed through five domestic offices and twelve overseas sales offices and representatives. In fiscal year 1985, ULVAC recorded non-consolidated net sales of 41.6 billion yen and a net profit of 2.8 billion yen.

13. This view is reinforced by the statement made by J. P. Lowry, director of industrial relations for the British Leyland group: 'Those who lose a war have a greater sense of dedication to rebuilding and a more disciplined approach, I think, than those who win.' Nancy Foy & Herman Gadon, 'Worker Participation: Contrasts in Three Countries', *Harvard Business Review*, May–June, 1976, p. 77.

Chapter 14

1. For more information about this project, see 'Large-scale National R & D Projects: Automated Sewing System', *The Japan Industrial & Technological Bulletin*, **13**, No. 6 (1985), pp. 9–11.

2. 'Yakudo Sekai Sports Sangyo' (Active World Sports Industry), *Nikkei Sangyo Shinbun*, 17 September 1982.

3. Nippon Steel Corporation Personnel Development Office, *Nippon: The Land and Its People*, Tokyo: Gakuseisha, 1982, p. 179.

4. Peter R. Cavanagh, *The Running Shoe Book*, op. cit., pp. 160–1.

5. Ibid., p. 161.

6. For more information on R & D in running shoe technology, see Tony Baer, 'Designing for the Long Run', *Mechanical Engineering* (September 1984); Richard Schuster, 'The State of the Art', *The Runner* (November 1984), pp. 96–122; Jonathan B. Tucker, 'Running-Shoe Technology Picks Up the Race', *High Technology*, **5**, No. 4 (March 1985), pp. 28–34.

7. A typical runner takes about 700 steps per mile. Research has shown that close to 80 per cent of runners are heel strikers. They land on the outer part of the heel, roll onto the midfoot, and push off with the metatarsal area (the ball of the foot) and the toes. The remaining 20 per cent of runners land on the midfoot. In heel strikers, the heel hits the ground with an impact that is two to three times the runner's body weight. According to Dr Barry Bates, the runner's entire body weight and vertical and forward momentum come down on a section of tissue and bone only a few cubic inches across. This impact occurs within less than a tenth of a second and comprises 90 to 95 per cent of the total shock experience while running. To prevent injury, the heel area must be well cushioned. Yet, because of the tendency to pronate, too much cushioning lessens the shoe's stability. As the runner's weight shifts from the heel to the midfoot, the leg and hip flex to distribute the impact, causing the foot to roll inward, or pronate. Most heel strikers pronate to some extent and those with low arches or wide hips tend to overpronate, so that the foot bends more than 10° from the axis of the lower leg. Shoes for pronators must be designed to stabilize the foot on impact and prevent excessive rolling. A small percentage of runners have very limited pronation, remaining on the outside of the foot through most of the stance phase. When the foot hits the ground, it remains on the outside, or lateral edge, so that most of the impact is delivered to the forefoot and outer edge of the foot rather than the heel. These runners need shoes that cushion the forefoot and restrict the outward role.

8. For further information about the performance of ASICS running shoes, see 'Tenth Annual Runner's World 5-Star Shoes Survey', *Runner's World* (October 1984), pp. 83–110; Alexander Weber, 'Produkt-Informationen: 20 Lauf-Schuhe im Test', *Spiridon* (Dezenber 1984), pp. 26–32.

Chapter 15

1. This figure came from the Japan Leisure Development Centre.

2. With increased leisure time, afluence and life expectancy, the elderly population is beginning to constitute a viable sporting goods market. By 1985, 10 per cent of the Japanese population were sixty-five or over and by the year 2020, over 20 per cent are expected to be in this age bracket.

3. A. L. Sandler, *The Maker of Modern Japan: The Life of Tokugawa Ieyasu*, Vermont & Tokyo: Charles E. Tuttle, 1937, p. 7.

Appendix

1. Kihachiro Onitsuka, 'The Theories and Practices of Japanese Management', translated by Sharon Domier and edited by Hiroshi Tanaka, keynote address

presented to 'Japanese Management', a conference sponsored by the School of Management, University of Lethbridge, Lethbridge, Alberta, Canada, 16–18 March 1983.

2. 'Matsushita Konosuke no Keiei Dojo', *Matsushita Seikei-juko-ho* (1 February 1983), pp. 8–9.

Index

Abe, Tetsuya 198, 199
accounting 44–5, 131–2, 133, 134
Adidas 148–9, 165, 168, 170, 205, 219, 234, 235, 236
adoption 10, 16, 172–3, 174–5
affiliated firms 98, 113, 115, 248
Akamatsu, Kumakichi 46
amalgamation 174, 177–88, 189, 190, 192, 203
  preparation for 177–84, 189
  reasons for success 189, 190
Amber Incorporated 205, 208
American influence,
  on management 70–1, 80, 133, 147, 247
  on sports 22, 28, 149, 150
Antarctic Observation Team 95
Aoki, Hanji 169
ASICS,
  administration 183
  athletic sponsorship 168
  corporate mission 245
  head office 237–9
  inaugural ceremonies 186–7
  managerial ideology 186
  meaning 1, 184–5
  organizational structure 190–4
  production sector 192
  shares 183
  strategy 193–4, 203–5
ASICS Circle 160
ASICS Distribution 218
ASICS Innovation (AI) 200–3
ASICS Research Institute of Sports Sciences 239–41
ASICS Sports Corporation 234–5
ASICS Tiger Corporation 135, 143, 235
ASICS Tiger do Brasil Industria e Commercio Ltda. 235, 236
ASICS Tiger GmbH 235–6
Association of Japan Sporting Goods Industries (JASPO) 189, 208
Association of Kansai Sporting Goods Industries 171
athletes,
  amateur 169
  professional 168, 169
atomic 208
atomic bomb 12
Austria 207, 208

Bank of Japan 108
bankruptcies 103, 107, 162
Bates, Barry 223, 225
Bessha, Akio 138–41, 201, 235
Bikila, Abebe 84, 92–3, 120
biomechanics 223, 224
black market 18, 19, 29
blisters 91–2, 227
Blue Ribbon Sports 145–6, 230
Bork, John, Jr. 143
Bowerman, Bill 145
bowling 111, 112
Brazil 236
Buddhism 72–5
business agreements, Japanese 144–5
Byun, Jae-bok 235

C. Itoh and Company 220, 230
C. Itoh Texmac Company Limited 213
Cambuci 236
Cavanagh, Peter 221–2
Chamber of Commerce, Kôbe Junior 107
Chatani Sangyo 230
Chin Woo Company 232, 234
China 206–7
Chung Chyun Industry Company Limited 231, 232
Chung Hsing Company 232
Chung Shyong Industry 231, 232
Clover Limited Liabilities Company 178
communication 57–8, 194
competition,
  domestic 30, 164–5, 178, 203, 218–20
  foreign 85, 102, 122, 136, 148–9, 165–6, 170
concentration decision 116–19
connections, importance of in Japan 26, 28
consumers 193–4, 215, 229

contracts 143–6
Cooper, Kenneth 142
corporate ideology 1, 77–8, 110–11, 115–16, 140, 191
corporate name 184
corporate sponsorship 168–9
Coubertin, Pierre de 22, 89
Credit Guarantee Association 33

Dachstein 205, 208
Dassler, Adi 168
Dassler, Armin 209
Dassler, Rudi 168
decision making 112, 181–2, 249, 250
delegation of authority 48, 51, 56, 57, 194
Descente 164, 203, 209, 218–20
distribution of shares 75–6, 78, 99, 115, 183, 248
    Matsushita 71–2
diversification 100–4, 106, 116–17, 160–5, 173–4, 220
Drucker, Peter 70, 116

Ellesse 163
Ellis, Joe 223–4, 228
Emperor Hirohito 12, 67, 120
employees 42–4, 146–7
    advancement 80, 81–2, 248
    ASICS 193, 199, 248–50
    dedication 56–8, 70, 75, 134, 140, 156
    expanding numbers 48, 58, 187
    female 155, 199–200
    firing 105
    first 27
    GTO 174
    in Korea 233–4
    in Taiwan 139, 140, 232
    Jelenk 177
    part-time 155
    recruitment 135–6
    resignations 105, 155, 238
    training 48, 58–65, 114, 133, 139, 147
    university graduates 58, 61, 81, 82
ethics 45, 249
examinations,
    entrance 61
    for advancement 81–2

factories 153, 191–2, 193
    fire 51–2
    first 48, 96
    Fukui 191, 212, 214, 215
    GTO 174, 184
    growth of Japanese 100

Jelenk 177, 200
Kita-Kyushu 212, 213, 214
Miyazaki 197, 212
Omuta 197
Suma 96, 97, 135
Taiwan 136–42, 201, 231–2
Takefu 191, 215
Tottori 6, 67, 135–6
Yamaguchi 197
Yao 184
finance 27–8, 33, 106–9, 113–14, 119, 120, 132, 133–4, 154, 203, 204–5
foreign market 84, 85, 101, 102, 121, 136, 142, 144–5, 148–9, 231, 235–7
Fuji Bank 109
Fujio, Masato 115
Fukuda, Sadako Kishida 5
Fukuda, Tokichi 4, 5, 6, 16, 49
Fukuoka, Masanobu 240
Fusalp 163
Fuwa, Shinji 235

garment industry 161, 192, 211, 212, 216, 218–20
Gelico 177
gemeinschaft 246, 249
Genzo Teranishi Stores Limited 173–4
gesellschaft 247
geta 90
Goldtiger Company Limited 163
Goldwin Incorporated 163, 164
GTO Incorporated 143, 170, 174, 178, 179, 180, 183–4, 186, 196, 197, 208

Hagiwara, Toshiki 27
Hamuro, Tetsuo 66
Hanasaki Incorporated 219
Hase, Yoshiaki 166
Hashimoto, Hirokazu 200
Hashimoto, Yoshihiro 178–9, 183, 186, 190, 239
Hartjes 208
Hayashi, Chikara 208
Hayashi, Kyoichiro 142, 143
Henderson, Joe 142
Higashida Company 17–20, 29, 44
Higashida, Shigeru 17, 18, 19, 20–1
Hino, Kinji 175
Hirao, Fumio 237
Hirose, Hisashige 107–9
Hiroun 112, 217
Honan Rubber 232
Hoover Corporation 208
Hori, Kohei 19, 20, 21, 22, 23, 26

Hsyu Tai Company 232
human revolution 72

Ichimoto, Shigeo 197
Ikeda Daisaku 79, 187
Ikeda, Hayato 100–1
Imagawa, Yoshimoto 117–18
industrial pollution 152
inflation 15, 103
information leaks 226
international expansion 121–2, 134, 135–
    143, 145–6
  Australia 237
  China 237
  Europe 235–7
  first attempt 230
  impetus for 85
  Jelenk 177
  Korea 232–3
  North America 142–3, 145–6, 230–1
  South America 236
  Taiwan 137–41, 231–2
International Track and Field Association
    168
inventory,
  control 204–19
  reductions 52, 105, 153–4
Ishibashi, Minoru 50–1, 58, 59, 99, 101–3,
    104, 110–12, 113
Ishihara, Takashi 24
Ishimoto, Takeo 209, 218, 219
Isohata, Shozo 42–3, 56–7
Iwai, Fukuo 186
Izuno, Katsuto 112, 217

Japan,
  Constitution 2
  economic growth 100, 133
  economic recovery 2–3, 119–20, 133, 246
  education system 4
  postwar conditions 18, 19–20, 24–5, 29,
    34, 36–7, 69, 134, 175–6, 242–3
  surrender 12–13
Japan Amateur Athletic Federation 92
Japan Amateur Sports Association 164–5
Japan Association of Retail Stores 79
Japan-Austria Cultural Exchange Associa-
    tion 208
Japanese Association of Track and Field 67,
    169
Jelenk Incorporated 143, 170, 177, 178, 180,
    186, 196, 197, 211, 234
Jin-yang 232
jogging 142

Johnson Rubber Corporation 136, 139, 231
Juvenal 184–5

Kaku, Hirotsugu 207, 239, 240, 241
Kanaguri, Shinzo 90
Kanban Hoshiki 202, 216
Kaneda, Hiroo 33
Kanematsu Gosho 50
Kangyo Bank 58, 106, 108
Kanzaki, Kazunori 57, 62, 64, 65, 80–1, 105,
    135, 201
Kashiwai, Kenichi 107
Kato, Akira 236
Kawamata, Terunaga 189–90
Keizai Doyukai 24, 195
Kim, B. C. 232, 233
Kim, Jang Kil 233
Kim, Seung Ryoum 234
Kim, Woon Ryoum 234
Kitami, Shoji 62, 64, 114, 134–5, 142, 146
Knight, Phil 145
Kobayashi, Kazutoshi 94
Kobe 1, 2, 9, 14–15, 17, 20, 23, 24, 27, 29, 34,
    35, 36, 41, 50, 54, 69, 80, 82, 99, 107,
    109, 112, 135, 139, 158, 160, 187, 202,
    209, 238, 239, 243, 244
Kobe Bank 33, 108, 109, 119, 157
Kobe Culture Centre 17
Kobe Shinbun 60
Kondo, Tatsuaki 215, 245
Korea 232–5
Kosake, Katsuharu 191, 215
Kostrubala, Thaddeus 142
Kunihiro, Kazuto 132
Kusaka, Hideo 108, 109
Kuwata, Mikio 236
Kwon, Dong Chil 233

labour laws, postwar 43, 64
labour–management relations 158, 196–9
lawsuits 144, 146
leadership 157, 183, 189, 190, 194, 244,
    249–50
Li Mu-hua 207
liaison offices,
  Chicago 142
  Europe 235
  Los Angeles 143
  New York 143
licensing agreements 136, 139, 232, 236–7,
    348, 349
lifetime employment 62, 134, 246
Liu, Peter H. 139, 140–1
logo 186

Lubalin, Herb 186
Lydiard, Arthur 142

Makino, Jiro 143
management,
    American and European 247
    Japanese 246–7
management by objectives 190
management group 156, 157, 181, 183, 191,
    194, 198–9, 244, 247, 249–50
    advancement 80–2, 199, 248
    and stress 242
    changes in 112–14
    composition of 114, 134–5
    goals 247–8
    resignations 110–11, 113
    training 58–9, 80, 114, 131–2, 133, 157,
    195
managerial ideology, postwar 23–5
marathon 84, 89, 90, 91, 92, 142, 167, 169
marketing 54–5, 132, 135
    'against-the-flow' phenomenon 35, 55
    'base strategy' 31
    Descente 219
    early attempts at 29–32, 35–6
    in postwar Japan 30
    'top strategy' 31, 94–5, 220, 236
Maruei Kagaku 202
Maslow, Abraham H. 71
Matsudaira, Yasutaka 149, 150
Matsumoto, Yukio 29, 31, 32
Matsushiro 11
Matsushita, Konosuke 8, 71–2, 76, 78, 237,
    250–1
Matsushita Electric Industrial Company
    Limited 8, 71, 171, 172, 250–1
Matsushita School of Government and
    Management 250
merchandise distribution 161, 217–18
mergers 57, 102, 113, 190
    see also amalgamation
merit system 80–2
middle management 58, 114, 140–1, 156,
    244
Mihara, Seiji 132–3, 134, 146, 158, 221, 240,
    242
Miki, Ryoichi 60–1
MITI (Ministry of International Trade and
    Industry) 68, 190
    automated sewing project 216
Mitsubishi Rayon 177
Miyata, Masayasu 235
Mizuno 164, 178, 203, 205, 218
Mizuno, Yotaro 91
Mobus Co., KG 235
Munsing 218, 219, 220

Murakami, Mamoru 239
Murakoso, Kohei 66

Nagami, Ishiki 174, 175
Nagami, Masa Maezawa 174
Nakamura, Kiyoshi 67
Nakayama, Kuramitsu 57, 64, 110, 135
Nekosu Corporation 162
nepotism 78–80
Nichidai Sports Shoes Company 137–42,
    138, 231
Nichiren 72–3
Nihon University Arctic Expedition 95
Nike 145, 146, 219, 223
Niki, Toshihiko 56, 63, 64, 135, 146, 242
Nishida, Tosaku 78, 163
Nishikawa, Yoshio 213
Nishio, Yuji 117
NPS (New Production System) 202

Oda, Kiyoshi 219
Oda, Nobunaga 117–18
oil crisis 152, 160, 179, 211, 246
Okamura, Teruyuki 156
Okitsu, Mamoru 99, 104, 113–14
Okura, Kihachiro 3
Olympic Games 22, 66, 89, 90, 95, 169, 177,
    210
    Lake Placid 205–6
    Melbourne 66–7
    Mexico 148, 150, 165, 173
    Montreal 164, 165–8, 170, 180
    Munich 149, 151, 161, 165, 167
    Rome 84
    Tokyo 86, 109, 119–21, 165
Onishi, Shinichi 174
Onitsuka, Emiko 49, 86, 243
Onitsuka, Fukuya 2, 9, 15, 28, 37, 69, 83
Onitsuka, Kihachiro,
    and union 196, 197–9
    associates' opinion of 35–6, 108, 112,
    115–16, 117, 160
    concern for employees 64–5
    dreams and goals 1, 20, 21–3, 28, 50–1, 75,
    86, 91, 99, 111, 142, 151, 185, 218, 239
    employee 17–20
    family life 45, 242–3
    father figure 57
    good health 241
    honours received 160, 207–8
    idea of diversification 101, 102
    illness 46–50, 52
    inner conflict 69–70
    internal and external concerns 194–5,
    203, 208, 209

lessons from military life 8, 33–4, 60, 112
marriage 38, 39, 40, 41
philosophy 59, 95, 100, 111, 114, 157–9, 179, 184, 195, 221, 245–50
search for happiness 69–75
shareholder 183
shoe salesman 29–30
successor to 244
theory of management 115–19, 187, 189, 244, 247–9
travels abroad 84, 85, 136, 142, 241
see also Sakaguchi, Kihachiro
Onitsuka, Seiichi 2, 9, 14, 37, 39, 44, 69, 82
Onitsuka, Takako 69, 243
Onitsuka, Tsune Tominaga 39, 40, 41, 49, 50, 69, 77, 85
Onitsuka Circle 96–7, 98, 105, 115, 119, 153, 159
Onitsuka Corporation,
appointed Olympic supplier 66, 164, 205
assets 26, 75
corporate mission 95
dormitory facilities 58–9, 63, 70, 132
establishment 26–8, 247
head office 48, 58, 59, 96
honours received 67, 68
revitalization of 119
strategy 104–6, 115–16, 116–19, 131–2, 140, 142, 151, 152–7, 159–60, 161, 162, 180
tax evasion 67–8
tenth anniversary 76–8, 99
works with Jelenk and GTO 177–9
'Onitsukaism' 244
on-line order system 215
Ono, Katsuji 93
Ono, Taichi 202
Onoda, Hajime 209
open management 68, 98, 100, 115–16, 156, 248–9
Organization for Economic Co-operation and Development (OECD) 121
organizational design 190–3
Osaka, Masato 79, 103
Oyama, Motoi 80, 243

Park, Ki Deuk 234
patents 229
Peter Brochause 208
Peter Steinebronn 205
planning 133, 190, 245
point-of-focus management 116–19, 131, 236
Port Island 238
product design 241

product development 41–2, 66, 86, 95, 132, 220–1,
athletes input into 31, 35, 91, 93
production 135, 139–40
automated 212, 212–16
multi-product, small batch 96, 98, 211
see also factories, subcontract factories
profit 55, 75, 95, 154, 157
distribution 24, 158–60, 235–48
functions of 157–9, 233
maximization 203
Puma 120, 149, 167, 168, 209, 235

quality control 147, 200–3

Rawlings 183
recession 103, 106, 152–4, 159
representative directors 183
research and development 87, 91–4, 97, 220–9, 239–41
retailers 35, 36, 54, 55, 99, 103, 115, 164, 196, 215, 217–18, 229, 236
retirement age 155, 244
robots 212

Sakaguchi, Dentaro 3, 5, 15, 98
Sakaguchi, Kame Takahashi 3, 15
Sakaguchi, Kihachiro 2, 16
adopted 16
childhood 3–6
military experience 7–14
see also Onitsuka, Kihachiro
Sakaguchi, Takako 80
Sakaguchi, Tokio 43, 79, 86, 228
Sakurai, Peter Tsuyoshi 142, 143
salaries 44, 158–9, 198, 199, 240
reductions 105, 155, 156
Taiwan 140
sales 48, 141, 154, 159, 193, 203, 218, 245
GTO 174
Jelenk 177
offices 56, 177, 193, 203–4, 217
performance improvement 203–4
sportswear 164
Samaranch, Juan Antonio 210
Sasada, Osamu 232
Sato, Kunikichi 9
Seiwa Society 171, 182
Senko Corporation 218
Sewon Company 232–4
shareholders 1, 24, 75, 78, 98, 99, 183, 248
Shibata Rubber Industries 107
Shigi, Toshio 166
Shimoda, Riichi 35–6

Shimonashi, Yoshiji 27, 48, 56, 79
shoe construction 88
    last 42, 92, 225–6
shoe ratings 145, 223, 228
shoe soles 66, 86–7, 89, 92, 94, 152, 224–5
Shoka Sonjuku 58
Shorter, Frank 142, 228
small group activities 200–3
social responsibility 1, 75, 78, 95, 157–8,
    159, 179, 245, 248–9
Soka Gakkai Sect 72, 187
Son, Kitei 90
songs 63, 77, 186–7
sports shoe production 30, 153, 203
sports shoes 84, 92–4, 120, 121, 142, 145,
    153, 165, 167–8, 220
    arctic boots 95–6
    baseball 160
    basketball 29, 31, 38, 84, 86, 87, 94, 116,
        151
    golf 160
    gymnastics 84, 120, 151
    leisure 135
    'Magic Runner' 91–2
    marathon 89–94, 120, 151
    running, development of 87–90; research
        into 223–9
    sneakers 88
    tennis 224
    track and field 67, 84, 116, 160
    volleyball 38, 94, 116, 150, 151, 170
    wrestling 84, 120, 139, 151
sportswear production,
    automated 211–16
    by Korean licensee 234
    GTO 173–4
    initiated 162–5
    Jelenk 175–7, 212
Steffner Company 208
Stock Exchange listing 99, 103, 105, 109,
    120, 152, 179, 180
    objections to 99–100
subcontract factories 41, 48, 96–8, 105, 153,
    159–60, 202, 214, 221, 232
subsidiaries 80, 135, 143, 197, 235–7
suggestion system 147, 200
Sugitate, Minoru 186
Sumitomo Bank 220
Sun Tzu 85–6
suppliers 98, 105, 107, 115
Suzuki, Sadao 105–6, 116

tabi 90
Tachibana, Shiro 53, 115–16
Taiencho, Noritsugu 191–2, 214
Taigon Chemical Industries 102, 113, 132

Taiwan 137–41, 231–3
Taiyo Kôbe Bank see Kôbe Bank
Tai-zong 188
Tajima, Hiroyoshi 160
Takahashi, Machiko 196
Takahashi, Yoshiyuki 62, 64, 110, 135, 181,
    201, 242
Takashima, Toshiaki 99, 112
Takeda, Harunobu (Shingen) 187
Takemoto, Hideo 43, 48, 56
Tanaka, Heizo 105, 136
Tanaka, Takemi 56, 64, 134, 235
Tanimura, Iwa Okamura 171
Tanimura, Yoshitaro 171
Teijin Limited 95, 179, 184
Teranishi, Genzo 173
Teranishi, Hikoji 179, 184
Teranishi, Mitsuji 170, 171–4, 178, 180, 194,
    245
    and amalgamation 178, 180–2, 190, 191
Teranishi, Shigekazu 179, 184
Teranishi, Yukiko 173
Tiger Dormitory 59, 62, 132, 135
    song 63
Tiger Rubber Company 48, 51–2, 57
Tiger stripes 227
Tokai Bank 109
Tokugawa, Ieyasu 245
Tokyo Onitsuka Corporation 56–7
Tomizawa, Yoshihiko 202
Torii, Tetsuya 95
totalization 161, 170, 180
Tottori Ichichu Middle School 4, 5, 7, 79
Toyobo Company Limited 220
trademark 45–6, 227
trading companies 230
Tranglobe Expedition 95
Tseng, R. S. 231, 232
Tsunemi, Hiizuru 17, 20
tyres 86–7

Ueda, Terutoshi 8–9, 10, 14, 15, 83
Uemura, Naoki 95
Uetsuki, Masaaki 61–2, 178, 186, 195, 235
unions 147, 156, 196–200, 201
unmeikyodotai 251
Usui, Kazuma 170, 174–7, 180, 183, 196,
    207, 244
    and amalgamation 177–82, 191–2, 197
Usui, Masaharu 179
Usui, Tamae 175
Usui, Tamajiro 175, 176
Usui, Toshiko 175
Usui, Yoshiharu 179, 184, 201
Usui Knitwear Manufacturers 176
Usui Textile Industry Limited 176

value added 158, 159
Van Corporation 219
Viren, Lasse 166–7
volleyball 150

Watanabe, Yasuo 216
West Germany 215, 235–6
Whatley, Ian 222, 224, 228–9
wholesalers 30, 54, 99, 115, 164, 196, 217, 229
Wongchang Moolsan Company 234
working conditions 42, 64, 136, 199
    in Korea 233
World Federation of the Sporting Goods Industry (SGI) 209
World War II 1–2, 7–14, 119, 120, 171, 174, 208, 246

Yae-yang 232
Yamada, Shoichi 209
Yamaichi Securities 99, 209
Yasuda, Harue 3, 49, 52
Yato, Masaru 43–4, 235–6
Yong, Soon-sik 234–5
Yoshida, Hitoshi 207
Yoshida, Shoin 58
Yoshida, Tadao 78
Yoshikawa, Torao 29, 45
Yoshikawa, Yoshizo 46
Yoshikawa Rubber Factory 28, 29
Young Man 174

Zensen Domei 196, 197
Zero Defects (ZD) 200
zori 90

7